Luca Collins is the author of three volumes of Children's plays published internationally, and has worked in the Australian Film Industry where he directed the short film 'FIRST,' which was screened at various International Film Festivals. He worked in the theatre industry over several decades. He is the author of 'WRITER'-a technical manual for emerging writers.

'Dancing With the Midnight Mare' is his first novel.

DANCING WITH THE

MIDNIGHT MARE

LUCA COLLINS

Based on real events

and

survivors experiences

This edition published by Luca Collins in 2025

Copyright © Luca Collins 2025

The moral right of the author has been asserted.

All rights reserved. This publication (or any part of it) may not be reproduced or transmitted, copied, stored, distributed, or otherwise made available by any person or entity (including Google, Amazon or similar organizations), in any form (electronic, digital, optical, mechanical) or by any means (photocopying, recording, scanning or otherwise) without prior written permission from the publisher.

Dancing With the Midnight Mare

EPUB Format: 9781764175418

Print on Demand Format: 9781764175401

Cover Design by Luca Collins and Kwik Kopy Design

Further contact can be made through Altamirawriter.com

TO HEDY, MADELINE AND CLARE

MAY YOUR DREAMS ALSO BECOME A REALITY.

BOOK ONE

'The difference between past, present and future is

only a

persistent illusion'

ALBERT EINSTEIN

'VOID'

The world has inverted itself,

Evil masquerades as the common good,

Forgiveness and compassion are now weakness,

Might and brutality are to be worshipped,

Time and its truth, has torn itself apart

And is no more.

The religion of fire and blood

Stands as a crooked cross,

Claiming to be a Saviour, a Messiah,

You may see his hollowness,

But he will take you before you can name it,

Beware children, run or be lost in the maelstrom

WARSAW SUMMER 1944

1

The sky gathered churning and dark, rolling in from the west, fulsome and threatening as the air all round lay still, humid and full of masonry dust and menace.

I slid out of the pipe, ruptured by explosions many months ago, which sat in a crater several metres from the house or what was left of it - on the broken street, in the empty ghetto, or what was left of that. Rat-like I scurried from one shadow to the next, covered in soot and mud and excrement. My clothes were frayed at the edges but the boots I stole from someone's window sill were still sturdy and strong. I flashed across space and into the darkness of the coal cellar and waited for him to arrive- my benefactor, or so I thought. Above, the dark clouds of a gathering summer storm promised a downpour and relief but for now held themselves in check.

He appeared over the rim and looked down on me as I stared up at him from the shadows, offering up a hopeful smile. This time there was a look on the face I had not seen before. Our one-time gardener Piotr now carried a determined yet franticly desperate expression.

'Where is your old man's money?' he hissed at me.

I shook my head and looked back at him bewildered, wondering what madness was this? The idea had formed in his mind that we managed to hide our money from the Germans and secreted it away somewhere in what remained of the Warsaw Ghetto. Only someone who had not felt the full force, the efficient cruelty and thoroughness of our enemies could conceive such an idea. But desperate men will create desperate delusions to stave off the calamity that engulfs them.

He thrashed about turning over rocks and bricks, certain that the family fortune was hidden somewhere in the rubble, the sweat pouring off his wiry frame. Coal dust rose all around him, blackening his face and hands. His search now more insane, his body jerking, moving in spasms as if he were possessed. And with each movement his anger grew. He had always been a disagreeable man but never a dishonest one, never vicious. Until now.

'He wouldn't have left you, just abandoned you, with nothing. I'm not stupid!'

Tearing at the broken stone, his sinewy muscles flexed beneath his singlet, as he hurled one rock after another out of the way.

'I know your bloody people, always hoarding something for the hard times.'

Moments later a shadow descended across his face. He stopped, glared then leapt the distance between us and took me by the collar. 'You goddamn liar, you know where it is.'

'I don't, I don't know.'

A large man, used to physical toil, his hair flew in all directions as the sweat from his brow flicked into my eyes and mouth; he raised his right-hand high slapping me hard across the face.

'You can't fool me, you lying little fucker, I know it's here somewhere.'

Then with both arms he held me above his head shaking me like a rag doll repeatedly, determined to make me tell the truth.

'Where is it?'

'Aaah! I don't know. I swear I have nothing!'

Holding me aloft by only one arm now, with the other he grabbed my hair, pulling my head back skywards. I was certain he was going to dash me against the broken stones that lay in the coal pit. Then like some animal caught in a trap, he let out a low guttural howl. It echoed up and down the street and in that instant our eyes met and we shared the same fear - what if the Germans heard and came for us.

He stopped, reason taking hold as instantly as his madness had and now, he put me down slowly and turned aside, no longer able to meet my gaze.

'I thought God had answered my prayers but no. You're as doomed as I am.' Slowly he collapsed to the ground. I couldn't be sure, but was he … yes, he was weeping? I backed away because this scared me the most, for years this taciturn man had been like granite but now he was crumbling before my eyes.

'Alright then, damn you.' He struggled to his feet and went to his burlap sack, tearing it open, his back turned to me. Breathing heavily, his shoulders slumped, he appeared frail, beaten. When he turned to look at me again, I saw a very old man, far more than his fifty years.

Perhaps it was Piotr's Catholic faith that got the better of him. Was he ashamed that the war had reduced him to this, a grown man roughing up a twelve-year-old boy? Still the anger, desperation, or hunger, whatever had possessed him before still lay beneath the surface. Though the madness was gone I felt he was still capable of anything, as he rough-handled me over to what remained of a staircase.

'Sit down, keep still. This might save you, you little shit,' he said brandishing a pair of scissors. And so, I sat, too frightened to move, in the cramped mouth of the coal pit that opened to the street, Piotr standing behind me. The pit was all that was left of the hovel we were once crammed into, after we were rounded up. The coal all stolen and now so too were all the people.

'You damned kids... always running through my gardens.' Snip, snip.

He said that as if our childhood games, among his vegetable trestles, was the cause of all his miseries; not the tanks or the guns or the useless Polish Army. The gardens lay overgrown and neglected and my family home, on the other side of the city, far from the ghetto, was now in the hands of Germans who had no further use for a gardener.

Worse still the Germans were coming for everyone, rounding them up in their thousands. No longer just the Jews but Poles of all kinds, for if you were not essential to our enemy then your days were numbered. Some said to help fight their enemies, slaving in military factories; others said just to be killed. I didn't know, all I heard were snatches of conversation that came drifting down to the sewer vents where I listened.

'Aaah!,' he drew blood as he butchered my hair. 'Stay still, you long streak of shit or you'll lose the whole fucking ear.'

Snip, snip. Yes, I am a long streak of shit, tall for a twelve-year-old and unnaturally lean. I look older than my age. My sister sometimes called me 'Fasolka Szparagowa - String bean.'

A little over a year ago the ghetto had been flattened and since then I've hidden for over four hundred days, roaming the streets in the dead of night in search of food, evading the patrols, and stealing clothes from washing lines. Piotr stumbled across me weeks ago and offered to help. But clearly the gardener had other ideas.

We met at the coal pit the times he came before, when he brought me food and sometimes medicine.

One last snip and my long unkempt hair was now a a girl's bob, the kind my older sister would have loved, if it had not been done so brutally, so carelessly. He pulled from the bag a washed-out blue dress, a faded pink pinafore, and a pair of buckle shoes. I undressed, stuffing my trousers, shirt, and boots into my rucksack.

'Why am I dressing as a girl?'

He shrugged but offered no explanation and in truth his manner was still too aggressive for me to challenge him. He had a daughter, so maybe these were the only clothes he could get me. I went with what was offered.

Piotr had been our family gardener and handy-man for all of my life. When he brought his complaints to our parents about the children damaging his flower beds, my father simply smiled and said, 'I will talk to them.' But he never did.

In the days when we were wealthy and respected, I heard my father offer to pay for his dying wife's hospital bills. But that was all gone, now it felt like some story I had written in my head. A tale so long ago and so far from my struggles, that the memories and longings merged even as the life I once led dissolved into darkness and smoke. I've tried to hold on with all my might to what was real from those days- all my family's faces, in the years before the war. Now time was stealing them away from me day by hundreds of days.

He watched me change and though I'd turned my back to him, I could feel his eyes burning into me. Envy, resentment, terror all there, in his intense stare. I'd seen those same expressions on so many different faces in the ghetto before they were taken away.

New clothes, girl's clothes true but new. I put them on willingly, glad to have something clean that didn't dig into me with its brittle creases, that didn't smell of gutter and death, something no longer stiff with dirt but soft and giving, smelling of laundry soap and sunshine. Still, they couldn't disguise the odor of my soiled underwear. He smirked as I turned to face him.

'Thank your Maker you weren't born with a big nose and dark curly hair, eh Jew boy.'

It's true, my hair was blonde and straight and my nose was small.

'Yes, I look like my grandfather, he was German.'

His face turned grey- black with rage and disgust, spitting a wad of nicotine phlegm that didn't quite clear his mouth.

'I don't know who I hate more, the Germans or your type!'

There it was again. I felt at once the resentment my older sister had felt. Yes, I am a Jew, though I'd never thought of myself as that until the war came. We did not practise a faith of any kind, in fact it was a matter of pride that we were atheists. We considered ourselves Poles … Poles with some German ancestry. But now the invaders made it an undeniable fact - we were Jews.

We stood, the broken man and I, for an awkward half minute in silence deciding together and independently if family business was finally through or not. He rolled a cigarette from the scrapings in his pouch, lit it, turning to go, with a grunt of dismissal, Piotr climbed out of the coal pit, full of broken stone and smashed floorboards, wheezing. For an instant I caught the whiff of his rolling tobacco and was back in his garden shed hiding from my sister and brother, the aroma lingering among his tools and pots.

Looking down from the rim he said, 'I've done all I'm going to do for you. You're on your own now, *shiksa*. It's too fuckin' dangerous. Besides there's no more food.' He threw that news behind him as he went. Shiksa was his idea of a joke.

'None of us will survive this, I know it in my bones. You were my last hope. Goodbye, you little bastard.' As he went, he muttered to himself; 'All those years I worked for them and I never knew they were Jews.' He spat again.

And that was the final time I ever saw him. I guess, he decided, having dressed me as a girl that he'd fulfilled any obligation he had to my family. With him went the very last of my previous life. It made me ache; I wanted to call him back - for as disagreeable as he was, he was a part, the last living part, the very last human from the world that was once mine.

My name is Bronek, Bron for short, that is all, no last name, my family, and its' name is stolen, destroyed and I may never get them back. So, I will not use my last name. I have a first name and my wits; that will have to do. Still he was right, I was on my own, just me and the rumbling sound of hundreds of rats moving from sewer to drain, street to street, one step ahead of the soldiers, the fire and the smoke, their feet rattling the cavities underground, their squeals ringing through the cavernous drains and broken pipes and up through the vents.

The street would soon be moonlit but was deserted for now. In the distance came the sound of soldiers scrambling over rubble. Climbing back into a nearby grate, through a broken fissure in the pavement, I followed the familiar echoes of the sewers, in the darkness. Strange how you adapt to the most foreign of worlds until they become normal to you; my ghostly sister, the apparition beside me in step with each move I made. Turn left, then seventeen steps, turn left again and continue till the rotting carcass; the body I was glad wasn't human. Step over and then right three times and with my hands I could feel the opening in the wall that had been my temporary home. Inside on a ledge sat my final two matches and the last of the prayer candles, stolen from the Catholic cathedral, days ago, though maybe it was months ago. All my time seemed to merge into one. Matches, candle stubs, Piotr – everything told me it was time to go.

In the dark, we all talk to someone. I talked to my friends from Dunaj Street, to my mother, even to God, in those moments when I tried to have faith, often against my better judgement, for he has given me few reasons to believe recently. And in that pitch blackness I also had conversations imagining my family was with me. I talked to my father, apologising to my parents for the willful things I'd done, asking their forgiveness though I have no idea where they've gone. I talked to my siblings though I know I'm just talking to the darkness, still I talk endlessly, in imaginary conversations with my missing brother Ryszkard, who never replies and to my dead sister who always does.

'Where will I go?'

You follow your nose. One way is as good as the next...or as bad, little brother.

It's true, death and luck walk hand in hand now and take their turns with my life. I pulled a bundle from my satchel, though in the darkness I could see nothing. In my mind I could bring the shapes forth and let my hands do the seeing - my boys clothes, hard and cold and smelling of urine, the clothes that once were new and clean and part of the world of all the senses. I stroked the dress I was wearing.

'What am I supposed to do with these girl's clothes Jana?'

You make a pretty girl; someone will take you in. You look like a goy, she said.

The darknesses subsided now, shifting and forming into solids. And there she stood in the shadows, her slender tall form, her bright sing-song voice. 'A goy,' even my sister now was speaking to me in Yiddish. This was the strangest turn of all, my dead sister who hated all things that reminded her of Jews.

How do I explain my sister … I cannot. Is it loneliness? Or madness? But she is here, the only remnant left of my prior life, oh not in physical form beyond an image in the darkness and a voice in my head. I am smart enough to question her presence, after all I'm not insane, there have been plenty of *them* shot by the Germans. But I'm also clever enough to know it will not help me if I become more logical and she disappears. So, I avoid my rational self, the one that I got from my father, the one that questions God. I know this can't be real but then fantasy is all that is left to me. Let talking ghosts talk, who am I to argue?

And I have always been smart; I was the smartest kid in my class. Clever enough to know that we should have left for America years ago, when the lunatic began to spit his poison. In the inky black I see my Uncle Wilfred back then, wailing at my father, hysterical and urgent, just before he fled. The fear filling our kitchen. I watched it take hold of my older brother and sister. I saw it turn my mother, my uncle's younger sister, into a pale mumbler. It terrified me. It is six years ago now but here in the darkness it is vivid. Back then I was yet to turn seven and only half understood what was happening but this was a year before Poland was lost.

'There is another pogrom coming, Harry. This Hitler will swallow us all,' he said to my ever-optimistic father. 'And this will be the one to end them all.'

Jana caught my eye and her expression told me she thought my father was a fool, that Uncle Wilf, as we called him, was right. And if Jana was sure then so was I. But my father who called himself Harry as my grandfather wanted, instead of the Herzl my grandmother had given him, would have none of it. We were safe, we were respected, we were honoured and successful, after all he was a professional, an engineer he argued. We had not been practising for two generations. We were Polish more than Jewish.

We were doomed.

* * *

The trucks rumbled overhead an hour ago, the Germans having intensified their roundups. Not long after that came woodsmoke and explosions; the air filled with brick dust that rolled through the sewers. It stung my eyes and coated my throat as I coughed up thick red-brown phlegm. The patrols were still moving on the streets above, as they have done for so many months: searching for the last of us subterraneans - relentless, unforgiving.

Back when the Ghetto still stood, they told us we would go to places where we could work and would be fed, but I refused to believe them. Some went willingly but then slowly terrible stories found their way back to us. Some denied that such things were possible and others knew it to be true in their bones. Finally, those still in the ghetto would take no more. People fought back, briefly reclaiming their freedom. By then my family was long gone but I watched the ebb and flow of the resistance through the grates of the city's sewers. I saw the broken half buildings, their doorways filled with rubble, every window shattered. And there, on the rooftops, people defiantly holding their position. Young men and women knowing they were outnumbered and that their hours were running out. No-one came to help us in the ghetto.

   In the summer this year it was the turn of the common people of the city- a second uprising in the streets of Warsaw, again I watched and again no-one came to save us. For days hundreds of German boots moved in every direction, as tank tracks rolled by, centimetres from my face, as I watched from below ground peering up from the drains. I heard the shouts of defiance and the curses in German but I could not see all the battle unfolding. It was like watching the world through a letter box.

   Off Miodowa Street I came to a grate that offered a wide view of the Market Square. At last, I could see what was going on. It was like watching a film but very real. Shots came from the opposite buildings; they hit the cobbled street and ricocheted. The young German infantrymen crouched behind what remained of a wall, pinned down in crossfire. I was mesmerised for hours. Finally, the soldiers stormed a building that held many armed Poles. You could see the progress of the Germans as flashes of gunfire appeared through the broken windows and walls. One floor at a time they moved up toward the roof. When the battle stalled on the final floor, three figures climbed out through a small attic window and stood on the slanting roof - a boy probably not much older than me, and two young women, one my sister's age and the other perhaps a little older but not much. The blonde woman, the younger of the two held a handgun, the darker one a machine gun. As useless as it was, the boy held what looked like a butcher's meat cleaver defiantly waving it over his head. Around their waists all three had belts from which objects hung, including bottles with rags stuffed into the necks. The boy picked up a pole that someone unseen had slid through the open window. Tied to the end was a red flag. He began to wave it above his head. For a moment they looked behind as soldiers scrambled through the windows on either side. Looking at each other, as one they took something dark and round from their belts and dropped them. Seconds later the roof exploded and was gone as four German soldiers cascaded over the edge and dropped five storeys. Gone too were the three young rebels. Masonry rained across the square and the red flag drifted down and landed just before my grate. I reached out and touched it. It wasn't a flag, it was a pillow case soaked in blood.

Every day was like this; more soldiers poured in and closed off the city and out of every street and building came Poles determined to defy them.

I could not tell which way the war was turning; all I knew was my subterranean world was filling up with frightened men and women seeking refuge. I could help none of them. Once more the Germans came searching underground. I have been the master of the canals and drains, a crisscross of tunnels and pipes that I learnt to move through swiftly. This was my domain, I ruled here but I would not let myself be slowed down by others. Instead, I pulled back into the shadows and watched them. Adults couldn't fit into the spaces I could and they weren't nearly as fast. Soon, most of them were caught or died in explosions. I'm not small for a twelve-year-old, instead I am long and agile. I managed to squeeze through holes and bend round corners like a contortionist. I am Houdini escaping from chains in a water filled tank. For months, more than a year, they've been looking and still not caught me. But I am running out of chances, for now there are more soldiers than there have ever been. And so, it's time to go and this time I must truly disappear.

You better hurry, it's getting dark. Don't forget the horse.

I nodded. Jana was right. And no, I didn't forget the horse. I clutched it tightly, my pewter keepsake that fitted into my palm - a cast figure of a cavalry soldier mounted on a thoroughbred, Sabre in hand, defying our enemies as our army had done in the autumn of Nineteen Thirty-Nine.

Moving along the last of the sewer pipes that hadn't collapsed, I squeezed through gaps that even I thought were impossible. Sometimes I had to labour for an hour, removing masonry and timber before moving on but sometimes it only took minutes. I pushed my head up into the open air, some distance from the coal pit, in the ghetto. My old home where Jana and I grew up, where Piotr had tended our gardens, was several kilometres to the east of the city.

High on the hill stood the burnt-out shell of the Royal Castle, telling us all, this is what happens when you stand up to the occupiers. The moon would not rise for another hour or more. It was one of the things you learnt when you lived in the shadows; you knew the fading of daylight and the coming of night, you knew how long it would last, you knew the phases of the moon like a calendar inside your head. Even underground you became aware of the lunar cycle, of twilight and of sunrise. You could feel them all in your body, like some instinct, like something a nocturnal animal would know, even in the pitch black.

This was Zelazna Street, in the dark with its doorways shuttered and many boarded up, still I knew it. The old brownstones, the tram tracks and over there had been the ice-cream vendor I would tease when he did not give me enough of a scoop. Was he dead, did he join our valiant sad army that rode out on horseback to meet the German tanks? Probably, ice cream scooper in hand, riding headlong into the might of the German war machine.

The first one or two drops of rain hit my face and ran down my cheeks, mixing dirt and sweat that ran into my mouth. Only the occasional building was lit and then only one window or a doorway. Here was another thing the Germans stole – the light from the bright dancing, laughing city. Now the city hid in darkness trying not to be noticed.

Ah but it was good to walk upright again, for so long and so far, street after darkened street; the pleasure of having a straight spine making me almost joyous. Upright I walked boldly, looking pretty in blue and pink, hoping that I really did make a convincing girl. Behind me the Germans brought down the walls of the Old Town as the last obstinate shards of red brick apartments that refused to yield, stood against the fire flare, like old rotten teeth.

In the final moments of twilight, a patrol appeared up ahead. Large, maybe fifty soldiers but they hadn't noticed me, being too busy climbing over the rubble of collapsed houses. I pulled back into the shadows and for the thousandth time, disappeared into the sewers, watching them pass by, through the grate. I waited ten minutes then came up to the surface. The sewer rat had done it again, given the Germans the slip. I turned a corner,

'Where are you going girl?'

Too late to hide. Luck and Death like I said. Glaring before me stood a young corporal, a boy really but still the oldest in this small group of soldiers. Cocky and belligerent, trying hard to be the kind of soldier he thought himself to be. You could tell by his swagger, he was determined to prove he was worthy of commanding these other boys. I knew the type, bullies, from the playground. He spat at me; it was clear I shouldn't be here.

Call his bluff.

I never changed pace only direction. He swallowed hard and I saw the pain flash across his face. He had ulcers in his mouth, I recognised this, I knew it well. Striding up to him I opened my knapsack and handed him my last lemon.

'Heil Hitler!'

'Heil Hitler!' he replied.

Before he could question me, I turned on my heels and headed toward the river. From behind, I heard the rustle of his rifle being raised and the click of the bolt engaging. Would he believe I am German? Or demand that I stopped and ask me for papers? Twenty meters to the corner. The rain was falling a little harder now as the street ahead glistened in the semi-darkness.

Would he shoot me in the back, like they did with Jana when she defied them?

Fifteen meters.

What was the punishment for accidentally killing a German child?

I did not look back; he did not call out. Only silence.

Ten metres. Five. Two. He never said a word. I rounded the corner.

The narrow alley ran down to the river's edge, I followed it as a light rain fell but it was gone within the time I had walked it. A summer shower as fleeting as Warsaw's liberty. The promised storm never materialised, it had moved somewhere to the north, leaving an open sky full of stars. All that remained was the steady run of rainwater pouring from pipes into the river. The moon was waning now and somewhere in the distance behind came intermittent gunfire. In a warehouse, stretching along a pier I came across a room full of rope, with large coils, each turn as thick as my arm, sitting in curling rows rising from the floor to waist high.

Climbing inside the one furthest from the door, I pulled a heavy tarp over me. I needed to rest, to catch up on lost sleep, to try to lose the exhaustion that ached in every muscle. I settled into the centre of the wall of rope, trying not to raise too much dust. The sound of chugging engines and the distant hoot of cargo barges merged with the gentle lap of water, somewhere below the floorboards. Quiet, no vermin; this was good compared to the sewers. Far too many nights I woke from sleep with rats gnawing at my feet or small almost invisible parasites nibbling at my flesh. Even the floorboards here seemed soft in comparison.

It was the high point of summer and the night air was so still and warm that it stewed the rope I slept in. The air was thick and stifling; the smell of Tung oil and brine reached into my lungs stealing away my breath. I woke gasping, flinging myself out of the coils and onto the hard timber floor, panting in a lather of sweat.

Get up, you can't lie out here in the open.

By three in the morning, I was on the move again, down along a pier where the trawlers and cargo ships bobbed gently, bumping up against the buttresses. Before daylight, I scaled the side of a river barge and hid in the hold. Finding my way to an open crate big enough for two or three grown men, I struggled over the lip and fell into a bed of hard brown potatoes, smelling of freshly turned earth. For more than half an hour I shifted them high up to one side and then nestled into a corner and stretched out, only to have the hill give way and dozens of potatoes roll down, lightly pummeling me but covering my body. I might stay undetected if luck held and no-one really looked hard. I stretched out as much as possible, with my hand in the pocket of my pinafore, clutching tightly to my horse.

'Still got it,' I whispered. *Good,* she replied.

Sleep took me again, a sleep as deep as it is possible to know, no dreams, no nightmares, just exhaustion. I rose out of the darkness and into the morning air. The light and the motion woke me. Above the scattered, scudding clouds coated pink with dawn-light, I gently swayed as if in a hammock. The crate hung suspended from a derrick high above the hold and was lowered onto a lorry, the load settling onto the tray as the potatoes fell to either side.

A broad unshaven man, a crucifix around his neck, a large knife hanging in a sheath across his shoulder, peered over the edge. Reaching down, he clutched me by the collar and held me aloft.

'Zegota!'

'Zegota,' I replied.

19   Dancing With The Midnight Mare   Luca Collins

LAST HOUSE 21ST CENTURY

2

Tara sat by the back door looking out through the window; it was 'toasty' warm up above the backyard. This was her favourite place in the old house. 'Madame' she called it and to her the old wooden house, surrounded by bushland, was a grand lady. A stately woman of undisclosed age but certainly no girl. The attic and its single window Tara imagined as a milliner's crowning invention. Then came her window eyes on the first floor, one of them being Tara's bedroom. From her window ran a veranda roof that ran out toward the yard, almost touching the spreading fig tree. A pitched roof but with enough room to sit outside the window unseen by adults. And finally, her widening girth at ground level with her huge bay windows, open verandahs, and wide wooden steps.

On the back porch, a flock of sulphur-crested cockatoos landed and were now tearing wooden strips from the handrails. 'If you see them, chase them away,' her mother said, but Tara couldn't take her eyes off them; their pillaging fascinated her. Were they sharpening their beaks? Did they enjoy being destructive? It wasn't like they ate the stuff. She wondered, if it hurt the old house to be feasted on like this? Perhaps she *should* shoo them away but *no*, her mother had asked and that was reason enough to ignore the request.

At this moment the house was hers and echoed with a pleasing soft murmur of distant sounds - no-one to give orders or demand her time, no shouting or tears, no parents. In the yard below, her brother was kicking a ball and conducting an ongoing commentary, in which he was simultaneously the announcer who was full of praise for himself, Cory Winslow, the player of the match. Ten-year-old boys lost in their own hero worship. She smiled at her foolish brother.

The sunset moved across the yard quickly, casting her brother into a late afternoon of dappled light and shadow. It would be another hour before her parents came home and brought with them their cold war. She watched the first of the flying foxes arc across the sky bound for the large expanse of fig trees just beyond the suburbs. 'Madame' was the last house in the street; beyond that was bush and beyond that, a half a kilometre away, was the quarry. A place where she was forbidden to venture; a place of towering cliff faces and flooded excavations. The place where she and her brother had been secretly going, since they were old enough to play on their own. Together they had turned the quarry into their landscape of imagination. The surrounding bush too was full of secret fortresses, battlegrounds, a great expanse of legends and reverence. Pock-marked across the hills and the creek were the wooden fortress and the sentry posts they had built over years, from fallen trees, nails and rope and all manner of found objects and discarded timber. A landscape of battles for a warrior queen and her companion, the boy who faithfully followed his older sister. Places that belonged to them alone.

"We will call this land and the fortress castle that guards it - Trelleborg,' she said with great pageantry and Cory nodded, thinking what a great word it was, yet not asking where it came from or what it meant.

Tara loved the quarry and the bush but it was the house that meant the most, the white pebble driveway that when you 'swivel walked' on it made a sound like maracas, the back stairs that when you double-stepped on each stair sounded like a snare and boomed under the verandah, like a bass drum. How when you opened the front door in spring and summer, and the back door was open, the whole house filled with eucalyptus and banksia scent and sometimes the smell of smoke from burn-offs. And after 'Madame' had been closed up for a winter's day, she would smell of old timber and rugs, leather bound books, and papers from Tara's father's library and woodsmoke from the hearth. She continually creaked and moaned on her foundations, as some of the rooms settled into a perceptible slant. 'Madame' was much more than just a house; She talked, but only to Tara. And Tara listened.

'Madame' was now full of anger and regret, emotions that Tara's warring parents had brought to it. They filled 'Madame's spaces with their accusations and hurt. Tara felt her special sanctuary had been poisoned. Now there were scars on the inside and today, on the outside. She watched the cockatoos for a few minutes more.

Why couldn't they be in the same room together? Why did they care for us but couldn't care for each other? Why are there no answers?

The first of two cars pulled into the driveway as she looked down from her eyrie.

'Crap, what are they doing here?'

Her stomach clenched into an angry knot. *How dare they come home early, stealing away my sunlit hour.* Madame shuddered and shifted in the wind that had come up.

*   *   *

Tara looked up from her plate and watched the dinner time dynamics. Her mother and father barely passed a word to each other, asking Cory and her to fill in the silence with what they had done that day at school. The meal turned out just as Tara expected - taut, unbending, falsely polite, all for the sake of Cory and her. *'Why bother sitting together at all if you aren't going to get on?'* Tara thought.

'I'm going to the den,' her father Ray announced.

'I'm going to the den,' repeated Cory, in an almost perfect impersonation of their father's 'Liverpool' accent. Tara smiled for the first time during dinner. She watched her mother, almost give in to Cory's larrikin humour but pull back, keeping her reserve. Kate smiled at her son but gave no reaction to her husband.

Ray ruffled his cheeky son's hair, then looked at his wife for a moment, her smile fading. She refused to return his gaze, so he disappeared into the den, tired and beaten. This sad little pantomime made Tara's heart ache.

For a few moments Tara stood at the door studying her father, as he watched the soccer replays, goal after goal. This used to be a time she loved, when they sat together father and daughter, sometimes all of them, Cory, and Mum too, following Liverpool FC, his team. She loved this ritual.

Sometimes he would turn the sound down and tell how he met their mother on the terraces of Anfield and fell for the blonde 'Aussie' girl, with the great laugh, who knew nothing about football. Who came to see a football game *'Cause that's what tourists do in Liverpool.'*

'So how come he picks up the ball?'

"He's the goalkeeper.'

'He's allowed to, is that right?'

'Yes, but nobody else.'

At this point Cory and Tara, who both played soccer would laugh and exclaim 'Oh, Mum!'

Tara made her father tell the story constantly. More than anything this seemed the most unfair, that the stories too were gone. She turned away and headed for the kitchen.

Her mother swayed, singing softly to herself to all the maudlin songs on the radio. Tara looked from that door now. Unaware of her daughter, Kate moved in a kind of waltz of regret, lost in a world of longing and sadness. Tara watched for a while and the longer she did the more the realisation came to her, she became certain her mother was dancing slowly in the arms of the man she once loved.

How Tara hated this time of the evening - a time when the requirements of the day were met, nothing more to do; when the starkness of the situation bit hard. When everybody was pretending that nothing had to be faced, that somehow the kids wouldn't notice it if it wasn't mentioned.

'As if? I'm twelve years old. I see everything.'

* * *

Tara curled up beneath her coverlet, the wind whipping the trees outside her bedroom window. The wild weather seemed to mirror what was happening downstairs. It started again, the same as so many nights before and she found herself clutching her coverlet to her and walking to the window.

Down below the son et lumiere of recriminations had begun, as the shadow puppets danced. She watched with fascination and dread as the lounge room light threw shapes through the big bay windows and out onto the lawn. She listened, caught in a state of pain and indecision; maybe if she knew why her parents were saying the things that hurt each other, she could find why and fix it. But what they said only made a half sense to her. Tara realised she didn't know enough about the grown-up world to make it stop.

She moved from the window to her other observation post, the landing at the top of the stairs, as the accusations once again came rising.

'All you ever do is think of yourself!' It was her mother. Tara could picture her, that resolute no-nonsense way she had of holding her body and face that broached no argument. It was that same stupid *business argument* again. The quarrel he never won.

She could see her father too in her mind. Why did he never say the right words to Tara's mother? He always knew the right thing to do with her and Cory. She liked her father best, she decided, knowing that somehow it was wrong to think that. Reproaches and defenses spilt up the stairs finding receptive ears, moving from Tara's room to the next - Cory's.

'I can't believe I'm hearing this…this is bullshit. I've bent over backwards for this family,' her father's sense of injustice echoing downstairs.

Silence, nothing from her mother and then a snort of disapproval. Tara bristled at that. The restraint they had maintained at the dinner table was barely there and receding fast. Tara could almost sense their body positions, her father open and pleading and her mother with arms folded, her defiant stance and that righteous indignation, that only fueled the intensity of his demands.

Clutching the railing, Tara turned to see her brother's half open bedroom door. Cory didn't notice her but simply climbed out of his bed and turned on his computer. With his headphones on, the all too familiar nightly ritual would become muffled and indistinct. The screen came up all reds and yellows, flashing and pulsing. Figures moving left and right across the screen, that did as they were commanded, that lived and died at a single keyboard stroke - a world you could control.

*　　*　　*

For a moment, Ray thought he saw a flicker of concession from his wife, something he searched for every time they found themselves at this impasse. But then it was gone. Kate stood resolutely. Ray could see his words weren't reaching her.

'I've gotta get out, Kate'

'To do what?'

Ray opened his mouth to reply but it was an automatic response. He struggled for an answer that would satisfy her. It was useless, how to find the words for something Ray could barely grasp himself. This restlessness, why couldn't he put it into words? Women were so practical. Men it seemed to him, were steeped in some deeper desire, some impossible need that was almost beyond explanation. He struggled to mouth it but nothing but more pleading came out.

'I don't know! But I do know the longer we wait the less chance I have of selling up.'

'Good,' she said with a vindictive finality.

Ray hung his head 'No it's not fucking good, Kate. It's destroying me.'

'You have to make it work. Grow up Ray. This is my family's money we're talking about.'

'You think I've forgotten that. Jesus, you remind me all the time. Kate it isn't going to grow. The market has collapsed; it's passed. We were just a little too late.'

'The story of my fucking life,' she said. He knew she meant it as much about him as her.

For a long while there was silence in the kitchen as they cleaned up after dinner, neither of them talking nor conceding ground. Tara still on the landing, imagined them standing as they had done so many times, not facing one another, task in hand, looking anywhere except at each other, aware of the other's sideways glance. So many evenings like this, of pain and accusation, and they always found themselves at this point, fighting for too long now to reach out. 'How stupid,' she thought and turned back toward her bedroom, wondering if she should get a pair of headphones too.

*   *   *

The house was dark and silent. A wooden staircase led to the second-storey. From the landing, bedrooms on either side of a corridor. No movement. The first sliver of the promising moon faintly projected through the corridor window; a rectangle of pale light like a watermark on the carpet outside the parents' bedroom. In the wash of moon glow, the house began to sing, softly, the kind of song that might be wailed at an old-world funeral - sung by the ancient, wise women of the village. It seemed to be words from some other language - foreign, European but somehow familiar. It called out to Tara but got no reply.

Out of the darkness a single beam of light appeared, then another and another, till there were six stark torchlight beams that momentarily illuminated six men in jet black with balaclavas. Six men gathered in that upper hall. The creak of leather shoes and the crisp swish of black trousers, at first were all that intruded on the song. Then came the soft, powerful panting of dogs, keen and alert, searching, straining at their leashes. The song rose again only louder, more demanding, still the house could not raise Tara. One of the men moved down the corridor, his torchlight flicking from side to side in quick darting arcs. The others followed.

The bedroom door burst open finding Ray and Kate sitting up in bed, silent with terror, pinned to the wall in the crossfire of all six torches. The dogs snarled, their threat echoing in the dark. Kate gripped Ray's hand tightly. Both were forcibly taken from their beds and brutally dragged out into the hallway. Dogs yanked at the leads, rising up on their hind legs, determined to savage the two. The house was screeching now.

Tara woke in a cold sweat, alone, confused and screaming. Inside her head the house was still screaming with her. Once more the phantasms had come for her. Her mother arrived at the door, shushing as she came to her side.

'It's alright Bubba, it's alright.'

*   *   *

Kate busied herself with breakfasts and lunches, her de-militarised zone clearly set out, these moments alone being a gift she gave herself. The clack and clatter of bowls and cutlery matching her brusque efficiency, sent out a warning that she was not to be intruded on. She turned away as Ray entered the kitchen. He flinched and came no further. They moved cautiously around each other, like two territorial mongrels.

'Tara woke last night,' she said.

'Nightmares?' he asked.

Kate could feel he was genuinely concerned, it created a break in hostilities and for an instant she dropped her defenses. It lasted long enough to offer, 'It's five weeks now.'

'No.'

Kate's look instantly hardened, fixing him on the spot. 'If you had gotten up more than once to her, you'd know that.'

'Sorry.'

She relinquished her gaze slightly. 'I have to take her to see someone.'

Ray nodded but any further thawing of the situation was interrupted by the arrival of a larger-than-life Cory. All hunger and swagger he dived into a chair and began to fill his bowl and half the table with cereal and milk. Their adult concerns now sidetracked by a ten-year old's focus on food.

'Mum, can I have two dollars? There's a show at school.'

'Ask your father. I'm broke,' she replied, far angrier then was appropriate. She threw the accusation at Ray but it was Cory who squirmed. Kate felt guilty for that.

'Sure son, what's on?' Ray asked in a bright, measured way that made Kate feel even worse. With more food in his mouth than humanly possible, Cory chewed and replied in garbled 'corn flake' but the answer was indecipherable to them both.

'Cory, go up and wake your sister. She'll be late for school,' Kate ordered, cutting them off strategically. Cory grabbed another two mouthfuls then sprinted out and up the stairs.

Ray turned back to his belligerent wife and chose the path of least resistance, placing his bowls in the sink, he moved to her, offering warmth.

'Kate?'

She turned again to the kitchen bench and began to cleaver the cheese block. Kate could feel Ray studying her back, waiting for her to turn, to give him an opening. There would be none.

The back door slammed and his car backed out of the driveway. By the time Ray had pulled onto the street, Kate was standing on the porch, too late for any words of appeasement. Instead, they fell at her feet in the wake of the Camry's exhaust. By now Tara and Cory had arrived. Kate gripped the railing, aware that both her children were watching her - the sadness changing back to that hard place that she always found herself in.

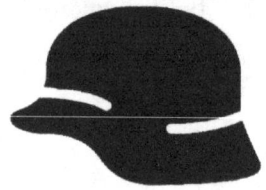

VIENNA WINTER 1934

3

It was cold and bleak on the city street, with the skies above threatening rain. The young man shivered and hugged himself, burying his frozen hands in his armpits but it was of little use. The threadbare coat offered as much warmth as this city had given him. Dresden now seemed sunnier, more hospitable, a thought he rarely had associated with his hometown before. Vienna, for all its fairytale facades, was a hard city and its romance had vanished for him some time ago. He knew he couldn't go back to face his landlord not with that much rent outstanding. He would have to sneak in after the old bastard was asleep. And so, for a young man without a pfennig to his name, the challenge was how to stay warm for the next few hours? The poster glued to the wall gave him his answer - a public meeting. God, even if they had no heating, a hall full of people would be out of the wind and the coming rain. They might offer a warm drink, perhaps a slice of bread.

An hour to kill, and so he walked the streets but only one, for when he reached either end it opened onto a wide boulevard, where the wind howled. It forced him again into the back street, a block away from the public meeting hall that sat in the centre of an exposed city square. Backwards and forwards he trod the footpath in an attempt to keep warm. Several times he stepped into a doorway only to be repelled by the smell of piss and shit.

Once he came across an alcove that was already occupied. 'Leave me in peace, I fought enough wars for you, you young bastard. Find another hole to crawl into!' spat an old man, his medals pinned to his grubby coat. His hands flailing up at the intruder, his leg stumps strapped to a makeshift trolley, made of an old crate and pram wheels. The young man recoiled and stumbled back into the street.

With fifteen minutes to go, he could stand the cold no longer and made his way to the foyer. The crowd was well-dressed and middle-class, men in large overcoats and scarves and women in furs and wraps. Some of the older men were holding forth on the evening's discourse.

The young man had never heard of the subject, 'The World Ice Theory' but clearly the assembled crowd had.

At exactly six o'clock the doors opened and the crowd filed in and took seats. The room had been heated for some time before their arrival and the crowd began to stand and one by one, take off their coats and fold them over their chairs. He decided to keep his coat on, for the shirt beneath was dirty and stained. At the back of the stage, on the left, stood the flag of Austria and on the opposite side the black, white, and red flag of the National Socialist Workers Party. Equal distances apart along the side walls of the hall, dressed in brown uniforms, legs astride, arms behind their backs, were young men all staring straight ahead.

A burly middle-aged man dressed in the same uniform but with more insignia, lanyards and medals, and a much wider belly than the sentries, stepped to the middle of the stage. He thanked them for coming on such a bitter evening and began to rattle off the credentials of the night's speaker. Published works, University in Salzburg, respected man of letters. Droning on for several minutes, it all made little impression on the youth as he used the time to search the crowd for unaccompanied beauties. None. The hall was as barren as his experience with the bars and the women of this lonely city.

The older Brown shirt finished and left the stage. A man in his sixties ambled on carrying himself like a university professor, white haired, pince-nez glasses, notes under one arm. He walked up to the lectern and gave an old-fashioned acknowledgment by clicking his heels together and slightly nodding his head to the audience. Still the disciplined men on either side of the hall looked forward, giving no recognition to the audience or the speaker. He cleared his throat and the general murmur fell to silence.

'This is not a Jewish theory, like Relativity. It is an Aryan fact. It does not adhere to the ideas of Freemasons like Newton or the decrepit statements of Einstein. This is visionary and belongs to the new world of truth and ideas.'

Some in the crowd clapped but not everyone. Throughout the crowd there were pockets of agitation, grumblings of discontent. The speaker took a long cane pointer and walked over to a screen. The lights went down and a slide appeared of "The Milky Way" followed quickly by an artist's impression of a cataclysmic collision between two heavenly bodies. In the darkness some in the audience gave an audible gasp, while others laughed out loud.

'The Solar System had its origin in this,' he said as he pointed with the cane.

'Rubbish' came from somewhere at the back of the room, much of the audience turning to see who had dared to disagree. The brownshirts came to life, moving now, searching for the voice in the darkness. The Professor continued, 'The collision of this smaller, dead, waterlogged star…'

'PROVE IT!,' came a voice from somewhere down the front as the men now changed direction and moved towards the lectern.

'...into this gigantic ice star.' From another row a voice cried out 'LIES!' And the militia changed direction again, as the audience began to enjoy the comedy unfolding around them.

'The impact was extraordinary, the huge explosion flinging pieces of the smaller...'

'YOU'RE AN IDIOT!' The comedy of the pursuers changing direction again, meant many in the crowd were laughing loudly now. The Professor chose to continue regardless, he raised his voice. 'STAR INTO INTERSTELLAR SPACE.'

Now the lights came up and the laughing stopped as the brownshirts glared into the audience, searching for some indication. Everyone sat as contrite as possible whilst some looked down, having difficulty suppressing their laughter. Finally, an old man, one of those who had been holding court outside, stood up and pointed to the man to the left of him. The brownshirts barreled through the first four rows, upturning chairs and pushing men and women aside, grabbed the man by the hair and dragged him up the aisle. Five soldiers set upon him, punching and kicking, but before they had travelled more than a few metres, his fellow hecklers burst from their seats and clubbed the brownshirts. The remaining soldiers ran from either side to the centre aisle, as other men and women joined from the audience. Someone shouted 'COMRADES!' and still more bodies entered the fray, from beneath their coats more clubs appeared and someone was brandishing a knife. A woman stood and screamed.

From the dais, the Professor kept up his explanation. 'THERE THE WATER CONDENSED, FREEZING INTO GIANT BLOCKS OF ICE.' But it was of no use, for now the hall was in uproar, the Professor trying valiantly but failing to be heard as the brownshirts hustled the first heckler toward the front entrance.

The young man stood up and began to walk out; he had seen enough. When he reached the foyer, he halted for out on the street the hecklers had been joined by still more of their compatriots and now they were forcing the brownshirts up the stairs, back into the hall. The comrades had gained the upper hand and won the first heckler back from the hands of their enemies. The brownshirts retreating, fell back through the front doors into the foyer, tumbling over each other. He ran to the glass doors and picking up a fallen truncheon rammed it into the steel handles and held the doors closed. Others quickly aided him, as those locked out railed abuse at those inside. Sirens sounded in the distance as both sides snarled at each other through the plate glass doors. Spotlights swept the square, shots rang out. As one the outsiders turned and ran. The police had arrived.

The portly sergeant at arms walked up to the man still bracing the door and slapped him on the back.

'What's your name son?'

'Horst. Horst Mueller.'

REFUGE   SUMMER 1944

4

The sailors from the barge hid me all day in a warehouse and after dark I was taken to the house of the man with the bowie knife who had pulled me from the potatoes. He stood in the doorway with me beside him and gestured as if to say look what I have found, another stray. His withered wife eyed me up and down. Silent, taciturn, the woman turned on her heel and the man pushed me forward, gesturing that I should follow.

The man's name was Tobiasz and hers Agneta. They were devout Catholics – members of Zegota, the Christian resistance, devoted enough to follow their God, to defy the Germans and among other things sometimes hide and save Jews. They did not openly do battle but worked quietly and defiantly. Whispers of them had come my family's way since the beginning of the Occupation. My sister and I talked about them often, as if they were part of a great adventure, like something we saw in the serials, at the cinema. This version was practical, far less romantic; I could not imagine Agneta swinging a sword or firing a gun against our enemies.

The tiny cottage was all on one level. At the end of the hall, she showed me to the spare room beside the kitchen.

"My mother has been dead seven weeks now,' she said matter-of-factly, looking around the room. And then she was silent again. Much of the old lady's clothes and her bible, even her smell still lived in the room. The scent of candle wax and lavender hung in the air while the old lady's urine wafted from her wardrobe. The room was cold. Despite it not being the sewers; its starkness reminded me of all I had lost. The dark oak furnishings offered no comfort at all and made me long for the warmth of my home. The bare boards were scrubbed pale and clean, no throw rugs, a single bed with a hard, straw mattress, sheets that scratched and a grey military blanket, like the ones we used to keep the geldings and stallion warm, when we stayed at our 'summer farm' in better days. There were no pictures on the walls. Nothing to distract her from her penance. I could picture this old lady and her daily prayers, as she prepared to go to her God. The room **was her**, a wooden version of her piety, bare and unforgiving. Worst of all, hanging above the bed was a large crucifix, with an agonised Christ nailed to it. I could not bear it. It terrified Jana too, she told me.

These Christians, why do they believe in pain, it's awful?'

The woman screwed up her nose and said 'But you will have a bath before you sleep in this room. You stink.' She handed me a towel and a nightgown and waited for me to undress. I meekly stood in the corner with the towel held against my crotch. The woman took me by the hand and pulled me to the bathroom and pointed to their solid iron bathtub and shook her head, then closed the door behind me. It was clear I was not to use it.

Instead, the man brought in an iron tub and placed it next to the family bath. They came in turn, the woman bringing cold water, soap and a scrubbing brush and the man bringing buckets of hot water from the stove. This took about ten minutes and in that time, they did not speak to me. The man had taken on the graveness of his wife. When at last they finished, I closed and bolted the solid oak door. As I lowered myself into the tub, I could hear them talking. They had no children and the arrival of a twelve-year-old girl would soon attract attention, it wouldn't be long before the authorities heard of me and came, she said as if lecturing the man. He simply harumphed in agreement. The Germans hated the Poles almost as much as they hated us, if they found me, they would shoot us all.

After the bath, I entered the bedroom determined not to look at the crucifix but to get into my bed and blow out the candle without making eye-contact. What was it the Christians called it, the Holy Spirit? I couldn't be sure this spirit wasn't an evil one. I had to escape its clutches and get under the covers. Only then I knew I would have a good night's sleep. As I lay in bed, I could hear them in the next room still discussing the situation.

* * *

* 'Skurwysyn,' she swore, the following morning. Then crossed herself for her sin, standing at the door with a fresh towel and looking at me as I stepped from the iron tub, for a second time. I had forgotten to bolt the door. The first bath was not enough to get rid of months in the sewers and she had boiled water for me again. But it was not my smell that made her curse. 'But you are a boy, you little liar.'

* Literal translation – 'Son of a Whore' but often said when one is tricked or surprised so also 'What the?'

I had not been quick enough to cover myself. Staring at where my hands clasped my manhood, she exclaimed 'But not circumcised. I thought you Jews … 'then she stopped and held her tongue, thinking it was better not to have this conversation. She turned away and seemed to be thinking now of what this new situation meant.

'It is probably best you remain a girl,' she added, handing me the towel.

'You cannot stay here much longer. We have someone coming to take you to the forest.'

I smiled a thank you at her. She grimaced. Her look said that now things had become even more complicated, more threatening.

I sat on the bed for most of the morning, reading the only book in the room- the old woman's bible. None of it made much sense to me. It was a series of battles and betrayals and wanderings through the desert but there were few heroes. I came across a boy who killed a giant and another who could interpret dreams but most of it seemed to be about a very angry god who punished these people. It was nothing like the folk tales I had grown up on.

They brought me some bread and a little dried meat in the middle of the day. The woman said nothing and left. Outside the door I heard another voice, a man's voice but not her husband. For a while they talked in a low murmur and then his voice exploded.

'Agneta, you cannot ask me this. I will not do it. No... no, not a girl.'

'Oh, she's more than a girl, let me tell you that. You'll find out soon enough.'

Then the two went quiet for a while and so I crept to the door and opened it just a fraction. I could hear him mumbling to himself, repeatedly he said no.

'This is not time for your grief; it has been long enough. The world has moved on and so must you.' She said that in a way that meant she had spoken the final word. He mumbled a few more words that were too muffled to make out and then repeated, 'But a girl.'

*   *   *

In the mid-afternoon, the door to my room opened and the woman entered. Behind her was a giant of a man, stooping at the lintel. Clothed in a large leather jacket covered in reworked leather patches, he wore a fawn denim shirt and moleskins that met huge working boots, buckled at the knee. He was as tall as he was broad, with an expansive belly. A full frontier beard grew wildly in all directions and a smile cracked his face with a gap-toothed grin. Bent over in the doorway, he looked out of place inside the bedroom. He looked like he didn't feel comfortable indoors at all.

'This is my husband's brother. He will take you out into the country. They have work for you. There are fewer patrols out there,' she said as she looked down at my crotch to see if it revealed much beneath the pinafore. Satisfied she stepped aside as the large man entered.

'I am Michal,' he said tapping his broad hunting cap, as if I was the lady of the house. He took my hand and led me out. I looked behind at Agneta but her face gave away nothing, I couldn't tell whether she had told the giant man I was masquerading as a girl. But from his behaviour it seemed like she hadn't.

He picked me up as if I was an infant and placed me on the seat and then climbed up onto the wagon. Smiling at me he said 'We have a long way to travel, girl.'

For the next half hour, he looked straight ahead and I studied his huge frame. Every so often he would talk to one or the other of the horses but always in the same way he had spoken to me- softly and reassuringly. The horses seemed to understand and would whinny back at him. We passed through several roadblocks and the further we moved away from the city's centre the less time they took looking at his papers. Agneta gave me her mother's papers, having scratched away some of the dates and then discoloured the paper with old tea leaves. The papers were folded in such a way that the creases fell across some of the dates so they became unreadable. She obviously had done this kind of thing before. In the city, such a ruse would never pass but out here the soldiers were less diligent. They barely looked at mine.

The town gave way to the countryside as our horses and dray pulled through the afternoon. We followed the course of the Vistula towards where it met the Bug, the two mighty rivers that pushed through the centre of Poland. The steady gurgle and tumble of the river calmed me, as the two 'old nag' horses mellowed into a contemplative amble. The danger felt as though it was left behind somewhere in the hard stone masonry and the steel stanchions that held Warsaw in their grip. And yet, no matter the steady, slow pace of our party at no time did Michal look at the river; he kept his

head lowered and his eyes always deflected. It was as if he feared seeing something there, in the water. It was a puzzle but I felt that keeping silent and not drawing attention to myself seemed the right approach and so I knew not to ask.

Out here the tall pines closed around us bringing darkness, so much quicker than in the city. Their branches carved the light into long parallel beams that looked solid above but disappeared into dust motes before they touched the ground. I took out my pewter cavalry horse and rider and let the rays of light catch and glance back at the dark trunks of the ancient forest, looking like fireflies darting about in the semi-dark. The horse was the only thing I kept from my family's house. I have lost everything I once loved but I will not lose this. Michal watched me, with a somewhat knowing look as I played with what was clearly a boy's toy. Did he suspect?

Off in the distance, wolves called out and replied to each other in the gathering dark. This broke the mood, unsettling me and the two tired old draught horses, who pulled our dray. Each howl from the woods brought a response from one horse that the other would then snort at in reply. I imagined them having an old husband and wife conversation about the forest. We stopped constantly to rest them, as the two, a mare and a gelding, were both way past their prime.

'They belong in the slaughterhouse,' Michal said shaking his head at them.

'No, they belong in a field, set free!' I offered. Michal looked down at me and smiled.

'True, in a kinder world it would be so.' He studied me for some time and then asked 'What is your name, girl?' I knew we would come around to this and I was prepared.

'Marianne.' I replied. It had been my mother's name. Actually, Miriam but she had changed it at my father's request. But I told him the more recent; he nodded and was satisfied.

The horses stopped as one, they simply would not go forward when the tiredness overtook them and so we waited by the river and I watched the barges plough the grey water well into the evening. We unharnessed the horses and let them graze. Still Michal kept his eyes downcast and always looked away from the shore. In the summer the light lasted as twilight for a very long time but with the darkness we bedded down. And that was the end of our first day.

*   *   *

The next day was much the same except for when we met soldiers on the road.

'Schnell!' they would bellow.

I would cower, saying nothing but Michal simply gestured to them to be patient, for Michal was in no great hurry, the war was a part of everyone's lives but not his. The soldiers bristled at his impudence but he paid them no mind. He moved neither faster or slower while they continued to bark orders. They demanded his papers and he got them out as if there was no urgency, no danger, as if their military efficiency and brutal manner were nothing not even a troubling minor irritation. His size meant that he stood out on the road and I'm certain it was the comical sight of the giant and the skinny girl that made the Germans stop short. Four times we were halted by patrols, who looked at his papers but asked nothing of me. I kept my legs clamped tightly together, turned slightly to one side with the dress pulled down to my calves and my head lowered. I got no more than a glance from each of the soldiers. Even in the heat and hatred of war, some conventions remained. A quiet, shy young girl was largely ignored as unremarkable. Especially a long thin homely girl, who had neither hips nor breasts. Whether by consideration or accident Piotr had offered me a workable disguise and for that I was grateful.

The soldiers would indiscriminately kill Poles when the mood took them. And yet they spared us. Perhaps it was the fact that his papers stated Michal was both a fur trapper and more importantly a timber worker and the Germans knew they would need his kind to bring firewood when the winter arrived, though I doubted our enemies thought that far ahead. They studied his double-bladed axe strapped to the back of the seat, not knowing that his hunting rifle was lodged in a hidden compartment behind it that had a trick opening.

….. He revealed it for me to use if he was taken and I was left alone. He seemed so unruffled by them and the threat of death did not carry weight with him, it was almost as if he was calling their bluff, daring them to do what they threatened. He was a man who carried secrets but gave nothing away.

'You are not afraid of them; most people are but not you. You are not afraid?'

I said it like a question but he ignored my query, treating it like a statement that required no answer.

'Well?'

He looked at me, surprised by my forthright manner, merely laughing to himself.

'I am not afraid, young Marianne because I am not afraid to die.'

'But why? Why aren't you afraid?'

'Because I have little left to live for.'

He spoke with such sorrow and finality that I did not probe further. I had many more questions but they became lost. For now, I kept the largest question to myself, that too would have to wait. War seemed to create puzzles, mysteries that had no answers. At least no answers that I could work out.

The first three nights we slept fitfully, for a few hours, bedded down in straw in the back of the dray, then we continued our travels. Just before drifting off, I would go through my day and find the blessings within. Even now I could find something to be grateful for: drinking water, the open road, the sad but beautiful old horses and my new protector. Things could be worse; things had been worse. It was something my mother had taught me and as I lay there listing my luckier moments Jana would chime in with those that I had forgotten, the three-day old bread Agneta had sent along with the dried, salted meat and green apples. It had been my sister's favourite ritual too. It brought us closer to our family, who we hoped were somehow safe but we feared were not.

The air in the middle of summer was warm but by three in the morning I found myself nestled into Michal's back. He grunted his approval, taking what meagre warmth, my bony body offered. The dray's hard boards barely held back the pre-dawn chill. The layer of straw was thin in the tray and offered little. They were just as merciless to our muscles and bones, so I never seemed to lose the aches that had come to live in my body.

And as for sleep, it was an elusive creature we grabbed and held for as long as we could. But it was never enough. Sleep like food, was just sufficient to keep you moving but no more. Once there had been plenty of both but that too had been stolen away. Now their meagre supply sat at the edges of my day gnawing at my body, with an ache that consumed me.

We were always on our way before sunrise, spurred on by the falling dew and the dawn cold. By the fourth day there were no more patrols, only the occasional convoy of trucks that forced us off the road and spooked the old horses. Convoys that always came at tremendous speed, without warning, some of them hurtling west and most of them heading east, in a desperate attempt to shore up defenses. The faces of the soldiers looked far more haggard on the ones heading east. They seemed to know something I didn't. That much I figured but in truth, I did not understand this war.

Despite his apparent indifference to the soldiers Michal seemed to know what was happening in the both the east and the west. 'One day our troubles will end' would be enough to say, softly. Its message was clear. Simply by a look, what was really being said was 'Do you know anything? How far away are the Allies? Have you heard any radio transmissions?'

Some answers were only rumours but those who risked listening to radios told us what they knew to be true. 'The Germans have lost the war in the east, that much is sure. The Russians are driving them back into Europe. The British and the Americans are coming too.'

I smiled, picturing my Uncle Wilf fighting for the Americans, though I knew he was too old. I watched the exchanges between Michal and those he met on the road and marveled at the guarded ritual they performed.

At night, bombing lit up the tree line. But when we came to a rise, we could see that the bomber raids were far off in the distance, looking more like a thunderstorm on the horizon. Planes were everywhere in the skies but still no sign of foot soldiers. Everyone on the ground, German, Pole, and Jew knew it was only a matter of time. On the fifth afternoon it started drizzling.

Michal looked up at the gun-metal sky and shook his head, 'No sleeping under the stars tonight.'

I nodded. 'Do you know where we are going?' Finally, I asked the most obvious question but still held back the one question I really wanted to ask.

'Yes eventually. I have been many times. I've hunted from there.

'What did you hunt?', I asked, imagining my companion locked in mortal combat with a bear.

'Rabbits, the occasional fox'

He looked at me but failed to see my disappointment.

'Bears?' I asked hopefully

'No, too hard to kill. Too damned hard to skin and smoke. Small animals are easier. I keep the furs but ate the carcasses. Some of the skins I take to my hosts, in payment.'

'Payment for what?'

'Payment for a roof overhead, sometimes just for company.'

I looked at him slightly puzzled but he kept his eyes straight ahead and shook the reins, pretending to be annoyed at the horses' slow pace. Finally, he answered.

'I do not like the world, young Marianne, it is full of people pretending to be something that they are not.' He looked at me solidly for some time, I squirmed wondering if he meant me.

'But even I cannot stay alone in the forest forever. Sometimes I want to hear another human voice. So, I visit the villages or I visit my brother and sister-in-law in the city.' He paused again, picturing those places and then shook his head. 'But I do not like the town, so I don't visit Agneta, except once a year. At Christmas. Or, to collect lost *girls*.' With that word he looked at me again from head to toe.

'You should be with your family at Christmas' I replied with an air of authority, trying to deflect what I felt was his unspoken enquiry. He didn't answer, instead his whole body seemed to slump.

'Yes, that's a good time.' he said but it sounded much sadder than it should be. 'I bring Tobiasz and Agneta a dray full of wood for the rest of the winter and fur to make mittens and hats.' Michal at last broke into a smile. 'One year, she didn't have *anything for me in return*. So, they both took me to the cinema, to see the moving pictures.'

'What did you see?' I asked, as cinema was my favourite pastime.

'I saw the moving pictures.'

'Yes, but which one?'

'There is more than one?'

'Yes, a different one each week.'

'But why?'

'So, you can go again and again.'

He looked at me as if I was crazy. 'Why would you go again. I would not go again. I've seen it.'

'Seen what?' I asked feeling that this circular conversation was starting to sound a little bit insane.

Exasperated, he talked to me slow and deliberately, as if I was a simpleton. 'I have seen these … these moving pictures. It is very interesting but now I have seen it, I have no reason to go again.'

Now it was my turn to look ahead and say nothing. We drove along in silence.

*   *   *

By nightfall we had found our way into a logging camp just off the road. As we entered the mess hall at dinner time, we found eleven men all digging into the evening meal, each man spooning mechanically, their beards resting in their tin plates so that the distance between food and mouth was the shortest it could be. They each eyed us then quickly returned to the task. But Polish hospitality being what it was, they still offered us a bed for the night.

'The bunkhouse is almost full, there is one spare bed,' said the crew boss, a burly man with a slash down the side of his face that had been stitched badly and had mended with a savage gash of red-yellow scar tissue. He looked at me strangely and then said, 'The girl can sleep by the stove in the kitchen.'

We ate in silence and Michal watched each of the men taking the measure of them. He seemed uncomfortable with where we found ourselves. One by one the men proceeded to get drunk and stagger off to their bunks.

'We will leave before sunrise,' confided Michal, as he too went in search of his bed.

*   *   *

Sometime in the dead of night 'Old Scarface' came for me. When I awoke in his arms, he was carrying me out of the cabin, off into the woods. I struggled but he held me firm with his hand across my mouth.

Jana, what do I do?

Hold still, wait for your moment. But do not hesitate. You must hurt him.

He threw me to the ground and for a moment I sat there dazed, among the pine needles.

'You be quiet now, my little happiness!' he said as he unbuckled his trousers.

MISSING 21ST CENTURY

5

The sun baked the day turning the air still, sticky, and close; Kate braced herself for the solid hit the heat would deliver when she stepped from the air-conditioned car. The property was a new listing and she was unfamiliar with it. The GPS on her phone had already sent her to one cul-de-sac and one street that ran the wrong way. That was the trouble with new subdivisions she thought, the order was created by the developers not town planners. She weaved through front gardens that were nothing of a sort, merely dirt, scaffolding and blue metal, where the landscapers hadn't given them facelifts yet. The thought amused her. Finding the street and the number, she opened up and waited for the couple to arrive.

*   *   *

…..Should I call? Ray fidgeted with his phone. Would it be the same as last time, her hanging up or just the cold request to leave her alone?

'That's just the way things go after twenty years,' Kate had said to him with a rigidity that broached no opposition. So final, no room to find common ground. Did she realise just where this was heading? He had seen it so often before, the last death throes of his friends' marriages. I don't want it to end like this, he thought. Not meeting each other meant no conversation, no solving their issues, no reason to stay together. Yes, there was the company and her father's loan but that was just the surface. He knew that their lives had conspired against their marriage. Too much time spent away from one another, too much neglect of one another's needs. It was so easy for it to happen without anyone intending it. But how to find their way back, that was the real question? No, the real question was, is there a way back at all? The damage was already done. It would take something larger than just talking it out, to bring them back to each other.

The sign across his office window read 'TARCOR'. He had blended his kids' names to make the company name. He liked the idea of it, but couldn't help shaking his head at the company motto – "When People Need To Talk." Ray dialed again but turned it off after two rings.

Oscar his co-worker, a decade older than him, watched with a look of fatherly concern from the other side of the office. 'You want to talk about it?'

Ray shook his head and sipped his almost cold coffee. He gathered himself up for the inevitable heart to heart he knew was coming. Oscar was not going to take no for an answer. He was a man who lived close to his emotions; it was something Ray had always liked about him. Not a typical male but still exhibiting that forthrightness that Ray found so beguiling about Australians.

'You and Louise okay?' Ray asked, knowing full well that Oscar would seize on this.

'Good as we're ever going to be, why?'

Ray nodded but decided to skirt the why and instead asked, 'You ever feel like throwing it in?'

'With Louise you mean? ... Numerous times.'

'So, what stopped you?'

'Well.' Oscar paused for effect. 'When I was young I still loved her and couldn't stand the thought of her ... and you know, another bloke.'

Ray watched his long-term partner, sure that Oscar saw that scenario lived out in his mind. 'And when I got older, I was just too fucking ugly to get another woman to notice me.' They laughed. Ray fell back into silence, then Oscar wheeled his office chair across the room like a school-kid on skates and smiled.

'You may as well tell me; you will in the end anyway.'

* * *

'Gotta go, I think I heard someone pull up' Placing her phone on the kitchen counter Kate turned to see her boss watching her appreciatively.

'Oh, it's you. I'm sorry Paul, the clients never showed. It was the McNicholls wasn't it?'

'Yeah, the McNicholls,' he offered but despite his years in real estate, right now he was not a good liar, 'they rang to cancel, but you'd already left.'

She watched him bridge the distance between them, his usual calculated charm attempting but failing to dazzle her. 'I tried to ring you but your mobile was probably off.'

Kate looked down at her phone knowing he was lying; there were no missed calls. But before she could call him on his story, he was beside her.

'I was hoping to catch you here,' he purred.

'Paul, this is a mistake, this should never have …,' she stammered, sidestepping him and moving backwards, till the kitchen bench prevented any further maneuvering. He put his hand on hers. Kate froze but did not pull away, instead she met him eye to eye. She hated him, she hated herself for what she had done. How could she have fallen into the arms of this, this … her words failed.

'Kate, it was no mistake. Neither of us was drunk. Well, maybe a little bit,' he laughed, 'We both knew what we were doing. Come on!'

'It was a mistake! And I am not going to compound it, alright!'

But Paul Tillotson, wheeler dealer and winner of 'The Ultimate Real Estate Award' two years running was not going to accept this equivocation.

'God, I want you Kate, I think about you all the time!'

Conciliatory words, Kate told herself, *careful how you step now,* knowing that her job might well be the price she paid here.

'Paul come on! This is momentary! It's not going to go any further. You're not going to leave Marissa even if I left Ray!'

'True she'd take me to the cleaners … Take half the business … maybe more!'

There in the new designer kitchen, the sweat appearing as patches at his underarms, she saw him as the needy child that he was. She watched him, as he thought of the enormity of what he intended to do and the consequences for his marriage. And then the doubt was gone. He looked her up and down, as his fantasies took hold and once more, he was the man of action.

'So what if it's momentary? Kate there's a bed upstairs. I have no expectations of this.'

A shadow crossed Kate's face and then a withering look that said all she wanted to say. Picking up her keys she headed for the door.

'There's a promotion in it, Kate!'

'Lock up behind you Paul. I'll see you back at the office.'

*   *   *

Ray looked across at Oscar who waited expectantly. They had built their business from a drunken dream one afternoon in a bar to what it was now, a struggling, mid-level telecommunications venture about to be swallowed up for just over half of its market value. But they had come this far together and Ray knew that he had to give Oscar something, their friendship demanded it.

'You still considering that offer?' Oscar asked.

'Yeah, but it's no longer what it was … it's ten thousand less,' said Ray

'Bastards!'

'He knows there are no other buyers. By next week he'll have dropped it again.'

'Then sell, I'll be Ok.'

'No, your job is guaranteed remember, Parker has no technical ability, he needs you … it's part of the deal, no matter …

it's just that Kate has me convinced that it's going to fuck up if I sell. That we're going to be on the street, almost.'

Oscar rolled his swivel chair a little closer. 'My old man said something to me once'

Ray looked up, for although he wouldn't admit it, he loved Oscar's stories.

'I was about ten. I woke up…dead of night, my mum screaming. My father rushes in and scoops me out of bed then grabs my twin sisters and rushes out of the house. The whole bloody place was on fire. Mum stood on the front lawn crying. The fire brigade went to a false alarm and by the time they arrived the whole bloody thing had burnt to the ground.'

'Shit!'

'The next day I sifted through the ashes and all I found was a half-melted sheriff's badge that I loved. But Dad lost everything, his books, his photos from the war, medals, my mother's love letters, the lot. I can still smell it. You know that bloody awful smell of burnt plastic and paper and clothes. I wandered round and round what looked like a bomb site. I was gutted but the old man put his arm around me and said, "Son, it doesn't matter…everything that's worth keeping is in here" and then he pointed to his head. "And in here." And then he hugged me like he was going to crush me.'

It was what Ray needed. 'Bloody Aussies' he marveled; he loved Oscar's matter of fact way of getting to the *'no bullshit'* centre of things, in a way few Englishmen ever did. He looked across at Oscar and simply shared a smile.

* * *

School was over but their parents were working late so Tara and Cory headed to the After School Care building. He danced along the footpath, glad to be released from the classroom, more energy than he could contain, circling his pensive older sister. The late Spring sat in the very atoms of the air, heat haze rising off the bitumen, magpies warbling, the day like a force holding them in its embrace, promising an even fiercer Summer.

Cory picking up her mood, slowed down and stepped in time to his sister's grave demeanor. It unsettled him when Tara was dark, when the world overwhelmed her. He wanted her to be alright, so that he knew that he would be.

'You wake up last night?' he asked.

'Yeah.'

'Me too.'

'What did you do?'

'Same as always, I put on "Destruction." I'm on level eight,' he replied, a note of triumph in his voice.' They turned to each other and pulled finger guns, bouncing with mouth explosions, gunfire and laughter. 'DESTRUCTION!!'they shouted in unison. They crossed the school playground and found their friends; immediately going their separate ways, as if they didn't know each other.

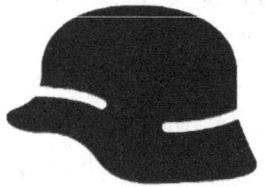

BROTHERS SUMMER 1934

6

Horst sat in the bar and waited for his friend, his non-blood brother who was also called Horst. *The other Horst'* had been the brother he'd always wanted. They met at school, shared girlfriends, went to political rallies, got into drunken scrapes together, fought their way out of several Dresden bars. They were inseparable except for the time he went to Vienna one winter. Their humour too was the same dark, slightly mocking brand. They poked fun at everything, jeered at old ways of thinking. But when it came to the Fatherland and their sense of grievance, then they spoke with a common sense of poetic purpose.

Dresden in the late summer seemed full of promise and the girls, he decided, were prettier and friendlier, then the ones in Vienna. Even the beer tasted better. He settled back with his second stein, in a booth at the dark end of the premises, and sipped slowly, it would be another quarter hour before his compatriot arrived.

There, in the other corner sat a man who despite the heat, wore a trench coat with a hat pulled down to his eyebrows. His head was lowered as if he were staring into his glass but it was clear that he was peering past the glass, watching the door. Something about him disturbed Horst; he felt certain he knew his face, that there was something familiar in his presence. By half way through his drink he had it.

Horst crossed the floor and stood before the man, 'Are you Helmut Voight?'

The man bristled and both of his hands shot down beneath the table, his drink wobbling and splashing foam out with the violent motion.

''I'm armed!' he snarled.

Horst stepped back and said in a conciliatory tone, 'It's Horst Mueller, we met in Vienna.' For a few seconds the man glared up at him then hissed 'Sit down quickly, but don't block my view.' Horst sidled into the opposite side of the booth and slid across to the wall.

'What do you want?'

'I...I just wanted to say hello. I'm Horst ...Horst Mueller, we went out after those Commie bastards that night last February, when they broke up your meeting ... I held the glass doors remember?'

Voight continued to watch the door and then he relaxed but only slightly, 'Yeah...yeah I remember.' Alert, he stared beyond Horst, never giving more than a glance at the man across the table. Nothing more was said until Horst asked, 'Is everything alright? Are you in trouble?'

The haunted man remained fixated on the door as if he was expecting that trouble to come bursting through it. Voight gave a hard and bitter laugh, 'Don't you read the papers, son?'

'Yeah, sometimes, when someone leaves one lying about. They're usually a day or two late. Something I should know?'

The other man drew in a deep breath and still seated, rose up to his full stature and for the first time Horst could see the Sergeant at Arms who had befriended him that night. The man took his eyes away from the door, long enough to address the question.

'You think we are going to be saved, like all the other fools in this country? Let me tell you you're not. Just because this government has found jobs for millions doesn't mean you can trust them.'

'Sorry but I don't know what you're talking about?'

Voight shook with rage and for a few seconds was unable to speak, his face contorting with a venom and hatred that made his jawline muscles go rigid. It looked like he was about to shout at the top of his voice at all who had betrayed him. Then he looked around and reined himself in, as if drawing attention to himself was not the wisest thing to do in a crowded bar. He screwed up his face and stared solidly at Horst and said 'Are you seriously going to tell me you haven't heard about us? About the S.A., about the Brownshirts?' Then added with a cynical sneer, 'What we were planning?'

Horst shook his head solemnly.

'Fuck, you must be the naivest kid in Germany!'

Offended by the outburst, Horst shifted uncomfortably, 'Look, I am not very good with politics, maybe you should explain this a little clearer....and slower. I do know that this country is a lot better off since we got rid of those idiot liberals from the Weimar.'

'Yeah, maybe we are….' Voight conceded. 'But there still needs to be people you can believe in, principles that you can trust, no matter how harsh.'

Horst looked at him bewildered. Voight sighed and decided to try another tack.

'The S.A. is finished. My brothers are either dead or like me, in hiding. Didn't you hear we were planning an insurrection. We were going to topple the government.'

'Oh, that!'

'YES THAT!' Voight snarled. He leaned in closer, 'No-one was plotting anything. Leastways, no-one I ever heard of in the organisation. But the newspapers said it, the radio said it, Goebbels said it and finally Hitler said it, so it must be true.'

'But can't you prove you're innocent?' Horst offered.

'Oh, fuck me, you really are a fucking babe in the woods. This country doesn't run on guilt or innocence, it runs on power, it runs on the strong commanding the weak. Like it should be. Complete control, nothing less. Goring wanted the army, Himmler wanted the police and Rohm stood in the way. BUT IT"S KILLED ME! I am just a walking corpse waiting to lie down.'

Horst sat there with his mouth open, unable to find the words that could refute this. Was this true? Was Hitler lying?

He'd spent *that evening* chasing communists and then drinking and telling stories in a beer hall, with these brownshirts till dawn. For the next couple of weeks, they had befriended him and given him food, clothing and a place to sleep. He never went back to his lodgings. But this, Hitler lying, the country misled?

'No, you're wrong, we are winning and the country is no longer dictated to, by the French and the British. You know that. I am sorry for you but like you say it's the strong who rule and we have got to be strong. This kind of talk doesn't help. I'll hear no more.'

Voight smiled a weary smile. And slowly shook his head. Just then Horst looked up to see his friend looking in at the window. Voight stood up and put his pistol inside his coat and slid out of the booth. Horst remained seated. He turned to Horst with a look like his father might have given him.

'I hope you live a long and prosperous life; I give you that from a man whose life is stolen away from him. It is dog eat dog in this country now. They have won and we've lost. I'd go with Himmler if you want to survive. He may not appear like much of a fighter but he's the cruelest, he will survive. Goodbye.'

And with that he gave the old-fashioned Prussian bow and left passing Horst's friend at the door.

'Who was that?' The other Horst asked.

'A man without a country'.

ROAD SUMMER 1944

7

The expression on his face said everything, as he reached beneath my clothing and found something different from what he was looking for. I couldn't help myself; his look was comical; I burst out laughing. But 'Scarface' did not see the joke. The energy of his lust needed somewhere to go, so he hit me across the head with his fist, slamming me hard against a tree trunk.

'You little bastard, what the fuck you playing at?'

He took me by the throat and held me aloft with one hand, his trousers around his ankles, his huge cock still erect. There would be a price to pay for my insolence. As he pushed me down, I gasped for breath but my hands found their way between his legs. I grabbed his balls and squeezed them like I was crushing two hard boiled eggs. His bloodshot eyes went wide with pain, as he doubled over collapsing to his knees. Letting go of my throat, he clutched his groin and went down to the ground, curling up in an agonized ball. I finished him off with a handful of dirt in his eyes, backing away from his moaning body. Lurching through the undergrowth, one after another of the low hanging branches whipped me, as I tried to put distance between 'Scarface and me.'

The horse! cried Jana and I reached into the apron pocket. It was gone. Behind me his groans sounded like an animal in a trap.

Scrambling back, I fell to the ground, narrowly missing my tormentor, as he staggered about blindly. Where was it? It had to be here. He would be able to see soon. Down on my hands and knees, I fanned across the forest floor with my arms in wide arcs, as he stumbled about, cursing and searching for me.

Hurry, hurry he's blinking!

Still nothing. But as I stood, I felt it under the heel of my buckle shoe, dug it out of the soft earth, turned and fled back toward the camp, my throat throbbing; I could still feel where his hands had been. Behind me, he was moaning and thrashing about wildly. On the veranda stood Michal, waiting. The rain had stopped hours ago and the horses were hitched to the dray. It was several hours before dawn and yet Michal was here, as if somehow, he knew I was in trouble.

'We've got to go' I shouted.

Looking back, there was no sign of my attacker, but I felt that any moment he would burst from the trees and then even my giant friend might not be enough to save me. Michal studied me and sensing my alarm said, 'Are you alright?'

'We have to leave.'

Michal looked down at my disheveled state and understood.

'Quickly!' I added.

For the first time the horses set off at a brisk pace. Perhaps it was the cold in the middle of the night, that made them want to warm their blood but I was glad of it. As we pulled away from the camp and turned the corner of the road, I looked back to see

'Scarface' staggering back to the hut, bellowing, still doubled over, as one by one the other men, carrying lamps, came out and looked up the road.

*   *   *

Across the distant horizon, through the breaks in the trees the first light was a soft blue-white wash against the dark sky. I sat close to Michal and watched the gentle repetition of the horses' movements, trying to calm myself. A couple of hours of travel had not quieted my nerves; I still imagined them coming after us, like some posse from the western serials at the cinema, 'Old Scarface' leading the other ten men, hellbent on revenge, a noose in his hands. As always Michal seemed undisturbed. Finally with the dawn I let the night go and leaned into my man-mountain on the seat of the dray and drifted off into memory.

In the months I lived in the sewers I came across fragments of the outside world. In that twilight life, with only the voices in my head, I longed for anything and everything that came from my old life. Ten-week-old newspapers floated by, a half a hardback book on chemistry, a romance novel where most of the ink had run and I could only read every sixth page. I filled in the missing parts from my imagination and what I remembered of the awful magazines my romantic sister left around our house. For a little while, I even named a rat, I called him *Nostradamus* for no other reason than it amused me. He seemed more curious than most and I came to believe he'd befriended me.

Loneliness is a strange bedfellow, especially when you have no bed to speak of. Often, I would sit in the darkness below the grate and look up on moonlit nights to catch glimpses of strangers walking by. Cradled in my hands I would always hold my cast pewter soldier on a horse, the cavalry officer with his sword drawn, as if he was leading the charge. It was the last and only thing I had from our house on Dunaj Street. I had risked capture to go back and get it.

One night as the moon passed through the grate and I watched the light jumping from my soldier's body, I heard churchgoers gathered on a street corner singing hymns, even an atheist like me recognised them. They sang of hope and peace and love of mankind and I almost believed their promises of being saved, of a better world. I watched them, from the manhole, until the Germans moved them along, telling them that gatherings were forbidden. When they were gone, I cried so loudly I feared that someone would hear but I couldn't stop. Even the Christians' God had abandoned me. For the next day I did not move, willing them to come for me, anchored in my despair.

As I sat there, the sewer trough gurgling below my boots, a sheet of paper floated by. The kind that had been secretly printed somewhere in Warsaw, the kind of pamphlet that offered a different kind of hope, but one that would get you killed, if you were found with it. It was a call to arms, encouraging all Poles to sabotage, to slow down the Germans, to defy their orders and when your life became too hot, too dangerous then it said it was time to flee and join the resistance. It talked of the Forest without ever naming where that forest was. All it said was bring warm clothing, weapons and food – all written in upper case. It was then that I decided to stop hiding, I would find safety and other Poles. And when Piotr came that final time, I knew where I would go.

And today I felt, even if Michal had not named it, that this was indeed where we were headed.

We travelled for a further two days, although 'Fred and Ginger' our draught horses had only covered half the distance younger horses would have. Jana and I had named them that, when we found that Michal had not bothered to name them at all, but merely called each of them horse. In all that time, we came across no German soldiers at all.

Perhaps the war is over. I knew this was stupid but I never argued with Jana, I'd done enough of that when she was alive. It was merely that we were on a backroad that was rarely travelled.

I studied Michal silently for some time. He was solid around the jawline with a heavily matted beard, now badly in need of a comb and trim. His hair swept back around his ears and down to his collar, in what you could only call a mane. There were soft flecks of grey, amongst the blond-brown. His frontier skin was mottled and scarred with heavy creases at the eyes and forehead. It was not the soft city face of my father but one built of earth and experience. He seemed both wild and placid, much like the animals he trapped - gentle with their own kind but ferocious if cornered. After a while I was sure he knew I was looking at him. But he allowed it and this prompted me to ask my first burning question, the one I had wondered about since I met Michal.

'Why are you doing this? Why are you taking me?'

He turned to me, placing the reins on his lap. The horses kept to their pace, neither faster or slower.

'Would you rather go by yourself?'

'No, I have nowhere to go. I have nobody. I have to trust someone and hope that they are taking me to safety.'

'I cannot guarantee that. No place is safe! Even before the war it was not safe,' he said this flatly. All the life went out of his voice as the sentence hung in the air, falling into silence and instantly he was somewhere else and I knew not to disturb him. Around him hung the ghosts of grief, of loss. I could feel them; I knew these things. Finally, he came out of the fog and found me still staring at him. He gathered himself and said, 'This war offers nothing but uncertainty. In the end, you have to say deliverance may come.... and take your chances.'

I wanted to ask him if *he* was my deliverance, but the words sounded Catholic and I felt strange saying them and so instead I asked, 'And who is your deliverance?'

'Deliverance? Harummph! I don't need to answer that question.' - he sounded full of violence and anger. I looked at him puzzled.

'Child, I make my own peace with the world, with this world and the next. At least I try to. I know only what I see and feel. What I had once *has been taken away from me* ... washed away. Now I live in the forest, perhaps for far too long, in the forest. We make our own way and we do what we can and must for others. But I have no answers for anyone. So, I try not to convince anyone else of anything. God expects me to find my own answers; he will not tell me! For this sometimes I hate him.'

I realised we were dancing around God and belief and pain and loss, someone washed away. And yes, even Christian kindness. I could see how much it hurt him to talk of being angry with his own God. It felt strange, for someone raised as an atheist, to be discussing such things but I had questions. Who was washed away? Had I replaced them or had he saved me because that's what Catholics do? Not the question where are we going but the why are you taking me? Was that what they were required to do by their God? But no, at that moment, I knew he did what he did because of *who he was*. And I loved him for that.

Afterwards Michal was silent but I felt we had reached an accommodation. He would be dependable in a way that others in my life had not been. Though I hardly knew him, this much was apparent. He was like his forest, forever solid and dark, in places like a path you could follow and in others impenetrable.

Throughout the day farmers nodded to us from their wagons, all heading in the opposite direction. It put me in the strangest of minds, it almost felt that Jana was right, that the war had left the earth, that I was heading home with my monstrous protector. But what of Michal and believing in your own deliverance? I knew I had to survive but was that the same as believing in deliverance? I wanted to find a positive way to see the dark world that had taken my family. All day I ebbed and flowed between hope and despair. The war would come to an end, like the one two decades ago had, though it killed millions. Would I survive this one, perhaps as the only survivor of my family. There was always the sense of foreboding, a strange feeling in the guts, like you couldn't help what was coming but you knew it would, as Uncle Wilf said, 'Swallow you.'

I thought of the day my father took me to see the Vistula break her banks, when I was five. We stood high above the river, on a third-floor balcony, watching the brown water roll and spin into every corner below, running headlong down deserted streets, splashing up against walls and falling back on itself, drowning the lower parts of the city. I squeezed my father's hand and he squeezed back. The river terrified me and even my father's presence, was not enough to make me feel safe from that unrelenting force of nature. Today felt like that.

We travelled through a corridor of trees, mostly poplars but every kilometre an oak marked the distance to and from the surrounding towns. I had been counting them. The light was fading and we knew we must rest the horses.

'We'll take the first side road that comes and bed down for the night.'

I nodded, almost asleep myself. But for the next hour there were no side roads. The twilight had come and gone and night was falling fast. Ahead in the distance, flames could be seen around a bend, a kilometre maybe two away. Out of the darkness, a figure stumbled toward us, charred and almost unrecognizable, his clothes hanging in tatters. He looked into our eyes and spoke something incomprehensible. Not Polish or German but some dialect I didn't recognise. In the throes of death, he was speaking his mother tongue.

I pointed out his boots to Michal; as unrecognizable as he was, he was still a Wehrmacht soldier. Michal immediately tried to turn the horses around, but 'Fred and Ginger' were too tired to

co-operate. The German soldier, burnt almost beyond recognition, collapsed against our dray, then lay by the roadside.

Run Bronek, run!, Jana pleaded.

Something deadly had happened here. Michal stepped down to force the horses back, while I held the reins.

'Hurry, someone's coming!'

The horses now faced back where we come from, as Michal climbed up but, by then, they were upon us. Several soldiers appeared out of the darkness, four men pointed their guns, shouting, cursing, two of them were burnt, though not as bad as the first but all had faces and hands covered in blood. Michael whipped the reins and the horses began to pull away. The closest of the soldiers shouted for us to stop, then fired. The bullet whistled past hitting the closer of our horses in the neck and Fred dropped, lurching to one side and falling onto the mare who collapsed under him. Ginger cried out in pain and fright, an animal sound that was almost human. I heard the snapping of bone.

The dray upended coming down hard on its side, splintering our seat and revealing the rifle. The force threw us into the ditch beside the road, where we both lay stunned as the soldiers looked down.

'Herausklettern!' yelled the leader, gesturing with his rifle for us to get to our feet.

Michal climbed out of the ditch and I followed. Then he picked me up like a rag doll, placing me down, holding me close to him. One of the soldiers smashed his rifle butt into the middle of Michal's back but he did not buckle. Instead, he took my hand and started hobbling up the road. Another soldier rummaged under the seat of the dray and brought out Michal's hunting rifle, in its hard leather sleeve. He stayed behind, as three of the four men walked us up to the road, toward the flickering light ahead.

DARKNESS 21ST CENTURY

8

The sky was the blue that only Australia in Spring could give. No clouds, the sun blistering down and there just above the horizon was the three-quarter moon, up early in the afternoon sky, waiting for the evening. From the window of the two-storey building, the sprawling suburbs stretched out till they met farmland and bush. Estuary Point Public School sat in the bend of the river, all of it visible from the Year Six classroom, on the top floor, where Tara daydreamed. Through the trees, past the wide expanse of water, she saw the blur; a fleeting movement on the far side. One, two and then four wild horses came to the edge of the forest, Tara squinted into the afternoon glare but they had disappeared again. So it was true! She wanted to tell the rest of her class but everyone else was busy working, she was the only one who had wandered off to gaze out the window. She would tell her brother Cory.

They had woven the wild brumbies into their imaginings; had made it part of the 'Broken Shield' history they played together. A history of warriors and journeys that had grown throughout Tara and Cory's childhoods. The story of untrustworthy allies and the dark enemies they fought or bargained with, in their elaborate adventures in the quarry and the forest.

She and Cory had looked for the horses several times on their holidays and weekends. Each day in the October school break they rowed across and searched for the brumbies. But Cory grew tired of the game and wanted to move on. Finding none, they decided that it was just a local tale. No-one else had seen them. But now here they were, Tara had seen them. And now the moment was gone, it belonged only to her.

In the schoolyard one, then two children were marking time outside before returning to the humdrum of whatever lesson was in progress. School was what you put up with, to play ball games

at lunch, that was how Cory put it. That had made Tara laugh, though school had never been a burden for her, it was once a place of knowledge, of discovery and of stories. That was gone, school had become a place without spirit, her parents' fights had made it so. Tara always felt tired in the classroom.

Miss Cork surveyed the class. The students sat in rows, some paying attention but a few committing the mid-morning crimes that being confined for too long created.

Some fidgeted, others doodled images in their books, one slipped a secret note to another. It was frustrating as a teacher but she persevered, deciding for now to ignore most of the transgressions. Even of those staring out the window. But not for long.

'Remember that the denominator tells you how many parts the fraction is broken into. And what does the numerator tell you? Ummm, Tara Winslow?'

Tara woke from her reverie and stared back at the teacher, looking a little lost but quickly returning to her seat.

'I am not talking Martian here? We did this last week.' The frustration in her voice evident as Miss Cork's eyes bore down on Tara. The class turned to watch knowing that one of the star pupils was searching for an answer.

What was the question again? How long had she been day-dreaming? What subjects were they doing now? But no one offered Tara a lifeline, each one secretly glad it was not them under the searchlight. She looked up at her teacher who she often found pleasant but it was the end of the school year and teachers grew grumpier as they got weighed down with exams and reports. Miss Cork was no different, she seemed determined that Tara must provide the answer. Tara's stomach knotted, as these thoughts began to crowd inside her head. What does she want?

'Ah… verbs are doing words, Miss.'

As one the whole class laughed.

Miss Cork frowning replied, 'That was the previous lesson. Where have you been for the last fifteen minutes?'

Tara sat silently, hoping that somehow the focus would pass to someone else, now that she had given some kind of answer, but the steely gaze would not relent. Tara waited saying nothing, just hoping that the silence would force her teacher to move on but no, she was not going to let this go. Tara knew her teacher often got tired of her class not paying attention. Miss Cork's dissatisfaction was raining down on her alone as Tara stared at the floor, not wishing to meet her teacher's stare.

'Well? … I'm still waiting!' she heard Miss Cork say.

The seconds dragged on in the silence, offering Tara nowhere to escape to. Desperate, she burst out of her desk, running from the room in tears. As she looked back from the door Miss Cork was standing, with her mouth open.

*   *   *

Ray Winslow struggled with his keys, as the phone inside rang, for the tenth time. Perhaps it was the sale, he cursed himself, why had he let his mobile phone go flat? Could it be the buyer on the landline? The door seemed to conspire against him, no not that key, nor that either. Finally, he dashed across the room lunging at the phone on the kitchen bench, shouting 'Hello' a little too loudly.

'Mr Winslow, it's Miss Cork. We met at parent-teacher night. I am sorry to ring you at home but I'm a bit concerned about Tara. Is this a good time to talk?'

'Is she alright?'

'Oh yes, she's not hurt or anything. It's other things.'

And for a moment, Ray thought there was a distinct pause, as if the person at the other end was trying to gather their words.

'She's always been one of my best pupils but lately her work is…well it's just not there. Sometimes she's off in a dream. But mostly because she just can't seem to stay awake. I am afraid I haven't been as sympathetic as I should', Ray heard her say. Ray slumped in his chair, his problems with the world of business disappeared; the nightmares, all Kate's concerns he thought were exaggerated came back to him. *My daughter's in trouble.* How much further could this family's life fall apart?

'I will talk to my wife and yes, we'll come and see you.' '*Enough,*' he thought, he knew what he needed to do and dialed out.

'Hello Parker, it's Ray Winslow. You still interested in the business? No, I'm not happy with your offer but maybe we should talk again. How about Friday?'

There he had done it. He sat thinking, this was not going to go well with Kate.

*   *   *

Cory was late from school, but no matter she would start the story without him. There, in the hollow of a broken tree stump that had been shattered by lightning the previous summer, she pulled out one of two wooden handled swords, carved and hand painted, its blade cut from the remains of an aluminium caravan and sharpened to a point. She took great care with the sword as it was as sharp and as lethal as any real sword. She held the longer broadsword above her head, announcing that the journey had begun. She was just a hundred metres above the lip of the quarry. The hill rose another seven hundred metres to the clearing at the tree line where their fortress and safety lay.

It had taken them over two years to build the structure, both becoming familiar with their father's battery drills, saws, hammers and ropes. Tara had even built a model from cardboard of how it would look. From their vantage point the lands of their adventures stretched out all the way back to the house and the beginning of the suburbs. And to the west until the ridge slowly descended to the river.

'This is the hand of the one true pilgrim. I am ready to go where you choose to take me,' she spoke to the sword. But this day the journey would not be far, there would be no guides and no puzzles to solve, no treasures and no rewards. For this time her enemies were ready. The shadows on all sides moved closer, rising up along the hillside. The armies of 'The Broken Shield' turned as one and stood their ground; it was obvious they would not come to her aid. Instead, they let the Dark Army pass among their ranks and come to the fore.

'Do not bar the way Dark Shadows.'

She turned to their sometime allies and spoke bitterly. 'And you… you have betrayed me before, my brother and I. We will not let it happen again.'

Still the Shield Warriors were resolute as they stood unmoving and the Dark Army, the true enemies passed. Where was Cory now that fate had turned so sharply against her? The dark hordes came forward and the first of them, their leader raised his hooded head. Tara could not see a face in the blackness of the hood. It was like looking into the darkness of a cave and yet there was a being within this clothed shape.

The Dark King spoke in a deep and thunderous voice that echoed against the steep cliff faces of the quarry -*Maiden, your path is denied. Do not cross me. This time we stand in great numbers, much more than before.* Tara turned in a slow circle and knew that it was true. The forest all around her had grown dark with menace.

'Do not think because I am alone, that I am without strategy or power. You would be foolish to underestimate me; I am the Falcon Wielder' she said. But the shadows paid no heed and moved in slowly, relentlessly. The distance to safety seemed immense. Tara crouched close to the ground and placed her open palm on the earth. And called on her protector to guide her.

'What should I do?' she whispered to the spirit that had helped her so many times before. She waited but there was nothing, The Forest Mistress, where was she now? Tara's bluff that she was not without strategy or power seemed hollow now; it appeared she'd been abandoned? Still, she waited and waited, until at last a sound came from a vast distance, a voice faint but growing stronger. The darkness was on the move now; the clouds swept across the sky and the temperature grew suddenly very cold. Still, she did not falter but listened intently to the message only she could hear and when her guide was done Tara said softly, 'Thank you.'

Her sword high above her head, she plunged it deep into the ground and leapt aside. The darkness descended on the sword and engulfed it in its' own fog and mist. But Tara was already scaling the steep incline above the quarry. Sanctuary lay several hundred meters ahead; behind her she could hear the laughter of the Broken Shield as they watched their new allies falter. Worse though was the cries of the Dark ones. She could feel the anger of the warriors of the Dark Army, furious that they had been tricked. Their cold rage came hurtling up the rocky trail, determined to envelop her in its freezing misery. She had covered half the distance now but she dared not look back for their fury was sparking in the air behind her. Ahead at the top of the ridge, among the tree line sat Trelleborg. If she could make it to their castle fortress before she was caught, she would find weapons and safety there. She was almost within reach of its sunlit battlements when she was struck. A large rock flew up from the ground and grazed her cheek, she stumbled but safety lay only steps away. She fell into Trelleborg and scaled the bush ladder to its ramparts. The darkness curled and boiled around the foot of the castle as Tara looked down. She was safe, but she knew that the stone had been hurled by them and it would seep into her like poison. Now the ache of her cheek began to settle into mind and body. She may have escaped the darkness for now but she would pay for it, as misery rose up and she could do nothing to keep it at bay.

*   *   *

Cory knew where his sister would be, found the break in the wire fence, hidden behind the low brush and belly-crawled underneath. They were often chased out of their secret place but somehow the security or a returning foreman never found their entry point. It was a matter of pride, for them both, as they snubbed the signs that read 'Private Property. Danger. Do Not Enter!' Outsmarting the quarry men was the part that Cory liked the best and he was sure his sister felt the same.

From the hole in the fence you could travel left down the fence line that led to the gate and into the quarry that had been carved out of the face of the hill. Inside the quarry were canyons that twisted and turned. The quarry wall stretched up crevassed and contoured more than seventy metres, casting long shadows into the pit below - a vast moonscape of rock mounds and hollows now filled with brackish rainwater. Here was the grey canvas on which a thousand adventures were painted. Here Cory had followed his sister to countless lands, the willing apprentice to the queen, the girl warrior, the captain of secrets and plunder. The sheer bluffs that pushed up from the quarry floor were the powerful backdrop to wherever they took themselves. Amongst the company of nomads and magicians, brigands and knights, the giant earth movers sat silently, the drivers having left for the day. Here was the land of the Broken Shield, where he and his sister had to use their wits to survive, one day at a time. Cory turned right choosing the hill that rose up steeply around the quarry, careful not to come too close to the edge. Everywhere on the steep ascent the rocks and soil slipped under his feet till at the top he found her.

Tara sat in the place she always did, on the lip of the quarry, her legs dangling over the edge, throwing stones into the abyss. Cory sat down beside her, perilously close to the rim. It made his stomach drop away and his legs go weak to look over the edge. But it was something he wanted to feel. He did not notice the gash on her cheek.

'I hate school!' he spat.

'I hate going home,' Tara countered.

'Yeah, me too!'

Cory looked adoringly at her, for she was the brainy one, big sister, the one who since he was a little boy had drawn him into her world of noble quests and honour. In the real world she was the one who always had the answers when he couldn't do or understand something. It was good to know she was around, good to have someone to ask, especially now that the questions had grown in size, had become monstrous. But something here was wrong, Cory could see that his sister had been crying.

'Sorry I'm late, I got kept in by Mrs Samuels'

'Again?' admonished Tara as she rubbed her eyes.

'Yeah, again!' he replied, angry at himself and the school.

'Tara, what do you think is going to happen?'

She knew exactly what he meant.

'I don't know. They're idiots! I hate them both!'

No, this was not the answer he sought; the hole was widening back home and Cory felt himself falling into it. He needed her to stop the uncertainty and the increasing noise. Tara had answers, so many of them, she had to have this one. She loved him and took him through the scarier places he feared, held him to her when they were forced to run through the darkness.

Now those dark terrors seemed childish but *this fear* – of what was happening to his home, this fear of where he and his sister were going, *this overwhelmed him.* Why were his mother and father fighting? Would they take one of them each and go? Is that what happens in divorce? The house was coming apart under his feet and he needed his big sister to set it right, to show him, like she had shown him before, that there was nothing behind the door at night and now to tell him that there was nothing coming for them and their family. He thought for a moment, did he really hate them?

'I don't.'

He waited but Tara said nothing; instead, she got to her feet sending cascades of dirt and rock down to the quarry floor. Picking up a smooth flat piece of rock, breaking it in two, she handed a smaller hand size projectile to her brother. Across the ravine, a large stick figure was painted onto the opposing wall, some thirty to forty metres away and several metres below the rim. It offered a suitable target. The two had always wondered at this because the graffiti artist must have scaled down on ropes. For Cory, that was more adventure than he had ever felt was possible.

'Betcha can't hit the old stick man' Tara challenged, determined to push herself out of sadness.

'Betcha I can.'

Cory's shot, spinning across the chasm, lost momentum, descending into the shadows below. Tara would better it; she didn't throw in that half-hearted way. She stood determinedly, dropping her weight into her thighs, leaning to the side, bending at the waist. She flicked the stone with the required kick in the release. Her grey and black disc sliced out across the distance, shattering, pulverizing, leaving a mark right at the point where the legs and the torso met.

'Good shot! Right in the doodle dah!' said Cory, using the baby talk he'd spoken as a toddler.

He looked at his sister - the clown once again had lifted her mood. He knew she loved the way he could always find the rude, crude, or stupid in everything and then would just say it, not caring what trouble it put him in.

'Doodle dah!' he said again, knowing he had got her.

They burst out laughing, then Tara turned.

'Race you to the bottom.'

Their voices echoed up through the canyon, as they ran helter-skelter to the quarry floor and out through the hole in the wire fencing, back to the world of pain, back to the world without answers - the world of adults.

RECKONING SUMMER 1944

9

We walked toward the flames, Michal still limping but staring off into the distance, as if he was willing himself to be beyond all this. He neither looked at the soldiers or at me but held my hand firmly as if to say I am still here. I stole a look at the soldiers: they were bloodied and burnt but most of all they seethed with anger: whatever had happened to them was now going to be repaid by us. Still Michal walked easily into the darkness. Despite the rifle butt welt, he held his head erect. I tried to gather strength from his disposition.

Stay close to Michal, I heard from deep inside me but I didn't need Jana to tell me just how much danger we were in.

A shot rang out from behind and then the frantic whinnying of the other horse. I knew it was Ginger. A second shot and she too was silent. Michal squeezed my hand harder, as I began to cry.

'Say nothing.'

I nodded. Round the next bend was a German staff car laying on its side, the flames were dying now but still lighting up the road like some ghostly sideshow attraction, the tree limbs illuminated, dancing in the darkness. A large hole in the road showed where a bomb had exploded. Beside the wreckage lay the body of an officer who must've been dragged from the car, his grey uniform soaked crimson with blood from head to boots. Ahead of that, a motorcycle lay on its side and another was a mangled mass of metal beyond the fence. The second cycle twisted completely out of its proper shape; the headlight still shining on rows of green, sitting in tilled soil. In the oak, just above, a soldier hung from a branch, as if he had been laid out to dry, his helmet hanging round his neck, like an oversized necklace. Without being told we stopped.

Despite all our danger I couldn't help ticking off the mechanics of the scene – the car was a Horch 108 and the bike was a Zundapp with a sidecar. Being the son of an engineer, I recognised all

this, for my father and I knew trains, planes, automobiles, even the first of the helicopters that were only experimental. Now these marvels of engineering were bringing monsters to kill us.

The last soldier caught up with the other three. One asked him about the horses but he shook his head. Grouped together they stood before the wreckage, looking at each other, considering what remained - they'd had a purpose, a destination, now that had been upended, just like the car. No-one was sure what to do. They were all privates, foot soldiers or rather motor cycle soldiers, now three of them were obeying a fourth, they must have decided would be their leader. He pushed us angrily to the side of the road where he gestured that we should sit with our hands on our heads. Then as one all four men began to talk loudly, clearly trying to figure their next move. The car and one bike were destroyed, three men were dead and four angry men were very much alive. They righted the second bike and side car but the forks were bent badly out of shape and it too would be going nowhere.

Six of us caught in the flickering light, stood in the middle of the countryside, the forest no more than half a kilometre from the road, just beyond the field, darkness all around, no transport. Too bloody impulsive, maybe you shouldn't have shot our horses, you stupid bastards I thought.

They are planning something, Jana offered, *beware!*

But I didn't need her to tell me that either.

Once or twice, they pointed as if deciding whether we were a help or a hindrance. Probably they were wondering whether we should end up like our horses. Finally, the leader got them all to stop talking at once and ordered one of them over to us. Michal looked up, as the soldier tried to gather up his meagre Polish and spoke in just single words.

'Gdzie…..miasto…..' and then a pause. 'Entfernung?' With this last word he gestured with his arms outstretched, running his eyes along an imaginary line, he had carved in space. The movement had an almost friendly feel. 'How,' 'Town' and then German that we understood to mean distance. Michal replied in Polish but it was clear the soldier made out none of it. Puzzled, the soldier looked at me and I gave the kilometres with both hands, opening and closing them twice.

'Zwanzig kilometre', he shouted to those behind. The others nodded while their leader shook his head and strode toward us.

Our usefulness over, the leader barked for us to get up, then walking away, with a clear movement of his arm, he sealed our fate. The young translator looked dismayed but raised his rifle with the other two, while the leader took out a cigarette and lit it. The three awaited his orders.

A shot rang out and for a moment the leader, his cigarette still in hand, stood there amazed, uncomprehending as a hole in his neck, almost at the collarbone appeared and began to seep blood. He dropped to the ground as the other three scattered.

The soldier, who had been our translator, hid behind the still burning car. We threw ourselves over the fence and shouting, ran away from our executioners toward the gunfire. Another shot rang out, whizzing past our heads, so we dropped into the rut between two rows of strawberries. All we could do was lie in the furrow and watch the gun battle in the flickering flames, as if it were some strange play. Behind us the translator fired back but his position was far too obvious against the flames and the next shot killed him.

One soldier cowered behind the oak, while the other private ran for his life toward the dray, the bodies of Fred and Ginger and the first soldier. For five minutes voices and guns remained silent.

All around us we heard intermittent sounds. Men moved in the dark, invisible, a footfall here and there, followed by panting and soft quiet grunts.

I lay still hoping that the Poles would know we weren't German and that somehow, we wouldn't be caught in the crossfire. A warmth grew between my legs; I was pissing myself. Only a few centimetres in front of me, I plucked a strawberry and brought it back to my mouth with the slowest, smallest movement. If I am going to die, then make my last moments a pleasure. It was sweet; sweeter than I had ever tasted a strawberry before. I reached for a second, as the night filled with gunfire again and the soldier behind the oak ran after his comrade, down the road. More shouting, then two shots, no return fire. Questions cut across the darkness and the reply came that they were both dead.

Even then, we did not move, we lay there in the dark, listening to the voices change from panicked shouts to questions and replies. Then finally Michal cried out, 'We are Polish. A man and a child. We are unarmed.'

The men in black, hoods over their faces, only eyes and mouths visible, prodded us with their rifles, then reached down and pulled us to our feet.

'Zegota?', gasped Michal indicating that he was Catholic and working against the Germans.

'Ludowa,' replied a hooded man.

'Ludowa,' replied Michal, recovering from his possibly fatal error with a sideways glance at me. I held my tongue.

Oh God help us, cried Jana, *they're communists!* I said nothing.

DARK KING 21ST CENTURY

10

Tara turned in her sleep, tangled among the bedsheets. Her cheek ached where the gash sliced her face. The night was hot and sticky and the air humid and close. Outside the wind dropped and somewhere, in the forest beyond, night birds were calling. She was softly murmuring in her slumbers, as if in reply.

The path was narrow as the forest closed all around them. Cory came up beside her and gave Tara a look of deep concern. This was not what they had anticipated. All around the shadow figures glided effortlessly whilst keeping some distance from them. Tara knew they were being corralled, shepherded in a particular direction but for now they did not resist the dark forms. The path grew steeper as the air grew rank with the smell of rotting flesh. At the tree line was a crest and beyond that a glow of firelight. Tara's cheek throbbed like a warning bell. She could feel the skin turning into scar with every step she took. The Forest Mistress passed among the trees some distance from them but this was of little solace; so many times, she watched over them but did not intercede. Tara knew they must prove their worth, without her help. They gripped the handles of their scabbard knives as one and quickened their pace. Still the dark forms kept up with them, forward scouts who would surely warn the Dark King that they were here.

Coming over the rise the trees ran down into a steep ravine that curved on either side of a wide circle as if they were solid sentinels for this unholy place. In the centre, a huge fire illuminated a hundred or more hooded figures. Each one looked up at the Dark King who stood above them on a large rock platform. He alone was staring at Tara and Cory as they entered.

'Welcome Falcon Wielder. Welcome young Sparrow.'

Cory bristled at what was obviously an insult but Tara placed her hand on his, as he clutched the grip of his weapon - bone handled with a six inch steel blade. A weapon that Cory was determined to use if challenged.

The Dark King smiled at the effect of his sarcasm, these two are easily manipulated, he thought then gestured for them to be seated and for his sentries to stand aside. The shapes glided backwards and formed a perfect circle among the trees. The Dark King gestured to his guests as if to say, you see the power I command then sat on his throne, stroking his chin.

'I know you think you have understandings with the armies of the east, the Broken Shield. But do not be fooled. I am the great power here. My people come from a thousand years of legend and we will rule when the Broken Shield is truly broken. We will rule for a thousand years to come.'

Tara and Cory looked at each other and smiled. It was the Dark King's turn to bristle this time but he held his composure.

'Join me, we are natural allies. Far more than your fair-weather friends from the east.'

Tara and Cory stood up defiantly and though he indicated they should be seated again, they shook their heads. Tara took her brother's hand and began to hum. Cory followed suit and, in the distance, off in the forest, there was a great rustling.

'I am not finished! The dark and the light will clash and we will extinguish the light. Our darkness will be the new light. You can share this with me if you are wise. Remember I once had dealings with the East too. They are not to be trusted. I am always as I appear, evil yes. But the best kind of evil, necessary evil.'

Tara and Cory remained standing, the rustling turned to what sounded like the ocean. Cory stepped forward and half drew his sword from its sheath. The dark soldiers on all sides crouched in

anticipation. The Dark King raised his hand and his forces stood down. Tara turned in a half circle and met the gaze of all who threatened them.

'We are not alone and will soon be joined by those who came once before. They are the sleeping giants of the west. Once they are roused, they will be unstoppable. My advice is to leave these lands and make no further claims.'

'How dare you address my people! I AM RULER HERE! You will show me respect' and with that he pointed to the pair. With finality he sliced his hand through the air. His soldiers moved toward them slowly in an ever-tightening circle.

Cory drew his weapon while Tara raised her arms high into the air and the sky above burst into movement. The Dark Army moved closer, like a tightening noose, as the two warriors stood back-to-back, the shadow soldiers failing to see that the sky was darkening *above them until it was too late. Birds of every description swept down in flocks that arced through the ravine, scattering the Dark Army in all directions. The black figures struck out but were no longer in formation. Ravens, crows, magpies - birds of every size and description swooped and tore at the dark army's flesh, as fleeing soldiers cried out in pain, covering themselves with their cloaks. Tara took her sword and ran at the King. Either side of her, two falcons with wings outstretched, dived toward him. The Dark King turned and fled into the cave that disappeared inside the end of the ravine.*

Tara disentangled herself from the sheets. The temperature had dropped for the moment and a gentle breeze blew at her curtains. Outside the dawn chorus, loud and exultant announced another day… another school day. Exhausted, she had survived one more night of nightmares, terrible dreams that she remembered all too clearly. Earlier came a fitful dream full of night terrors that only vaguely consisted of fragments and then the last one, clear and concise, in which she had spoken to the Dark King. She would tell Cory what deal the Evil One was trying to make with the two of them. She dragged herself to her feet and wearily made ready for school.

* * *

Tara came back from lunch to discover her teacher Miss Cork had written two lists across the board. The first was a list of countries the children's parents, grandparents or even great grandparents had come from, some Asian but many more European. She knew this to be the start of a term long project, finishing with an International Food and Culture Day.

School had been so hard for her over the past month or more. She hadn't slept well and that turned her class into a drudge. But here was something Tara had always loved, remembering the previous year's festivities, and for the first time, in some while, she felt connected to the present.

'This will be ready for the final week of the term - a multicultural display. You can investigate any of the aspects in the list on the right, with any of the countries on the left.'

Most of the class wriggled with enthusiasm and the energy caught hold of Tara too. This was the kind of schoolwork she could become consumed in and hopefully put her troubles away for a while.

'You may work independently or with a partner, but no more than three to a group. You can discuss with your friends what you want to do.'

From across the other side of the room her newly arrived friend Katya gestured, pointing to herself and then to Tara and finishing with a broad smile. Tara nodded in reply.

Tara put her hand into the air and Miss Cork turned to her and smiled. 'And yes, Tara you can present dioramas as part of your display.'

Everyone laughed, for it was common knowledge that Tara loved building worlds out of cardboard, balsa and paint. Tara smiled back knowing that whatever Katya did, her own role was assured. It felt good to have a partner, someone who would make her forget the troubles of home. Perhaps this time her work would even surpass her model last year of "The Oracle at Delphi. "

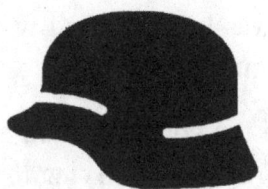

MESSAGE WINTER 1938

11

The corporal stood in the cold hall, stamping his feet to keep warm. Across from him in the alcove, the radio operator decoded the message and signed off at the bottom of the sheet with a quick signature and the date, then placed the details in the log. Everything must be notated, accounted for, this they both knew. One day the great history of the Reich and how it transformed the world would be written and even a small part like this would be scanned and discussed by countless German scholars. This, their leader had told the gathered members of the brotherhood only the previous night before they sat for the evening meal in the great banquet hall. The radio operator admired his handiwork and smiled at the importance of even his small part in the great endeavour.

'Here Mueller,' he offered the missive to the corporal who stood by the door.

The SS soldier looked at the paper from a distance not daring to take it. He stood far enough away that the radio operator would have to get up to give it to him. Corporal Horst Mueller regarded it, as if it was a snake.

'Is it good?'

The radio operator shook his head but said 'Some good, some bad.' Horst knew he was being played with and bad news could have unpleasant consequences.

Scheisse!' cursed the corporal shaking his head. 'You take it,' he said stepping further away, trying to prevent the note being handed to him. But the radio operator just shook again, gesturing that this was his base and that he couldn't leave his station.

What bullshit, thought Mueller, if I wasn't here, he'd have to deliver the bloody thing himself.

'Arsehole!' He snatched the sheet out of the operator's hand and walked down the ancient steps, no wider than a single man. A vagrant cold wind whipped out of nowhere, chilling him to the bone. The old castle played on his nerves as four centuries of ghosts and misery seemed to hide in its shadows and like the wind, it clawed at him. It was grim and unrelenting, despite the inspirational talks at night. This wasn't what I signed up for, he thought.

At the bottom of the stairs the wing opened out into a large long corridor that ran to the next tower facing the valley that ran off into the west, with a meandering river and quilted farmland. The corporal climbed the narrow spiraling staircase to the final floor, where long oblong windows stood evenly around a circular room, each shuttered and darkened with heavy drapes. Smoking coals and small flickering flames that rose being the only light. They gave an intense red glow that accentuated the deep crimson and black of the swastika flags that overwhelmed the room with their hanging magnificence. The leader liked atmosphere. In the centre of the room striding back and forth, his dark uniform and polished leather boots shimmering in the firelight paced Hitler's right-hand man.

Horst Mueller came to attention, the folded piece of paper shaking slightly, in his hand.

'Herr Obergruppenfuhrer, this was just received from the Tatra mountains.'

Heinrich Himmler stood in the middle of the 'black sun' motif that stretched in marble across the floor of the west tower of Castle Wewelsburg. It was cold within the walls of this old renaissance castle and he had ordered two burning briars to be placed either side of the insignia. Their bright flames cast light that danced up the smooth walls. The figures on the ancient tapestries moved, shifting in the firelight, as if desperately attempting to return to the cities from which they had been stolen. The images made the young corporal shudder, only adding to the terror he felt standing before the second most powerful man in the Reich.

What was it the Brownshirt Voight had said 'Go with Himmler. He's the cruelest.' Now he understood what the ill-fated sergeant meant.

Himmler always took messages here. The symbolism pleased him- the tapestries taken from conquered lands, the furnishings given up by those who now obeyed their masters or were dead. But most of all, the marble mosaic that formed a black -green circular disc beneath his leather jackboots, with twelve zigzag bolts of power radiating out to an outer ring - that symbol was centuries old and meant some kind of connection with the power of the nobles that had once built the castle and ruled this land. Mueller too recognised how much pageantry played into their world. Himmler appeared to draw energy from the alchemy of the castle; it seemed to course through his body and heighten his senses. To Mueller, he appeared larger than life.

Himmler's mission, the castle's regiment knew was to find 'The Source', the validation of their right to rule their inferiors and the Brotherhood of the SS were the bearers of this great tradition.

'Our future is written in our past,' Himmler declared to his assembled men and for Horst and those around him, each one felt sure that all he decreed would come to pass.

'This noble cause is justified by history; our race stretches back in purity for a thousand years. As it will for another thousand.' Only the previous night at the regiment banquet he declared himself to be the reincarnation of a tenth century Saxon King. Horst had never heard of Henry the Fowler and didn't understand the idea of reincarnation but so many wondrous things had come to pass in the last few years that he held his skepticism in check. Every night he and his fellow soldiers marveled at the gains Hitler made for Greater Germany, defying the French and British - re-arming the Rhineland, unifying Germany with Austria and recently liberating the Sudeten Germans from the Czechs. Anything seemed possible. Perhaps Himmler really was the embodiment of an Ancient King he thought. Miracles seemed to happen for my superiors he thought ... I will wait and see.

Horst also remembered the tirades when things did not go to plan. Always keep in your head that a transfer to some less elevated position was a possibility, he reminded himself. He just wanted the war to start so that this grinding routine could end and his life become more animated.

Himmler had tried so many times now, from Tibet to Iceland, sending his scientists and soldiers in search of the mythos of the Aryan lineage, to trace the great German people back to their roots in folklore and legend. Maybe this time it would eventually reveal itself Horst hoped, as he observed closely the look of anticipation on his leader's face. Keep the faith Horst told himself but remained a good distance from the man who could make or break a soldier. Nervously, the corporal studied Himmler, wondering if he might escape the infamous fury his master meted out to those who displeased him.

Horst stepped back a few steps, as Himmler opened the note slowly, sure that their leader was savouring the moment of triumph. The Half-Moon Cave, the legends, the old myths all had to be true, this was the latest mission that all in the castle had been discussing, wanting to believe. It would lead to the fabled Underground City of Agharta, to Shambhalla the subterranean world. The opening that once belonged to the Buddha but now would be Germany's. Once the Reich had mastered them all, all the lesser races and set them to work in service of the glorious fatherland; once they had cleansed the land of the impure - the Jews and Slavs, the Gypsies and all the other degenerates. Once they had set up the new world order, then the mystic paths would align with the occult master that was their leader - Himmler.

Horst quickly read his face and trembled. Again nothing. The expedition had not found Shambhalla, the world beneath this physical plane. Nor even the entrance to that world. Horst took several more steps backwards in slow succession.

Himmler screwed up the radio operator's typed message and tossed it to the floor. It rolled to Horst's feet but the leader seemed oblivious to the fact that he was not alone.

'No matter,' he muttered to himself, 'We will make our will felt. After all I am the Lord of Atlantis'.

Horst breathed a sigh of relief as Himmler walked away, without dismissing him.

FOREST SUMMER 1944

12

The communists quickly and efficiently ransacked the car, taking food, ammunition, the officer's pistol, and the soldiers' rifles.

Although we were unarmed, Michal and I walked ahead of the group; six men in all, the first of which kept his rifle trained on us. As I turned back to look at him, he grimaced and gestured for us to keep moving. Why are they treating us as if we are the Germans?

Another carried Michal's rifle and it didn't seem they were going to give it back. No-one spoke to us; no-one told us where we were going. Or why it was necessary to keep our hands on our heads? It did not feel right to Michal, I could see it in his face. We were Poles just like them, not Germans. But then perhaps *they* were not just like us.

I tried to pretend that it was like being in trouble in class, when 'Old Man Petrol' forced us to stay in at lunchtime, with our hands on our heads. Our classroom teacher Mr Petrov would finally relinquish and send us off to the grounds about twenty minutes in. Everyone knew it was because 'Old Petrol Pump' got hungry for his own lunch. We loved making fun of our foolish teachers, talking in the few American words we knew from the movies. Words they didn't understand. Perhaps our trouble was like this. Would a walk in the forest end on a happier note too? Neither Michal or Jana was optimistic.

After a couple of stumbles, we both put our hands by our sides and the guards said nothing. I think even they could see how unrealistic it was. The forest grew darker the longer we walked. The light wasn't fading, instead the trees grew closer together. After a while the light began to change again as the trees thinned out and we slowly rose, heading up to the tree line. I tried to watch our paths. Yes, I was almost certain. We had tracked back on ourselves, every so often. I broke off a branch, threw its budding leaves to the ground. Ten minutes later we crossed the path again and I watched Michal tread the buds into the earth. It was as I suspected, they were doubling back on themselves every so often, to cover their tracks. The soldier behind me pushed me hard in the back. It was a defensive strategy; a short loop back around might bring you around to where you might confront an enemy if you were being followed.

'Oh, this one is smarter than she looks!' he offered to the man who was their leader. He grunted in recognition, then spoke to me.

'You know the forest girl? You know country ways?'

The others all sniggered at the innuendo.

'No, I am from the city but I am smarter than *most fools* give me credit for. I watch and learn.'

They all laughed and even the leader, knowing he was bested, chuckled. *Winning respect is done by doing the job beyond expectations*, my father always said to me. *Failing that, humour works well.* Perhaps I had won this man over, just a little.

It grew dark and again without a word they stopped. We set up camp, while there was still light. All the men fell into various roles like clockwork as they had done a thousand times.

'Get firewood and don't get lost.' It was the leader as he looked me up and down, still distant, still dismissive.

As I walked away, they were tying Michal to a tree. Me, they seemed to trust. A half an hour later I returned with more wood than any girl my size could be expected to carry. Nothing was said. My father's advice did not have the desired effect.

By supper, Michal had been untied and we were sitting around the embers of a fire. He remained silent, watching, studying their leader, fleetingly looking across to me. Perhaps we would make a run for it in the middle of the night. I had no idea what Michal was thinking but we had heard things about the communists, things that now seemed ridiculous but I wondered. Try as I might I was unable to catch Michal's eye for more than a second. It was clear he was being cautious, weighing things up.

We were fed. What little they had was shared between all of us. Was this a good sign? Then the four men passed a flask between them, but did not offer Michal any of it. The other two were on watch. Beyond the fire their leader studied me, long and hard. He had been watching, without any comment, for some time.

'So, what's your name girl?'

Damn this, I've had enough! In the glow of the fire, I stood up and kicked off the buckle shoes. *Stupid shoes, they were never made for walking in swampy forest anyway!* I pulled my pinafore over my head, by which time every eye was upon me. I lifted my dress and pulled down my underwear.

'My name is Bronek... what's yours?'

Leave them laughing my father said. If the Germans had arrived at that moment, brought there by the roaring laughter, they would have found four men, no five for even Michal was laughing, five men rolling on the ground aching with the pain of it. When they had almost come back to sensibility, I took my penis in hand and waggled it at them. And they collapsed again. Finally, the two sentries came back, to the camp, to investigate and soon all seven men were laughing, until they cried. I stripped buck naked and pulled my old pants, shirt and work boots out of my knapsack. No-one looked away. As I pulled up my britches with my back to the fire, I wiggled my arse at them and they were off again. We laughed together for several minutes more, each time they thought they had control, another one of them would set the whole group off. No-one was on guard.

As we settled again by the fire, the partisans one by one peppered me with questions. Where had I come from? Where were my parents? How had I escaped? Michal listened just as attentively, though I thought his look seemed to say, *I knew all along*. So many questions that brought nothing but exclamations and admiration for my ingenuity and boldness. The Wehrmacht had arrested so many of the professional class, my father being an engineer, I explained and at first, they used him in some factory, utilising his engineering skills. My father would not talk about what they were making him do, all he said was, 'For now it was keeping us safe.'

Then one day he came home saying that they no longer wanted him and he feared for what would happen next, I told my attentive audience.

But I kept some parts of the story to myself. I heard my mother and father wondering aloud as to whether the Germans had discovered our family history. The Germans didn't need an excuse or reason in Poland; they seemed to be intent on finishing us all off. Practicing Jews first, families that didn't even consider themselves Jews anymore and then the rest of the Poles. Though the Partisans laughed and praised me, I still did not give them everything, not the ghetto, not the first uprising, not the biggest secret. I didn't trust these communists yet.

At the end of the night their leader grabbed me by the arm and still chuckling he said, 'If I live, this is a story I will tell over a hundred, no a thousand beers for the rest of my life.' Stepping back, he studied me for some time. 'My name is Jakub. You are a Jew like me, aren't you? That explains the masquerade.' I nodded and he smiled but he was still puzzled.

'But you have not had the cut?' he said, pointing to my crotch.

'No, we were raised as Poles but never as Jews. My father would have none of it.' He smiled, understanding probably more than the others. 'Made no difference to the Germans, though. They found out. They came for us.'

Something altered in Jakub then, maybe my story was just a little like his. I saw him soften, no longer guarded and resolute but perhaps a little like we all had once been, before the war had changed us. He looked at me in much the same way that Michal did, it was reassuring. He held his finger to his lips and shook his head slowly, adding 'We will not talk of this again. You were lucky not to be raised with religion; you should thank your father for that.'

'If he's still alive' I replied. Jakub nodded a look of serious intent on his face.

When we went to bed that night, neither Michal or I was bound. Michal looked across and realised that it was me who had worked some kind of magic here; that these communist partisans saw us differently now. He smiled a deep thank you. I felt for the first time, that we were not going to be shot.

Before dawn we rose, dressed then walked on, though now we walked among them. Michal striding ahead in his half a league boots and me wherever I chose in the line. Often, I would walk with Jakub but just as often I trailed at the rear.

You see Jana, these communists are not so bad.

We shall see, nothing is certain in war.

That much I could not argue with and Michal's rifle had not been returned to him so perhaps Jana had a point.

The day hung with grey diffused clouds high in the sky, high enough that it didn't feel like rain. All around us animals could be heard, scattering unseen, spooked by the arrival of men. The birds moved from branch to branch either side of our single line, constantly calling out, announcing our presence. Nature seemed to have no time for us or for the war.

The forest trails most often took us far from roads and villages. For hours on end we walked in total silence, never stopping, merely passing the water canisters back and forth along the line. Each time I thought we were completely alone, men would appear out of nowhere, as if they had dropped from the trees and would then walk beside us. Sometimes words were exchanged as we walked in tandem, other times it felt more menacing, the unspoken message being *'you may move through our territory as long as you keep moving.'* Despite a common enemy, solidarity was not always a given. If we halted it would be only briefly, while Jakub spoke to them. I caught only fragments of what they were saying, always pretending to appear disinterested. Jakub offered what he knew of German troop movements, the others told him what they knew of the Allies and the Polish Government in Exile. Jakub said no more than he had to, not identifying his ideology, mostly he simply grunted or nodded. In the end safe passage was negotiated though some other militia's area and we moved on. Many of these encounters took less than a minute and then these ghost men were gone, disappearing as if they had never existed. I wondered where they lived, did they live in the trees or underground? Nowhere did we ever come across tents or wooden structures.

The deeper into the forest we went the colder it became, the warmth of the day forgotten, as soon as the sun moved toward the horizon. One of the sentries from the previous evening, Marek took a liking to me and asked me more questions about my family in a low voice, so that Jakub would not hear at the front of the line. I told him how had I escaped and in return I asked him personal questions. Where did he come from, was his family alive, how long had he been fighting?

'Jakub and I grew up together in a village in the north. We have been timber-getters all our lives. It is why we can find our way through these forests.'

'Michal is a timber-getter too,' I added. He just grunted. A child they might take to but not the man, that much was obvious. I had won no favours for my friend.

'Where are we headed?'

'It will do no harm to tell you, you are going to a camp and you will work. As for your big friend, we are not so sure. He is not one of us.'

'A communist you mean?'

'Yes.'

'Why should that matter?

'Oh, it matters, it matters a great deal.'

As if I had insulted the cause they were prepared to die for, he walked away without another word. I watched him move further up the line, leaving me to keep the rear

The forest grew quiet during the afternoon; sounds from the outside world wafted in. A truck changing gear up a hill, a herd of goats moving along a country lane, the bells around their necks clanging, the sound of convoys travelling east and west at great speed. Most seemed so far away they presented no threat. Some sounds were so close I felt certain we would run into them around the next bend but I came to realise how deceptive a forest could be. In the quiet the sounds seemed to travel great distances so I could never be sure how far away danger really was. Still, we remained in single file keeping a constant pace. No-one spoke to me for the rest of that afternoon; each man lost in his own world. Our thoughts were only our own, a steady rhythm of breathing, motion and contemplation that melded together.

The sewers seemed a long time ago. My family home seemed even further away as a deep ache grew inside me, welling up in my chest and shoulders, tightening my throat. I tried to sense if my family, my mother and father, my older brother were still alive but I could get nothing.

Don't cry, not in front of them. Jana was right. I held the pain back inside me and pushed it down.

What others were thinking I could only guess; still I imagined that they also thought about home and family and probably how closely death walked with us. It made me feel connected for the first time.

The tranquility around us all day made the noise that entered our world in the early evening sound so jarring, it felt monstrous.

First a single roar then another layer of engine whine, then an entire cacophony of screaming internal combustion madness. Like a drone of wasps moving in every direction. It froze us to the spot.

'There's a road nearby.'

'Sounds like a convoy.'

'Motorcycles at the front!'

'They're DKWs with sidecars. I know the sound.' They stopped and looked at me. It was as if I was standing with my pants down again.

'My father had one, he'd take me in the sidecar. I know that sound.'

Marek, who I had insulted only hours before, let out a low whistle of admiration. The world always seemed to be doing that, under-estimating me, never realising that though I looked like a clueless boy I was not. I had a brain that had kept me alive when all the rest of my family was probably dead. Jakub slapped me on the back, as we all moved on in silence, once more walking in single file.

Close to dusk, in the almost complete darkness we stopped as a grazing doe in the distance offered itself. Jakub gestured and they all spread out raising their rifles. Michal looked across at all of them and called out in a loud whisper.

'No, do not all fire. If there are patrols near, they'll investigate.'

'Fuck you Zegota, I'm hungry!' said Marek.

Michal strode to the nearest partisan and took his gun. 'I will do it. One shot!'

Jakub quickly turned his rifle on Michal, clearly not pleased that he had taken a weapon from one of his men. Michal ignored him but stepped to a tree and leaned into the trunk and closed one eye.

'Don't miss frajer * or I will drop you!'

* frajer - dickhead

As he steadied his aim so too did Jakub, at Michal's head. His anger was burning now but Michal barely acknowledged him. One shot was all it took; the animal fell instantly. He handed back the weapon and moved toward it. We all strode forward but Jakub followed us, still looking furious.

Gathering in a half circle, we watched as Michal leant over the doe's body muttering softly. All of us standing there, uncomfortably invading his space. The partisans all shifted toward each other, looking perplexed. 'What's he doing?'

'He's thanking it for giving up its life for us.' How I understood this I didn't know but somehow, I was certain, for it seemed the kind of thing that Michal would do.

They turned to me, all of them disturbed by the strange ritual -'It is what hunters do.'

'Only the ignorant ones!' spat Jakub, standing behind us. He glared at his men and one by one they shuffled out of his orbit.

'Be careful.' It was Jana, she was right. Michal got to his feet and Jakub pushed him forward back to the trail. As he did Jakub gestured to the others to carry the doe. They jumped to attention and did his bidding. Michal moved forward his head held high, perhaps he was proud of his marksmanship but the damage was done for all the goodwill we had won ourselves was gone now. In one action we were back at the beginning again.

Dancing With The Midnight Mare   Luca Collins

SYRENKA 21ST CENTURY

13

Tara began with a piece of ply board painted black. She measured out the dimensions of the old market square in Warsaw according to the scale. Something she was able to do from a helpful online site that gave information in English.

Her friend Katya suggested Poland - she would supply the traditional costumes and some of her parents' photos, together they would cook Pierogi and Tara would build the diorama. Tara was pleased with the arrangement as it allowed her to create all the buildings; afterwards she would get her friend to help her paint the facades. They both wanted to be the best in the class.

From the modern photos, the buildings were now painted sky blue, orange, green, red, brown, pink and various shades of creme, butting up against each other in long rows that took up each side of the square. Some were four storeys high but most were five, many had attic windows and steep sloping roofs. Periodically there were laneways that led into the space, either at corners or midway along a side. The surface of the square was all cobbled bricks in neat rows crisscrossing in tessellated patterns. In the middle was a round fountain inside which stood a rectangular granite plinth and on it was mounted a statue of a semi naked mermaid, brandishing a sword and shield. Tara would make her from clay, baking it in the sun and hand painting it a stony grey-black. She thought about the mermaid and wondered why the people of Warsaw had chosen such a creature for a city built on a river and so far from the sea. Did it have some special meaning? She would ask Katya.

* * *

'Oh, but they belong to rivers also. She's from the Vistula, a Syrenka - a mermaid and once she was caught by a merchant who wanted to sell her but then was rescued by fishermen. She is a protector now…of the city I mean.'

It was Saturday morning and they would spend the weekend working on the project. Katya had come to help paint the buildings and to teach Tara how to cook Pierogi. She'd brought some of the pastries along for them to eat while they worked.

'It's very beautiful! Miss Cork will be pleased' complimented Katya and Tara just smiled.

Tara thought that this diorama might be better than the 'Greek' one she had made for Miss Campbell, for a library display the previous year. They worked on the project all through the day and when it was done, they backlit the buildings, placing small tea lights strategically around and inside the structure. The effect was transformative. The Old Market Square came to life, as if it had been 'Touched by God' Katya said. Tara wasn't religious but she liked the idea of an unseen hand helping them. One by one they blew out the candles and went downstairs to cook. Katya's mother had packed all the ingredients they needed for the pastries. Katya stayed for dinner and then left, promising to return early the next morning after Mass, to work on the courtyard.

Tara stood on the battlements of Trelleborg and sniffed the air. There it was again, the smell of woodsmoke but mixed with something else? Not something everyday but potent enough to be familiar. And then she knew - the smell of rotting flesh. Fear coursed through her body, her heart raced. They are coming!

Cory was out patrolling the perimeter. She scanned the bushland in a wide arc but he was not in sight.

'Cory! Cory! Come back!' but there was no answer. Though they were still some distance off the sound of marching feet - rhythmic and menacing shook the foundations of the fortress. Still no Cory. Opening the portcullis, she slid underneath leaving just enough space to return and then lower it quickly. She climbed to the closest hill and there scaled an angled tree trunk jutting out from the hill, which led to a rope ladder and an observation deck. From there she could see almost three hundred degrees and a half a kilometre down to the rim of the quarry below.

There they were, in the growing dark, brandishing burning torches. Strangely their numbers had swelled; there appeared to be twice as many as previously. How was that possible? Where was Cory? The dark forces entered the quarry, their firebrands illuminating the black granite walls, casting their hooded cloaks in long threatening shadows.

Now the first of their line was rising along the path that led to the top of the escarpment, like a winding illuminated snake. And there was Cory moving across the top of the ridge some fifty metres further up the hill, still he hadn't noticed their presence. Tara leapt from the platform and landed on the slope below, hurtling forward toward her brother. She did not call to him for fear of drawing the dark army's attention.

As she ran down the hill Tara lost her footing and tumbled forward, rolling uncontrolled toward the escarpment. Pummeled by rocks, whipped by branches she fell headlong rolling forward *as the precipice loomed. Five metres, two metres. From one side a figure flashed at right angles to her descent and crashed bodily into her, flattening her to the ground.*

There in a cloud of dust they lay- Cory and Tara, as the first of the burning torches appeared on the rim. Silently they scrambled to their feet and disappeared back into the trees above. A minute later they slipped under the portcullis, lowered it and climbed up to the battlements.

'Why is there so many of them?' asked Tara

Cory stared down at the moving ripple of lights that swirled up the hill - a tide of terror, glowing in the darkness. 'Look, they are the same number but they are carrying a torch in each hand.'

'NO! They are going to burn us out!'

Tara climbed onto the roof and turned on the tap of the old water tank that sat on the hill just above their fort. Even as an empty vessel the tank had taken them several weeks to drag and roll into position. But the stream of water was much too meagre to have much effect. From here she could see the first of their enemies lay a burning branch at the foot of the wall. Then the next lay another firebrand and then came another and another. Against the wall grew a bonfire, as each soldier threw one of the branches and waved the other over their head in demonic glee. Cory, beaten back by the heat and smoke climbed up beside Tara. The thick plumes stung their eyes and took away their breath....

Tara woke from sleep to find her room glowing red against the grey clouds of smoke that hung low across the floor and around her bed. The diorama was on fire. Balsa and glue, paper and paint feeding a fire that now spread from one side to the other engulfing the whole Market Square.

Desperately she looked for something that would put it out. The table it sat on was not alight and for now neither was the ply board base. The rest of the room was safe. There, on a chair lay the two oven gloves and the empty metal tray that she and Katya had carried up, that earlier had been full of pastries. She slipped both gloves on and began to pat down the flames but each time she lifted her hand the fire took hold again. As if it had a will of its own the flames were determined to continue. She clutched the oven tray and brought it down hard on a whole row then moved around the corner to the next row and the next. When she had put out the entire fire, she filled her waste basket with water from the bathroom and poured it all over the display. She did it three times to be sure, then opened the window and closed her bedroom door firmly and placed a rolled-up blanket at its base.

Amazingly, no-one had woken and as she looked at the desolation she wondered how she would explain it to her parents. Worse still, what would she say to Katya?

FIRESIDE 1944

14

The stars came out, vast across the sky from one corner of our world to the other, below them on the horizon hung a low cloud bank. A monolith of granite rose out of the woodland and all that afternoon we scaled it, determined to make the summit by nightfall and get our bearings.

Now shielded by two hard sheer rock walls, we built a substantial fire, confident that its glow could not be seen. A moonless night meant that the updraft would be relatively invisible too. I watched the smoke curl and turn like some ghostly serpent, thinning and disappearing as it rose. The men sat around the fire except for one on watch. Some talked of home, one or two simply stared into the fire content to let the flames and embers reach into their minds and take them into reminiscences. For a long while Jakub and Marek argued politics, each in turn more determined, more cutthroat than the other. Certain that the war would end within the year they agreed that what Poland would be, would depend on whether the Americans arrived first or the Soviets returned ahead of them. They both agreed that the Russians were closer.

We all salivated at the scent of frying meat. Michal cooked as much as he could, cutting it into long strips and searing it. He had even found some wild herbs earlier that day that now made the deer smell like it was cooking among vegetables. I longed for the taste of them too as we devoured serving after serving. He wrapped all that was left from the meal in leaves and handed an equal amount to each man. Michal secretly smiled at me as I stuffed it, at the bottom of my rucksack, next to my metal water canteen and the girl's clothes I carried just in case. I knew he gave an extra-large piece to me.

The last person he handed a package to was Jakub, who said nothing as he took it. Then Michal returned to his fallen log, pleased with himself.

For a few minutes we all sat in silence. It was Jakub who broke it.

'You think that deer's gone to God, hunter man?'

Michal and Jakub locked eyes. Everyone stopped mid-mouthful.

'You think that doe is resting in the Lord's bosom?' The anger, mixed with contempt and sarcasm, rippled through the air.

Michal said nothing but I could see he was stung by the words. It challenged his way of seeing the forest, his life and how he saw his place in Creation, I knew enough of him by now to know that. I stiffened, waiting, knowing that they were armed, and Michal wasn't.

'You think it had a God…you think my family had a God? What about his?' pointing to me.

'Do the Germans have a God? Does Hitler?'

He wrenched up a wad of phlegm and spat it into the embers where it sizzled loudly.

'I have no God ... but I have a rifle.' Jakub met each man's eyes in turn and each of them turned away looking at the ground. 'And I'll shoot the next fool who lets this bastard take his rifle from him.'

His anger was his true weapon at that moment and he battered each man in turn with it. He looked briefly at me; *I am the leader here, you remember that,* the look said. I swallowed hard.

'Talk to the sky all you like bumpkin kraju * you'll get no answers.'

Michal and Jakub remained like two wild cats staring at each other, defying the other to make the first move; the atmosphere crackled with resentment, while those around them squirmed. Marek met my eyes and shook his head. The silent message was clear - do not interfere.

* country bumpkin

Both remained silent, squaring off against each other. For Jakub it was a question of leadership but for Michal I didn't know. Perhaps, as he was so tall and broad, he had never had to back down and now he simply did not know how to. There appeared to be no anger in it on Michal's part, he just saw no reason to move; he remained as solid as the rock we sat upon.

One by one we slowly and silently retired, trying not to disturb the stand-off. Making ready for bed, none of us made eye contact with the two adversaries. Pissing against a tree trunk I looked back; only Jakub and Michal remained seated. There, in the soft circle of embers each returned to staring into the fire. Quietly, Michal got up.

Are they going to fight? asked Jana.

When Michal finally replied, he spoke softly but firmly, without aggression. 'Perhaps God has left the world. I don't know.' Then he moved away from the firelight and added, 'But if he hasn't I hope he is watching over us all from behind some tree.'

Jakub remained seated. He spat once again into the fire but did not look up.

We walked all the next day until once again the temperature dropped with the coming of evening. Jakub looked around, unsettled by the forest. He spoke to one of the partisans who took another man, each of them moving away on opposite sides of the main group.

Something is wrong. Jana observed, she had been absent from me all day, now she was back from wherever it was she lived, no, lived was the wrong word, wherever she existed when she wasn't watching over me.

'We'll go another half a kilometre, if no-one comes out of the trees we scatter and go to ground … and await my orders.' The others nodded around their leader, Michal nodded too. It seemed that he too knew something was wrong. I caught up with Marek, he looked frightened, the little boy showing through his face and body. He looked down at me and as I opened my mouth he gestured for me not to talk.

'We are home. But no-one has come. No sentries have stopped us.'

'SHUT UP!' ordered Jakub.

I dropped back to Michal and fell into line again. We walked another half -kilometre and still nothing. The two scouts returned and simply shook their heads. And with that several hand signals were given. Move silently, spread out, slow down, rifles cocked.

Now more than ever Michal and I felt helpless and vulnerable. Michal strode up beside Jakub and followed closely behind him biding his time. We reached a stream and looked for a way to cross. Michal turned to Jakub, he was not demanding but he was firm.

'Give me back my rifle; give the boy a gun too!'

Jakub thought about it for a moment but shook his head, apparently still unwilling to trust him. Michal stopped and stood his ground at the point where a tree trunk straddled the stream, the only point at which they could cross. His huge frame blocked their way. It could have been a defiant gesture but Michal had no aggression. I marveled at how he could do that, no matter the situation.

'I don't share your politics and you don't share my God. But if you give me a gun, I will fight to save your life, as well as mine.'

Jakub stopped and so did the others, their faces all turned to their leader. Michal folded his arms and met Jakub eye to eye, standing before the fallen tree. Again, though he was resolute there was no belligerence in his actions. Michal demanded to be considered without the other losing face.

'One day we will bring these butchers to heel. You will need men like me by your side. I would not betray you. I am Polish.' He said the last three words with a sense of pride, that spoke to them all, regardless of politics or religion. It was enough, Jakub lowered his canvas sack and gestured for the man beside him to do the same. The gentle clink of metal sounded as the bags unfolded on the ground. Michal smiled and stepped aside.

They each took turns to cross on the wide mossy log. Michal opened the bags and took out his Heym SR 30 and handed me one of the dead German's pistols, a PO 8 made by Mauser. He showed me how to cock it and I held it facing it down to the ground, afraid to raise it, my hands trembling. Michal threw the sacks on his back and we crossed in silence. 'Made by Mauser,' I thought to myself, 'you are such an idiot, maybe you are going to die and still you rattle off this useless information.'

Yes, you are an idiot; pay attention, Jana chimed in.

Reaching a break in the trees we found a small collection of camping bags and blankets. Jakub crouched down and put his hand inside the closest bag then went to the fireplace and moved aside the top layer of ash, placing his hands on the charcoal below. Then he shook his head and it seemed that they all knew the truth of what was happening here.

'This is a breakfast fire. Ten maybe twelve hours old.'

We spread out again and began to walk up a gentle slope that then descended into an even denser copse of trees than where we had come from. All of us crouched low to the ground as if the weight of evil was crushing us.

From some distance away a rifle shot rang out, then shouts in German. Through the bushes came a crashing sound, the swish of undergrowth and the face of terror. A boy-man maybe eighteen no more, falling, scrambling up again, turning this way than that, as more shots whistled past him. He didn't see us lying flat on the ground, as he rushed up the hill toward the camp. He reached the top, silhouetted in the half-light for a moment, he hesitated not knowing whether to turn right or left. A single shot rang out and he jerked violently, then dropped as a dead weight. Several slaps on the back congratulated the German sharpshooter as, laughing and joking, they disappeared back where they came from.

We lay there for some time, barely breathing, as the darkness came down all around us. As one we rose and moved deeper into the trees that closed in above but spaced out from each other at ground level, as old forests do. The thickly wooded landscape became as black as a cave now, but in the distance a battery of lights lit rows of conifer trunks, stark in silhouette. Four troop trucks stood in a line, their engines running and their headlights illuminating a long trench. It stretched the distance of a football field but no wider than a single body length. At times it curved around a tree trunk but then ran true again. The Germans stood above the pit that was almost filled in, smoking and talking. Here and there a leg or a hand, but never a head, protruded from the soil. The bodies had all tumbled head first into the pit. On the rim lay the bodies of the last of those that had dug the elongated grave. The Germans began to throw them in.

The soldiers numbered maybe fifty, possibly seventy, it was difficult to count as they moved in and out of the shadows and light. Certainly, there were enough to fill four troop carriers.

'What do we do?' asked Marek.

Jakub looked out beyond the trucks into the darkness and I knew he was assessing the land like I would have done; thinking how to make the forest work to our advantage. 'We move out and we wait up ahead.'

One of his men was sent back quickly to the encampment. Jakub signaled for the rest to follow him. Michal looked at me and I could almost speak his thoughts. What could seven men and a boy do against seventy?

WAR AND FOG 21ST CENTURY

15

Katya laughed. 'Oh, it doesn't matter. We will start again. We'll say this one is what the city was like at the end of the war. My grandparents left us pictures. Let's name it 1945 and use the photos.'

Tara was relieved. 'Yes, and I have the other half of the plywood, we can do it again and tell the story of what happened next!' she added.

Katya looked at the wreckage and thought for a moment. 'Yes, but this time let's do the cobblestones and the fountain first…'Cause, they will be the hardest.'

Tara was glad to have help, they would share the endeavour and her friend would tell her how such a beautiful place came to be destroyed.

The smell of smoke still lingered from the night before but was quite mild. Her parents were sleeping in this Sunday morning and were none the wiser. Later in the day she told her parents that this wreckage was always intended, as an accompanying piece to the one they were now working on. Her mother looked displeased, saying she was unhappy with fire in the bedroom but did not object to them continuing. As she left, she looked up, remarking that perhaps the smoke alarm wasn't working?

Tara and Katya took the greater part of the day to rebuild the old town market square and paint it. Any paint left over was mixed together to make blacks, browns and greys and these were added to the bombed-out shell of the square in 1945. Katya came with two traditional Polish costumes and they tried them on while they waited for the paint to dry.

'You wanted to know how the square was destroyed, yes?'

Tara nodded. Katya placed two chairs facing each other and gestured for Tara to sit. Before she began, she sat quietly and appeared to be gathering herself together, in order to begin the telling of the ordeal.

The story of the uprising in Warsaw was something her parents and grandparents told as almost a ritual, certainly a story of national pride and Katya relayed it with great earnestness and a sense of tradition. Tara sat silently absorbing it all.

Finally with a deep breath Katya concluded, 'But Warsaw wasn't the only one, oh no. On both sides, the people rebuilt their streets and buildings in both Poland and Germany, just like they remembered them from before the war. It was good for their souls, my grandmother said.'

Tara thought it had been a perfect day until the evening meal. It came with a familiar sense of unease; a feeling that unsettled Tara and Cory. They exchanged looks across the table triggered by their parents' subdued hostilities.

As it was a school day tomorrow both children went to bed early.

A thick fog hung along the quarry floor and swirled around Tara's feet as she made her way to the winding path up to the bushland. She could not escape the feeling that she was being shadowed. The forest above was covered in a blanket of low-lying mist, through which saplings and small bushes pushed their crowns. From the corner of her eyes, movement flashed and was gone. The slope was steep and the terrain was tricky when she could not see what was at her feet.

'Have you come to see my handiwork?'

Tara jumped, the question appeared to be right beside her. Deep and demanding she knew it to be the voice of the Dark King.

Look!' he commanded.

An object sat on the hillside, an island in a slow turning grey sea of fog. It was a seated man his legs drawn tightly together and clasped at the shins by his wrap-around arms. His face stared off into the distance, immobile like a stone gargoyle. Was he dead? Tara wondered.

She knew the face she felt sure but from where? He acknowledged nothing but she felt certain he was still alive, frozen in position. Off to the right and a small distance above the first living statue were two more. Each in the same position - legs together, hard against the chest held by the arms, head looking away, lost to this world. She knew these two; it was the butcher and his assistant from the shop in the next street. And the first one she now felt sure was the postman who came by swiftly on his bike. 'Not so fast now!' came the Dark King's sardonic voice.

Further up was a solid group clustered together, all mute and staring. Tara shuddered, her stomach clenched, a cold sweat forming on her forehead. The first of these was Miss Cork and the second the librarian Mrs Campbell. Behind them were all the teachers of her school. Gathered they looked like the pieces taken from a chess board. Her head reeled and terrible thoughts began to take hold. A fear she did not want to give credence to, as the terror charged her legs into motion. She ran to the next island, it was Katya and beyond that her mother and father who for the first time were staring straight at each other, yet still not seeing.

Tara was running now, stumbling as she went, knowing that the worst was to come. All around the hills were ringing cruelly with the Dark King's laughter.

Oh, please no! He must be here somewhere. But there was nothing but the grey fog churning, flowing around the trees, as Tara disturbed it with her frantic movements. He was not here and yet she knew somehow, he was. He must be! The fortress stood almost at the top of the ridge and at its entrance at the portcullis was a shape. An elongated shape in the distance, alone, abandoned. It was not like the others as ripples of mist fingered the contours, like they were trying to wake it up. It had fallen over. Tara reached the body and reset it upright. As it rose out of the cloud she cried out; it was Cory.

'Aaaaaargh!

The sound echoed throughout the house as 'Madame' shifted again on her foundations and she too began to wail with the sound of timbers grinding and splintering. In among the trees high on the ridge the Forest Mistress turned toward Tara and the house and closed her eyes as if in prayer.

On the second floor, the light came on in her parents' bedroom.

124 Dancing With The Midnight Mare Luca Collins

RETRIBUTION SUMMER 1944

16

Jakub disappeared toward the trucks that spotlighted the horror among the trees. Their cabins were empty. Three minutes later he returned with four petrol caps and a jerrycan.

'Let's hope they don't notice these are missing,' he said to all and no-one.

Anger and hatred fueled us all. Even against such odds, we now walked with our own, almost certain death beside us, determined to make the enemy pay. Michal carried the same need for revenge in him, his whole body seemed to go rigid.

The other partisan came back from the campsite with four single long sticks wrapped in pieces of clothing. Jakub laid them out in a straight row and doused the bound cloth with petrol.

'We have three lighters, we need yours,' Jakub said. It was a request not an order.

Michal nodded and pulled his carved wooden pipe out of his inside pocket then brought out a beautiful Ronson silver lighter, long and sculpted like the plinth of a statue with geometric deco designs. A lighter for a playboy not a woodsman.

Like the one our father used to have. I choked when I saw it. Yes Jana, just like our father's. The one sent by Uncle Wilf, all the way from America.

The instructions were clear, 'No shots unless you are certain. No two shots from the same spot. No two shots in succession.' We all nodded as if we understood but I doubted we did. If Jakub had a plan in his head, he told no-one, perhaps because there was not time, perhaps because it was only half a plan and might not work. I could see we were expected to take it on faith. I wondered how we wouldn't all end up dead; seven against seventy, eight if you counted a boy who had never fired a gun. How could we possibly win? Was this the kind of folly that only a communist would conceive? Did he intend to make a futile sacrifice and try to take down as many Germans as he could before we were all killed?

We waited in the trees, four of us perched in the branches unseen. The other four men were somewhere on the ground, hidden. From our positions there was a clear view up along the road but only to the next turn.

You can see why he is leader, Jana offered, the admiration brimming in her voice. I couldn't see it; I thought we should get away as quickly as possible before we all ended up in that long pit. I seemed to be the only one.

And then we waited….and waited. My mouth went dry and I began to shake. Fear took my whole body; my muscles ached with the tightness. I tried to distract myself; I must have checked my handgun six, maybe eight times. I watched nightbirds arrive in nearby branches; they did not notice me. I watched some of them tear away the bark and find small insects inside. Forest life moved around me, speaking gently to each other, perched on branches calling out to partners in other trees. Only the constant hum of the engines reminded me that a great crime lay below us. The night seemed to stretch on forever. It was another hour before the soldiers returned and climbed into the trucks, turned the engines over and pulled away.

I was the last and furthest out of those sitting in trees as four sets of headlights appeared and disappeared among the branches with each turn in the road, flickering, flashing, ghostly apparitions of these monstrous criminals. The trucks changed to second gear moving at no more than ten kilometres an hour on the rutted country road. Two men sat up front, a driver and a passenger while the other soldiers sat in the back enclosed in the canvas shell. The road turned and twisted among the trees and the trucks moved slowly, not shifting out of second gear.

By now, I was resolved to punish these men for all they had done to my family and to my life. Despite the hatred that consumed me it didn't replace the fear that gnawed at my insides. The first battle was with myself.

You must do this, Bron. There is no other way.

Yes, Jana I know; everything had been leading up to this. But still I struggled.

The night was moonless, dark, and cloudless. Seven men and a boy against seventy, the numbers kept running through my head. Part of me wanted to run, it seemed stupid to live like a rat, fooling the Germans for more than a year and a half only to die facing an entire company, with only a handgun. The trees held us in their embrace, as if to say we will hide you. It seemed the earth was crying out against the terrible thing that happened here and all I could hope was the forest would conspire to help us.

The first in the convoy turned the corner beneath me and then *there they were*. Four men moving, out of the woods just as soon as each of their target trucks slowly passed. Momentary figures running, illuminated by the firebrands they held at waist height, then bending low they disappeared, beside the trucks, shoving the fiery branches into the mouths of petrol tanks and then dropping flat to the ground and rolling away. The action took a second or two only. The first explosions happened in unison, the lead and the last truck, throwing their rear ends high into the air, both looking as if they were doing fiery handstands. The third catapulted sideways throwing burning men and canopy into the forest. The second ground to a halt, penned in by flaming debris but inexplicably there was no explosion. Twenty men, maybe more leapt from the tray as a commanding officer climbed out from the passenger side of the cabin, shouting orders. He stood there defiantly, in the middle of the road attempting to bring discipline and order where only fear and panic ran. Burning men careened in every direction, colliding into tree trunks and rolling among the pine needles, screaming. The first shot rang out and shattered the windscreen of the second truck, the driver thrown back hard against his seat, then slumping against the wheel, the horn blaring.

The soldiers as one dropped to the ground, in the forest and on the road. All except the officer, his long black leather coat and medals shimmering in the firelight. Another shot and he too, dropped like a stringless marionette. I could not be sure of the first shot but the second was Michal, I just knew it.

Soldiers everywhere panicked, clambering off the road and into the forest. There was silence from the able-bodied. Among the badly burnt, muffled groans escaped from them now and then as they desperately tried to stifle their pain for fear of snipers. It was several minutes before any soldier moved.

My body shook uncontrollably; my mind racing I tried to deal with this strange mix of emotions; terror, hatred, exhilaration - first one then the next in quick succession.

There were no commands, no order - just the desperate soft rush of terrified breathing and the almost hum-like groaning sound of suppressed pain. The one constant was the crackle and roar of burning canvas, rubber, and metal. Immediately below me, came the rustle of a soldier pulling himself to his feet and engaging his rifle. Invisible, hidden by the crisscross of branches, moving very slowly. I strained to see him from my position more than half-way up.

'WOHER?' a voice rang out somewhere further off, both terrified and angry. Only one word. No answer came back. I knew enough German to know he was asking 'Where ...where are they?' I also knew no answer would return; no-one was prepared to give their position to the enemy. Here in the darkness, with the power of the unknown, we could be whatever we wanted to be. A unit, a company, God's avengers, the armies of hell.

'Sechshundert,' a voice rang out. I recognised it, it was Jakub, possibly speaking the only German he knew. Six hundred, why not? Yes, why not? Jakub was toying with them. 'Psychological leverage' our card playing father used to call it. Below me the soldier appeared, hiding in the shadows; from above I could see his helmet as it caught the burning truck's flickering light. I steadied my hand as best I could, but I was shaking, unable to hold the gun still. Fear and doubt fought with me. He did not move but neither did I, for I was directly above him. Part of me didn't want to pull the trigger. From there, I knew, I could never go back.

Shoot Bron. Shoot. Do you think the soldier who killed me hesitated? No, he did not!

I squeezed the trigger and the weapon recoiled throwing me hard against the trunk, my ears ringing so loud that every other sound disappeared. But when I gathered myself, I could see the soldier below was spread across the ground, lying very still. I watched his body but there was no movement.

He is dead, said Jana with a level of certainty only she could know.

I looked at him for a while, trying to understand what I was feeling. So many times, I wanted to kill them, these invaders with their brutal commands and cruel indifference, their new clothes and well-fed bodies. Their guttural, snarling voices and beautiful clear skin. I hated them for what they did but also how they looked. They stood clean and crisp while they had turned me into a cellar rat, dressed in rags. And now I had killed one, like I had wanted to do for so long. I had always felt certain that when this moment came that I would be triumphant, that I would feel powerful, no longer afraid. I wasn't sure what I felt but it wasn't that.

"No two shots from the same spot." Jakub said so I climbed to a new position, wondering if this deadly, tactical game of hide and seek would go on all night. I wasn't sure if my nerves could take it. Five minutes later another shot rang out, a man screamed and that was enough. Soldiers' broke ranks from every point and began running through the forest crashing into branches, yelling and cursing, hurtling away from the burning wreckage and the invisible six hundred.

The evening star was almost down, the pale sky light coming up behind fir tree silhouettes. The air hung heavy with the smell of burning gasoline and rubber. Heat in the air and the ground disappeared quickly as the night moved into morning. Somewhere in the woods grown men were slowly dying, some whimpering, others calling for their mothers. Even this did not satisfy me. I thought I wanted to punish them all, for what they had reduced my life to, for my family, for snuffing out my blazing red sister, the one I loved best and turning her into nothing more than a voice.

But the moans of these dying men hurt me as much as their masters had. I found no pleasure in listening to their deaths, though I so much wanted to. It confused me.

It is good you haven't become a monster, Bron.

Marek pulled the dead driver to the ground then swung up into his seat. At last, the horn stopped. Jakub surveyed the landscape one last time and then climbed into the passenger side. We watched from the roadside, as they moved back and forth pushing and nudging the burning debris off the track. As the road ahead cleared, we piled into the back and settled in. Jakub looked at the empty frame of the split screen window, his side was still protected. But the bullet had also passed through and shattered the small window, behind their seats, between the cabin and the back. I could look right in.

'We'll drive as far as we can in the darkness, then pull in off the road,' Jakub said.

He looked once again at the empty space and observed, 'It'll get cold, we'll take turns.' Marek nodded and tugged his cap down over his ears.

As we pulled away, I looked across at Michal and smiled. But wait, I was up on my feet and banging on the rear cabin shell. Marek slammed the brakes on.

'We forgot something!'

A few hundred metres back in the darkness, back past the last burning truck and one or two of the soldiers lying somewhere in darkness, groaning and getting acquainted with death, there I found what I sought. I scooped them all up and ran back to the truck. By now they had all clambered down watching me approach in silence.

'You are going to need one of these.'

I handed Jakub all four petrol caps. He smiled and studied them for a moment then handed one each back to Michal and me.

'If we live comrades, I will get these turned into medals and you can wear them when you march on liberation day.'

Marek removed the failed tree branch and replaced the cap and we pulled away into the darkness. *If we live comrades.* The camp, the sanctuary we had been depending on was gone, its' people lying in an unmarked long shallow grave, somewhere in the forest.

If we live comrades, Jana repeated. *Where are we to go now?*

BIKE 1944

17

Four in the morning, the world beyond the broken windshield was fleeting and alien, as we raced away from the lost camp and the murder pit. Michal drove with me beside him, Jakub by the window. Unable to stay awake at the wheel, Marek had retired to the back. Outside the darkness gave away nothing; we could see no more than five meters in front of us. A pothole here, a frightened deer or rabbit skittering off there. Jakub was meant to be navigating but exhaustion had taken him also and he lay slumped against the passenger door. As there was only one route, we decided to let him rest at least till we came to the next crossroad.

I watched him sleep and wondered what kind of a man Jakub might have been had war not altered his destiny? What does it mean when you tell yourself you probably don't have a future, that even if this war ends you may not be alive to see it? Do you still believe in the communist life you want for your country, while you are certain that you will have no part in it? What does it do to you when you decide you must kill in order just to last another day? I knew that last question could be asked of me.

At first light we hid several kilometres up a side road, covering the truck with branches so that it could not be seen by land or air. We slept under it for most of the day taking turns to stand watch. And that is how we moved for four days on the contents of the three jerrycans that were in the back of the truck, driving at night, sleeping by day, till we arrived in an area where they hoped to find other communist fighters. We were closer to the Germans than either Michal or I wanted to be. But we had no say in where these partisans chose to wage war.

'I wouldn't have thought it possible, to travel so far and not be stopped,' offered Michal.

'Maybe there is a God,' said Jakub, half sarcastic. Michal just smiled back.

'If there is, he's looking after you, mountain man,' said another partisan who had barely offered a word to either of us before. They all chuckled. I looked at my companion, appreciating the joke and the man. It was something I had called him myself. Yes, he really was a mountain.

That afternoon, we abandoned the truck, having finally run out of petrol, and set off into the woods. Michal seemed to be as much at home as Jakub or Marek. The forests here were different, the colours and shapes, no longer marshy scrubland but now alpine, no longer mottled browns and bottle green but the constant deep green of pine forest. Jakub and Michal took turns leading on the forest paths, each deferring to the other when the route narrowed. It seemed they had reached an understanding, despite their differences. The others fell into line.

'Where are we going?' I asked the young man who had only just begun to speak to us that morning.

'Don't know…new territory ... caves I heard.'

I wondered how they knew where to go or how their compatriots knew they were coming.

Six men together would always be seen as a threat and would be arrested or killed. Carrying guns was an offence punishable by death. Some, of course, were on the run, the sons of families the Germans had demanded offer themselves as labour for the war effort. The forest was the only place where these men could walk free.

Jakub answered many of my questions about freedom fighters and who the people we met in the forest were, some of whom I knew to be Jewish partisans. When I remarked we had no radio, the reply came that finding one when you were stopped and searched would also have led to execution on the spot. These men would never allow themselves to be stopped and questioned, the idea was absurd. They would fight to the death. Perhaps it was just that a radio was hard to come by and too heavy to carry when what you wanted to be was fleet-footed and deadly. Marek said it was not something they needed, as long as they knew troop movements and how far away the Soviets were. Ammunition, food, cigarettes, maps, compasses, even radios were dropped into the forest by bombers in the night. But not for the communists if the Allies could help it, he said bitterly. The Government in Exile persuaded the British to supply the partisans but they were particular about who they supported. Still, what fell from the sky could just as easily fall into any group's hands, right or left wing if you were in the right place Marek said, chuckling to himself. When the war was over it seemed that the partisans would fight each other for control of the country.

Travelling armed in a small group was dangerous but provided an independence and level of invisibility the larger groups couldn't achieve. They managed to skirt all the patrols up until now. Any contact with the Germans was destined to end in a gun battle and having joined together, I guess they were all willing to fight to the death and probably expected us to do the same. The question was how long before it came and how many would they take with them? There was a fatalism about these partisans that scared me, they were all willing to die for their cause while I was determined to live for no cause whatsoever. Just to live, seemed enough to me.

I wondered if Marek or Jakub were weighing up the same things, asking the same questions. Or Michal who seemed to share their fatalistic approach to life also. The unknown terrified me, I wanted to know all I could about a situation, everywhere I went I tried to weigh up its potential to kill me, always measuring, always assessing; perhaps it was the engineer's mind I had inherited from my father.

You are so like your father, much more than your dreamy older brother.

Yes, Jana I am not much like my brother Ryszard, that's true. The war had made me a boy with an old man's mind.

We crossed an open field full of stubble that lay fallow for the season. Across its' rutted surface the first shoots of lucerne were appearing among the loose soil and stones. I looked around to see the others, stark against the brown rows that rolled over one sloping hill into another. Out here we were more exposed than ever but our luck held out. We merged back into the woods and disappeared.

Late in the afternoon we entered one of the caves the young man mentioned. It was large and airy, with a break in the dome that let in the sunlight. Directly below the fissure sat a fire pit and I was immediately given the job of collecting firewood for the evening.

I filled my rucksack with kindling and dry leaves, then dragged larger logs into a clearing. *When I have enough, I'll get 'The Mountain' to carry back the bigger ones.* We'd have all we needed to keep us warm through the night. Satisfied with my pile I wandered off to find mid-size branches.

Sitting beside a trail a hundred metres from a rutted country road was a Zundapp 600. My father and I had seen only two such motorcycles in our street before the war. We had stood before them admiring them both, like they were beautiful twins. Back then, German engineering was something we marveled at. The engine cover was off and beside the frame sat a leather pouch laid out flat with a series of socket spanners sitting in pockets, in descending order.

Where was its owner? Where were the Germans? Why had the repairs been interrupted? Did the soldier's company need to move on forcing him to abandon his motorcycle? Was this a stolen bike? The insignia marked it as military and German. Not Polish that's for sure, we Poles were more likely to have horses, like we were still living in the nineteenth century.

I slipped back down the dirt road to where it met the main one and hid in the bush and waited. No-one came along the road in either direction. Just how long had it been sitting there? Perhaps it was left yesterday. Maybe it had sat there a month; It was not covered in leaves so maybe it had not been here long or maybe it had and the wind had blown the leaves away, I couldn't tell. It scared me we were so close to something belonging to the enemy. Several minutes passed. Convinced I was alone, I walked back and stood before the machine. Had someone really abandoned such a beauty?

Checking the arc of the sun, yes, there was enough time to spare an hour to pull it apart before I went back with my wood.

I put down the handgun that Jakub had given me and began. Unscrewing the bolts, I laid them on the leather pouch and removed the first part of the engine. I did as my father had taught me. *Place the parts on the ground in the order you undo them, put their nuts and bolts beside them, corresponding to the holes they each went into.* I could hear his mechanical, methodical instructions inside my head. It filled me with an otherworldly pleasure to once more be following his commands.

An hour later I was sure I knew what was wrong and put the engine back together, all except for the cover. Completely absorbed, I didn't notice the lengthening of the shadows till one of them moved across the tools and I looked up.

'Was machst du Junge?'

A German corporal dressed in motorcycle fatigues, his goggles hanging round his neck was standing over me. He was not armed, but he was hostile, incensed that I was touching his beloved bike, then his look changed from indignation to curiosity. He brushed me aside and kicked the bike off its stand. Bracing it, he straddled the frame. A smile lit his face when he kick-started it just once and it roared into life.

'Du?'

I nodded my head and he gave me a look of pure admiration. Glancing over his shoulder, then he turned to me, gesturing urgently to run.

'Schnell!'

But it was already too late. A Wehrmacht officer and six more armed men appeared.

'Was geht heir vor sich?' the officer said. His gestures made it clear he was asking what the hell was going on?

The young soldier smiled apologetically and pointed to me and then to the still running motorbike, explaining that I had got it to work. The officer strode forward to take a closer look, as the six behind him shuffled in, intrigued by yet another wonder of this war. I slowly backed away to the forest edge. Quietly, no swift movements keeping my eyes on them, as they talked excitedly beside the Zundapp. *Soon the officer **must** see my gun lying beside the tools.* Almost at the tree line now. Alarmed, the officer turned quickly to me and pointed. I fled into the bushes.

Behind, I could hear him shouting orders. I heard his foot soldiers crashing through the undergrowth. I could run faster than any fully laden soldiers, all I needed was a clear path. Out of the woods, I ran down the country road, away from my partisan compatriots, away from Michal. I was gaining distance as the foot-soldiers struggled with their rifles and boots. A gun shot rang out, shattering a branch just ahead of me that fell to the ground. A second bullet hit the ground beside me, raising dust within an arm's length.

STOP BRON! They have your measure. The next shot will kill you.

I took Jana at her word and dropped to the ground, covering my head with my hands. As the soldiers caught up with me, I heard the rumble of a truck approaching. The Wehrmacht officer pulled me to my feet almost lifting me off the ground. His face was red with rage and exertion as he held the gun at my face.

'Woher hast du das?'

I knew at once why he was angry; this was not just a German gun; this was a German Officer's gun. Shaking me violently, again he demanded, 'Woher hast du das?'

'Znalazlem to!' I screamed that I found it. But he understood none of it. He threw me to the ground and kicked me hard. I pulled myself up to a seated position and scrambled backwards on all fours away from him. Taking his pistol from its holster, he pointed it, then paused. Would he shoot me on the spot? The officer looked beyond me, the surprise showing on his face, as a new wonder appeared.

Michal stepped out of the woods, with his hands above his head. The soldiers ran to him, surrounding him on all sides. He walked toward the officer ignoring the raised rifles; the shuffling soldiers, crab walking along, attempting to stay in position. It would have been comical if not for the possibility we were going to die. Michal pointed to me and then to himself and spoke.

'Ojciec.'

The officer understood none of it.

'Vater.' Again, indicating with gestures that he was my father. The officer strode up to Michal, holding the gun in his palm as evidence.

'Du?'

Michal nodded. The officer was incensed. Michal began to mime finding a gun, going through the whole act oblivious to the soldiers' rifles. They all looked on in astonishment, at this giant's apparent disregard for them. When he was finished, he stood before the officer, his hands wide apart, as if to say, there is the explanation take it or leave it.

The officer was flummoxed, not knowing what to make of this strange little play they had witnessed, while his men stood watching, just as taken aback and dazzled by Michal's charade.

Regaining his composure, he walked up to Michal and struck him across the head with the gun's handle; Michal barely buckled, instead he held out his arm toward me and in a strange kind of deference, the soldiers parted and allowed me to come to my protector.

'Vater,' he said again to them all, a large gash across his forehead now running with blood.

Nothing more was said as we were bundled into the back of the truck. The motor cycle was being wheeled towards us, its rider looking dismayed at how things had turned out. The officer looked in at the two of us and laughed.

'Wir haben einen Elefanten und Maus gefangen.'*

The soldiers all laughed as they climbed in, still enjoying the joke as they chained us to the seat and loaded on the bike. Opposite us sat nine soldiers but not ordinary infantrymen, these were SS troops. Michal sat resolutely, the blood still pouring from his wound. Staring at the floor as we pulled away, I could not bring myself to look at him.

Oh God Bron, where are we going?

* 'We have caught an elephant and a mouse.

HELL 1944

18

Michal sat on the hard board seat across from me with the motorbike lying on its side in the centre of the floor. He kept his head low though he still towered over the two soldiers that were either side of him. The bike's cover was not properly attached and though I was chained in place I felt the urge to crouch down and fix it.

You stay where you are. That damned bike and your curiosity has landed us here.

Jana was right. I had condemned myself and I had taken Michal with me.

Through the back flap of the truck the forest moved away and the open road disappeared behind us into fields of grain and cattle grazing behind neat wooden fences. Briefly came a village and a town and finally a city. We travelled all that night and all the next day till the late afternoon, stopping for maybe an hour while the truck refueled, and the soldiers were fed. There was nothing for us. Poles were still walking the streets as it was not yet curfew but passed us on the far side of the road some distance from the truck. Just before we pulled away, I heard someone call out in Polish the word 'slaves.' Then there was much shouting in German and I could hear the voice fading, along with the clatter of footsteps. In my mind I could see the defiant Pole running from the Germans. That same voice but further away shouted as it ran, *'Escape!'*

Manacles looped around the steel frame of the bench held us both, in a seated position. One of the soldiers across from me watched us, with great intensity. I'd tried so hard to stay one jump ahead of them, to be smarter than the Germans. In the sewers and the streets, I could always outwit the patrols but a moment of inattention had given me away. Now I no longer had control over my own life and it made me want to cry out, in bewilderment and rage. *Escape-* there was no way and nowhere to run to.

An hour before dawn we entered the underworld. A soldier pushed me viciously, then unshackled my chains. We climbed down from the truck and walked through a barbed wire fence held up with cement posts that curved almost like half-finished question marks, passing along a rough stone road to the wooden roofed archway that stood on solid stone uprights. It almost looked like a railway station. Above on the arch were three words in German, though I did not know what they meant. On both sides the same kind of fence, cement uprights, and barbed wire. Equal distances apart soldiers patrolled back and forth, with guard dogs at their heels. The fence was not so high that a man couldn't run at it and scale it if he was prepared to be cut. From it came a continuous hum and the pungent smell of ozone- the fence was electrified and for a moment it brought me back to the electric train set my father had bought me for my eighth birthday. Crowned with long curled waves of barbed wire, the fence stretched off into the distance in both directions. All the grounds within were illuminated by large lamps on tall gantries, like those in a sports stadium, bathing the open spaces in harsh white light, like daylight without warmth and casting the towers and fences into long frightening shadows. At this hour it was quiet except for the distant sound of the generators.

I tried to take my bearings but the further I walked, the more this world closed in. I counted the guard posts, the towers, the number of soldiers on duty, many with large snarling dogs -all watching my moves, straining, hungry to give chase. On every side, cement and steel, tin and wood, stones and dirt, not a tree or a blade of grass anywhere. I looked up to the sky where tiny white cumulus clouds caught the moonlight, drifting to the south and freedom. I stumbled. Look down, fool. Focus.

Yes, focus. There is death in every corner of this place, focus. This is where they were taking us the first time they came for us. Jana spoke and for that moment it was reassuring to hear her voice. She had been silent for some time.

No food or drink, nothing for two nights and before that, what we ate in the forest, was barely enough. We stood in the open just within the boundary of the camp, the guards ignoring us except to make it clear we were not to move in any way. Just before sunrise the camp became active and I looked up to see three men dressed in striped prison clothes and old shoes walking towards us with a small sack. One of them, the one with the beret, carried a rounded slab of wood with a crudely fashioned handle. The guards pointed us to a room at the end of a long, low building. Cold and empty, it contained no furniture. Against the wall were a series of pipes, open at their spout, every three paces along the wall. At the end of the room was a handle, at waist height, that connected to the pipes.

The guards stood lazily back against the wall while the three men ordered us to undress. Our clothes and shoes were placed in a bundle by the door. Pushed down onto our knees, our heads were shaven. The youngest of the three came for Michal's beard but Michal quickly got to his feet. The guards raised their rifles, as the leader of the prisoners struck him in the groin with his truncheon. Michal doubled over and slumped to the floor. For no more than ten seconds he groaned in pain, before the other two attempted to pull him to his knees. But Michal was far heavier than these bird-like creatures could lift. They both looked to their leader, who appealed meekly to the Germans.

'Oben,' the guard shouted, gesturing up with his weapon.

Michal struggled up and after a few moments the boy began again. When the beard was gone the Kapo, the one with the beret, stepped up to inspect the boy's work. Michal met him eye to eye and hissed one word.

'Zemsta!'

The older man just smiled; for a moment it looked as if he was going to say something but quickly glanced at the guards and thought better of it.

They pushed us back against the wall under the open pipes. The young man at the end, turned the handle and a spattering of water came out - cold and meagre. We stood under the shower for only long enough to get wet, then were ordered to turn on the spot while we were coated in a white powder. Its stench made my head spin and my stomach heave. We dressed into the clothing of prisoners, striped and worn, and were handed shoes that weren't our own. I looked over to my clothes pile, as the young boy was gathering them up. The sound of pewter clanging on the cement floor made a dull thud, as my little cavalry horse fell from the bundle echoing in the hollow room.

One of the guards came over, picked it up and looked at it for some time. Everyone in the room watched him. As he held it, it seemed that some memory had taken hold and he was no longer with us; he had disappeared somewhere far away from the war, to a place where soldiers on horses were noble and valiant and perhaps a little boy might have dreams of being a soldier - someone brave and decent. Then he looked up to see all the eyes in the room watching him, for a moment there was this look of disappointment that this was his soldier's world, not the one of the cavalry man on horseback. He closed his hand tightly around the horse, as anger rose in his body, then he strode across the room to me. By now the faces of the prisoners were lowered. He held it out, gesturing with his hand for me to take it. I did not move. He counted at me loudly in German down from five. When he came to one, he held it just that little bit closer.

'Null.'

I knew not to disappoint myself or give him any satisfaction or possibly a chance to strike me for reaching out; I remained still. He shrugged his shoulders as if to say it's your choice, then he closed his hand and placed it in his pocket.

We were ordered out; as we passed the prison leader said softly to Michal, 'You want revenge giant man, then live.'

'Shut up!' said the guard as he shoved the Kapo in his back.

Outside the sun had just risen and the parade ground was full of people, if that is what they were. SS troops stood in straight lines their attack dogs by their sides, sitting obediently. Kapos, the men in berets, stood at the end of each line of prisoners, every one of them holding a small baton or a clipboard with papers.

'We are in Hell!' said Jana.

The towers, the dogs, my thirst and hunger, the sickly chemical smell of the strange white powder made me stagger and stole away any hope I might have felt. But it was the prisoners that undid me.

A ragged army of ghosts stood in the open space between the wooden huts, clothes hanging off them, soiled and in tatters.

Sleeves held in place with strips of cloth that did not seem to belong to what they were wearing. Some were barefoot, others had their shoes tied together in the same way as their clothes. Despite the warmth of the day many stood shivering in the morning air. I had never seen such creatures. Where did they come from? Had the Germans invented them as something to frighten their enemies?

No, these are our people. Poles, Bron. This is what they have done to them; I've heard stories of these places. This is one of them.

Standing on a raised dais the commandant spoke slowly and deliberately as if he were talking to small children or as my father used to call them, to the feeble minded. The soldiers, who had brought us, stopped and we did the same. The officer, addressing the prisoners, raised his voice only once but continued that way for a full minute. I understood none of it except that he finished every sentence with 'Ist verboten' and I wondered how many of these scarecrows understood what he was saying. His speech over, he disappeared into the only well-built building – brick, two-storeys with clean windows and stone stairs. The building sat next to the parade ground but faced away from the huts, as if it did not want to look at these ghouls they had created.

Entering the quadrangle, we were shoved to the back of the lines. Most of the prisoners kept their eyes down but the few who looked up met us with such a strange look that it disturbed me, no it frightened me. All of them looked like they wanted to take our bodies for their own. Not really eat us but wanting our bodies just the same.

A loud coarse command rang out and the men marched away, though their movements were more like staggering. We were pushed to one side, then shoved towards a man sitting at a table in the open air. He smiled at us briefly and secretly, then spoke in Polish. He was not a soldier but also not like the camp officials with the clubs. Balding and bespectacled, his skin was not the grey-white of the others, not sallow and pockmarked. His collar and cuffs were discoloured but his clothes, though shabby, did not hang in tatters. He took all our details - name, age, what city we came from, what skills we had. He told us we would be mining.

Michal looked sideways to see how far away the guards were. They all seemed disinterested in the daily routines these privileged prisoners administered. He spoke softly, 'Chlopiec?' *, indicating me with the smallest of gestures.

* The boy?

The clerk didn't bother looking at me but merely repeated what he had said before, 'Mining'

Dismissed, we were ordered back into line to follow the others. Moving away, I noticed one of the soldiers go up to the desk and talk to the clerk in German. The balding man nodded very attentively with his head bowed. The soldier pointed twice toward Michal and me, as the clerk made notes. It was the motorcycle soldier I met in the forest.

BOOK TWO

'OSOWKA'

Take what is mine, I give to thee

A sky of radiant blue

And clouds that drift for eternity

Gold crest and crimson hue.

And if you are asked to tell of love

In a world of black despair

Say that a life was lost and saved

In a promise given there.'

DRIFT IN MANY TIMES 1937 -1944

19

The days ceased to be, the world shrunk away and existence changed only from light to dark and back again. The summer was fading gradually but there was nothing to mark it. It was almost impossible to find an anchor, some kind of normal life as days of misery and hunger faded into one another. I knew that despair and madness were waiting. I could see it in the faces of those that had been beaten down by Osowka, a death camp in everything but name.

In those first weeks I made myself a vow. Even in the labour camp, this place with so little hope, I decided on a number of strategies. I told myself that I would find some sign of life, some beauty in this place. And it was there each day waiting for me - the clouds. Resplendent at sunrise with a beauty in gold and purple and again at dusk with the eternal promise of return. Every day they changed shape and colour and rolled off into the distance to a place where it was warm and free, somewhere to the south. This would be my gateway, my door to a world sometime in the future. Beyond my initial despair, I told myself that the war would end, that the Germans would finally be defeated and that I must stay alive till then.

A second strategy was to stay close to Michal for though he was wasting away he was still larger than all the prisoners there and this offered me some protection.

My third strategy was to learn the names of those in my hut and out on the yard, the names of Kapos and those who knew their way around. Some I kept my distance from, the vicious ones but others I offered the only thing I had to give - humour. Dark humour true but even here we would laugh at something just this side of death. I did impersonations of guards and a particularly mocking one of the commandant's speeches. All gibberish mixed with German and Polish swear words and every sentence finished with 'Ist verboten.' My hut would gather round me in the darkness at night to watch my 'Black Cabaret.' They tried to contain their laughter so passing guards would not hear but that only made it funnier. Make them laugh my father had said. It was the only light in our very dark world, a world that repeated itself day after day without reprieve. I lost count of the day or the month but tried to retain the year, as I and all those around me were ground slowly into dust.

All I could do to gauge the time that had passed was to count the full moons. One, two, three and more. I added to them what little knowledge I had of the time of year from my days in the sewers and streets of Warsaw. As we walked out from the camp each day I would zero in on certain deciduous trees and use them as an indicator of the changing of the seasons and the dropping of the temperature. It was inaccurate but it was all I had.

The desire, the very thought of food was the strongest thought of all. I stood in line waiting for gruel.

'Zundapp!' I heard from behind me, as I was shoved by a soldier. I fell into the man in front of me, who collapsed to the ground. Those around him helped the other man up. I got to my knees but I kept my eyes down. We all knew enough not to make eye contact with our tormentors. He grabbed me and pulled me to my feet, slapping me across the back of the head. Then he turned and walked away. I kept my place in line, slightly stooped, took my watery gruel then returned to the hut's steps. I sat far away from searching eyes, pretended to cry, doubled up in the corner. Reaching down inside my shirt I brought out a hambone with some meat still on it. It was my motorcycle soldier; I knew it the instant he said the name of the motorcycle. The others probably thought he was swearing at me, using some German word they had not heard before. I remained curled up in a ball gnawing at the bone. If the guards had seen me, I would have been shot for stealing and if other prisoners smelt it, I could also have lost my food.

There was an unwritten rule inside the camp, you did not steal another man's food. We all knew what happened to those that did. Others got up in the night and came to the bedside, they held the perpetrator down and smothered him. It did not happen often, but enough to send a message, to remind all of us of what was wrong, what was unacceptable even for those who had nothing. Our strength lay together - we would live or die but we would do it together. In the morning the body would be carried out and the Germans would make a note of it.

I had stolen from no-one. But this was different I had no idea what another prisoner might do if they discovered my secret? This was not a mere bowl of gruel, this was lifesaving. I had a benefactor and I wondered if he would come again? I thought about that while I gnawed at the shank and wondered at his motives. It could not simply be that he had been impressed with my mechanic skills. I knew enough to keep this secret. When I was finished, I buried the bone for later and filled my mouth with soil to cover the scent.

We walked through the series of fences and out through the gates into the countryside. I walked with Michal for we were in the same detachment of workers. The foothills of the mountains came up to meet us and from there we trudged along the rutted road, its muddy tire tracks collapsing at the edges like scars and wounds. It was just after sunrise and even some of the SS troops were half asleep. Only the very slowest received the butt of a rifle, the rest of us maintained the pace. When we arrived, we separated though sometimes we worked in pairs. Sometimes I was with Michal and sometimes not. We had been carving out a tunnel from sandstone for several months but this new one was gneiss, as hard as our lives had become. And with every shovelful I could feel it draining my life away.

We filled the ore cars till they almost overflowed, then two of us pushed them along the rails and deposited the rock in a slag heap some distance from the tunnel entrance. Several who dropped in their tracks were ordered back onto their feet, and when they did not obey they were shot where they lay. Then their bodies were bundled onto the top of the ore cars and taken out with the next load. Others who lasted till the end of the day but were failing to work as the Germans wanted were rounded up and sent away. We never heard of them again but we didn't need to; we knew exactly what had happened to them.

Inside the camp Old Frederic, a German Jew, would sometimes laugh with me, sharing in quick and guarded amusement. He saw our jailers as fools. They had not discovered he was a Jew somewhere in his past. He was no older than my father, perhaps in his forties but it was impossible to tell his real age. Life in a labour camp made everyone look ancient. He'd lived in Poland since he was a boy. He told us all he was a bootlegger, a distiller of illegal whisky who had run afoul of German officialdom. When the Germans first arrived in the city of Krakow, he kept his knowledge of the German language a secret and thought he could stay a jump ahead of the district governor.

'They assumed that I was an illiterate Pole, nothing more, but I was clever. I said nothing but watched. I watched everything. I never raised my head up. I always walked slightly stooped. Like this you see boy, so my ears are level with them. And I do the same here. I can pick up even a muttered word. I intend to survive' His cunning smile turned quickly to a laugh. A sense of humour could keep you alive longer than bread.

The following day, he told us of what he had overheard but this time the humour was gone.

'The monster is coming. Three days from now, for an inspection,' he said.

He needed only to tell a couple of us, soon the news spread through the camp like a forest fire. At first, I thought they meant Hitler but from their reaction, the look of horror on their faces I knew I was mistaken. It was worse than that.

The hut across from ours was being boarded up by prisoners, while the guards stood a healthy distance away. From inside came the sound of fists pounding in return and a great despairing moan. Finally, "Typhus" was painted in large black letters, in dribbling house paint across the door, that was now nailed shut. Though different in Polish, it was the same word in German as in English. Regardless of what you spoke, everyone in the camp knew the word and what it meant. I wondered how long before the disease would find its way to our hut?

On day Old Frederic, the German speaker, stopped me in the yard as we gathered for the early morning work detail. He looked suspicious.

'Hey Wozniak, where are you from?'

'Warsaw.'

He looked at me curiously, trying to add it up. Like me, Frederic knew that knowledge helped keep you alive and he was determined to get the measure of me.

'But your old man he is not from Warsaw?'

'No!' I said knowing he was talking about Michal, whose rural accent probably gave him away. He studied me as I moved away from his prying eyes. He gave a slow smile.

'Wozniak, that isn't your name.' It wasn't a question, it was a statement and with that I could feel the ground shifting beneath us. I turned and walked up to him, meeting him eye to eye.

'It doesn't matter. We have no home, no country. You can call yourself anything that you like.' I was sure where this was going now; I decided to cut him off.

'Catholics bleed the same as any other.' It seemed to work. Just then Michal came and stood beside me and looked at Frederic as if to say what is going on? Frederic shifted uncomfortably, then shuffled away.

The agonising rock walls were determined to destroy us; the ore seemed to be harder with each day. All around me, men and boys died where they fell or staggered out at the end of the day never to return. The gneiss broke us one by one. The Germans had some deadline that we were to meet, that much was clear, for we worked at a pace that never let up, first dynamite while we covered our ears and then the soldiers demanding we remove the rubble that filled the ever-lengthening tunnel. Every guard seemed to be alert and watching, ready with a rifle butt, a boot, or a bullet. As the last of a rock wall gave way, we made it through and joined a larger cavern that was wide enough to hold a truck perhaps a tank. For the next two days we worked relentlessly, our guards not even stopping to smoke, as we levelled the floor of the new chamber, with hard packed dirt. In the centre was a huge shape covered in a large tarpaulin. It had been weeks of this ordeal and puzzle but it was only when the news of "The Monster's" arrival that I understood what it was that we were doing.

The thirteenth day in the new tunnel I pushed the remains of a final ore car, with Old Frederic when he stopped, a look of terror on his face. He pulled back into the gloom and lay on the ground, in a crevice, jerking me to the floor beside him. It was the prophecy he told us of, three days before. A group of German officers were marching in single file along the one hundred metre corridor, holding torches and lanterns. Just behind the first lantern was Heinrich Himmler. Though I knew I mustn't, I lifted my head to see the man the camp had called "The Monster." They passed our abandoned ore car without noticing us. I thought how short and toad-like he seemed, with his double chin and a receding jawline. And though his uniform tried to hide it, he had a paunch. I'd imagined someone like an ogre, but he was more like a troll. I laughed quietly to myself as Old Frederic jabbed me, fear wracking his whole body, his terror almost beyond his control; he pissed himself where he lay. Frozen in one spot, we were unable to flee. Their voices echoed in the cathedral-like room, as the commandant proudly pulled away the covering, displaying the object in the centre. Standing in the middle of the great cavern, Himmler walked around a large bell-like machine that towered several metres into the air.

All talking at once, I could hear the excitement and delight in their voices but my German was too poor to understand much of it. The commandant signaled, they fell silent, as Himmler addressed them. His voice was shrill almost hysterical, not the voice I'd imagined for the man who held Europe by the throat. He reminded me of a whining old woman, complaining about the price of cabbage. Once or twice, he spoke in English with a slight American twang as if he had watched too many movies. 'Geiheimwaffe' he said then 'Wunderwaffe'. Himmler was putting on a show. 'Secret Weapon' then 'Wonder Weapon' in a mock gangster manner. Sometimes he sounded like Edward G. Robinson and other times like the other gangster the one who tap danced. They all laughed, some laughed far too hard and for too long to be believed. Frederic looked across at me and I could tell that he had understood every word they had said. His fear now looked more like madness, as his grimacing face made him seem like a stone gargoyle, in the half-light.

Together the officers stepped back, while the sound of an engine engaging echoed against the hard rock surfaces. Each man put on their protective goggles. The bell, turning on its axis, created a wailing noise that rose as it picked up speed. The faster it moved, the louder it shrieked and the further Himmler and his men moved away, behaving as if it was going to explode. The commandant grinned and clapped his hands together, like some delirious child at the circus. The sound became a constant roar as the cylinder reached maximum speed. Himmler laughed wildly, raising his arms above his head - a magician summoning an apparition from a stage table. It was like something I had seen in one of my fantastical comics or one of my books by Jules Verne. But it also reminded me of real life; of something I knew from early childhood but I couldn't place it.

The commandant raised a single arm to some unseen assistant and now the sound of the engine was joined by a low steady hum and a pulsating glow. And then it came to me. My grandfather kept bees and he would remove honey from the frames with a spinner inside a barrel. I was looking at a giant centrifuge but, with its wailing engine roar like a banshee, it was more than that.

The air around the cylinder began to crackle and splutter with electricity, arcing and curling across its surface. The blue-white lightning sparks flashed in wild frenzy, making the shadows and cracks in the walls dance madly overhead. It was becoming much more than just a centrifuge. Himmler stood with his hands above him, as if he were the conductor of this mad machine.

My father had taken me to see just such a thing when it first came to the National Museum in Warsaw. I was ten years old; it was the most magical thing. But for Old Frederic this was not a "Van der Graaf generator," this was a weapon from hell, in the hands of "The Monster." Frederic's face contorted, he was losing his mind and about to do something impulsive, like get up and run. I reached across and held his shoulder, pinning it to the floor with the length of my arm. It was brotherly, but it was also insurance.

'Stay still, they don't know we are here.'

That seemed to quiet his nerves and he looked at me as if to say, I trust you, please get me safely away from here.

Half an hour went by before they left. We watched, unseen from the shadows, they strolled past, the commandant walking side by side with Himmler. Later Frederic told me what they had said.

'Your Cagney impersonation was very good.'

'Better than Goebbels?' asked Himmler.

'Much better,' replied the Commandant.

After they left, the prisoners filed back in to begin work again. Somehow, we managed to join them and leave when it became dark. Numbers were counted at the beginning and end of the day, when we returned to camp, so no-one realised. No-one knew what we had seen.

It was the first part of the day, deep within a tunnel. Many of the guards were still half asleep and were not meting out the cruelties that they would inflict later on in the day. But one poor Pole had already fallen foul of the SS. In the semi-darkness, I looked over his body to see if there was anything I could salvage but his clothes were in a worse state than mine. Still, I tore away his sleeves, they came apart easily at the seams and hid them inside my shirt and went back to the ore car. In the darkness of the tunnel the motorcycle soldier came out of a connecting shaft and pulled me aside. I left the ore car half filled with rubble and the rest filled with the dead Pole's body and moved into the shadows.

'Do you speak English?' he asked in what was a very passable accent.

'A little!' I replied as he shoved some stale bread into my hand.

'We are losing. Will you help me escape?'

I stepped away and studied him in the semi-darkness. It was the motorcycle soldier - 'Zundapp' He was shaking uncontrollably. Perhaps it was the immediate fear of being caught talking, making plans with me or his terror of what would happen when they finally lost - what the Russians would do when they got hold of him, perhaps it was both. He was a tall, gaunt, skinny youth but still a little too well fed to be mistaken for a Pole I thought.

I nodded. 'We will help each other.'

He smiled saying, 'I want to make it to the English or the Americans.' So, it was true then, the Americans were coming, my heart lifted in my body. And with that he held out his closed fist and dropped my pewter horse into my hand.

'I won it back for you in a card game. I am a very lucky fellow.'

And so, our contract was sealed. But he would need a lot more than luck if he was to live through what was coming. So, would I.

Footsteps further off in the tunnel ended our conversation. He disappeared, moving deeper into the darkness while I returned to pushing my ore car; as he moved away, he whispered his name.

'Horst.'

One day we were ordered back to our hut. The door closed and from outside we heard hammering and we knew our time had come. From within, I could hear the slap of paint on the outside as it spelt words across our doorway. By that evening "*It*" was in my body and I reacted with fever and delirium. My existence slipped in and out of grasp, images, fragments of the past welled up like pictures from newsreels then disappeared as if they were magician's tricks in a theatre. Pain and thoughts jostled inside me for position. I lost myself, my body burning, cutting loose from the world, until a memory hard and strong, anchored me back here. The past and present mixed together as if they both lived in the same place, as thudding blackness kept me in its grip for

what could have been hours, possibly days. *Here in the typhus hut. Here, where they had left me to die.*

Mist. Image. Inside the ghetto. A picture somewhere in the haze inside my head, it was Hebrew writing, something I had never been taught, something I had only been vaguely aware of. The words were only fragments, written on broken stones strewn across the road in the ghetto. For months the synagogue, at the far end of the street, lay in rubble. For many it was the proof of what was to happen to them; it was there to break Jewish spirits, we all understood that. But it did not have quite the same effect on our family. The words themselves meant nothing to us; we children Ryzkard, Jana and I had never learnt it. Not ceremonies or bar mitzvahs or circumcision, nothing. Our parents never took us there, for we were atheists, all of us. My father and my older brother and sister held their atheism as a matter of intellectual pride. I had heard teachers and others talk of God but it was always the Christian one and I made a point of learning as little about Him as I did the Jewish one. I made my own logical investigation and found both Gods wanting. I entertained the idea of a God briefly when I lived in the sewers but that was when I needed to talk to someone and God was just one of the voices but I never got any replies. I took my father's position, considering the idea of talking to invisible forces, as foolish as the idea of fairies and goblins. My father and I both prided ourselves on being scientific and rational.

And yet inside my head was Jana, my invisible guide and protector. I pictured her in earlier times when she was flesh and blood, entering our house in her grand theatrical way.

We had lived on the upper side of the city for generations, among the wealthy professors, lawyers and doctors of Warsaw, far from anything remotely Jewish. Together, Jana and I always sent up the old Hassidic men we came across, with their long locks and silly hats, not knowing that we were distantly related to these strange men. We knew that mad people rocked themselves and these 'Hassids', as we called them, did the same. We mirrored them moving back and forward like two insane jack-in-the-boxes faster and faster, until we fell about laughing.

In March 1943 we were rounded up and found ourselves among them, not the orthodox ones with their strange clothes and hats, they had disappeared a long time before we arrived. But we were among Jews none the less, living in what Jana and I could only believe was **their madhouse**, in the *'Jewish Ghetto'*. *Jana felt extremely resentful. She blamed the situation on their peculiar antics, thinking of the long gone 'Hassidics'..*

'If they didn't act like fools the world wouldn't hate us.'

I wanted to believe it was so, that sooner or later the Germans would realise that we were not like them, that they had made a terrible mistake and let us go back to our old life.

Five days had passed now since they nailed up the hut. Some like me had caught the disease, the rest waited. Boarded up together they would all fall prey soon enough. I watched from my upper perch to the far end of the room as the hut came in and out of focus. One of the men in the last bed in the bottom rung was dead. Another crawling skeleton lying on the floor, pulled himself up, struggled to the side of the final bunk and removed the body, dragging it all the way to the door. He left it there as if it was the laundry or the refuse the town took away. Returning he claimed the dead man's place. No-one said a thing.

My muscles ached in every part of my body and my head pounded relentlessly, blocking out speech or coherent thought. And yet my mind would not stay still; events played across my half-closed eyes like the Saturday matinee newsreels that Jana and I always endured impatiently, waiting for the serial or the main feature.

Forty odd men dead now, piled up against the door; the door that might never be opened again. Michal had moved to the bed closest to me and one level below, in the days when he was well enough to move. Now the mountain of a man lay diminished, his six-foot frame, that once had hung over the end of the slats was now shrunken, a scaffolding of skin and bone like all the rest.

An hour later another body dropped to the floor two bunks away. Behind him a man appeared, from the ground, rolling him out of his place. The first man was not dead but much too weak to fight the second. The second, for what remained of his own life, stole the bare comfort of the other's bed. A bed which appeared to have more straw than his own, even though another two men lay in it. Perhaps he would remove them too if he lived longer than them. I knew the names of all those in our hut but as the days passed it became harder to recognise each one, or even who slept where as their faces all transformed into the same death mask.

All of this came to me in a soft fog, as if I was looking through gauze. Jana had gone now; she no longer lived in my head as the constant drum of pain had driven her out; the relentless rhythm that now struggled with my thoughts. My mountain, my Golem who had protected me from every imaginable danger, he too drifted away from me, his voice stolen, returning only as a dry rasp. Death waited for us all somewhere in the shadows and the stench.

'I want to die too,' I heard myself say, though the words didn't sound like mine but like a voice from the bottom of a well. Michal looked up and with a surge of strength reached out and touched me with his thin bony hand.

'NO, DON'T DROWN!' he cried but he said it as if he were far away, somewhere else. A cry from deep in his heart.

Then his voice returned to the room. When his eyes met mine, he spoke very slowly, all his physical effort bound up in his words, as if they were all that was left of Michal.

'No, Bron. We've come too far,' he said, pushing the words out into the stifling air, denying the fact that he was dying. My mountain was going and now what I feared most was being alone.

I tried to cry out but I had no more strength in me than he did. He gathered himself and sat fully up, an effort of strength I felt only he was capable of. His death mask face changed and the human I loved began to come through. Now it was animated with deep concern, as he listened to my plea for release.

'I want to be with Jana. With Ryszard. With Mama and Papa', the words ached. I felt certain they were gone; that my parents must have come to a place like this.

For a long time, he said nothing but fixed me with his eyes. Silent, immobile yet stronger than he had been for days. He seemed to be searching for something inside himself. When finally, he spoke again, his voice was slow and rasp-like, yet there was something commanding and full of love. I listened, transfixed, my world coming into focus. What he said was the strangest thing I had ever heard. But I would need to think on it for some time as his tale made little sense. What could he possibly mean when he said 'A white horse is coming?'

I dry-retched for a time, barely bringing up bile. My head crashing into a wall of pain every time I moved. As I lay there exhausted a new image passed through me, just as real as the night it happened. *An empty street in the darkness, as I looked into the distance, from an upper window.*

They came sometime after midnight; you could hear the trucks rumbling in from beyond the barbed wire. I could see them from the tiny attic window. We lived on the top floor in a single room with five other families, barely enough room for us to sit or lie down. Though we didn't share names, we shared each other's terror. All around us was the frantic clatter of floorboards and roof spaces being moved and treasures being secreted away. The crying and wailing began before they arrived; before the first barked orders rang in the night. But within seconds, of the trucks coming to a halt, everyone within the buildings was silent. Only the heavy panting of their black attack dogs remained. Silence, desperation, hatred and fear swirled in the enforced silence till it was broken by orders shouted through a megaphone, heartless and shrill. After that, came the stamp of boots up the creaking wooden staircases, the smashing of doors and the shrieks of women and children being separated from the men. Men were dragged downstairs first and the women and children followed.

Huddled among the men, I tried with difficulty to put on my second shoe without a sock, when I looked up to see Jana, standing slightly separated from the other women. My sister was no longer a girl; she was a woman of twenty. Even from that distance I could read her face - confused, frightened but growing steadily into that stubborn resolution only she had. Perhaps that's why she acted the way she did. Perhaps she did not understand the instruction she was given but I doubt that. No, regardless of what they shouted, Jana was determined to defy them. She walked in the opposite direction to the others. I believe this was the moment where she reclaimed her life but I cannot be sure; it all happened so quickly. I called out but she never heard me above the megaphone and the hysterical crying. Everyone watched as the tall crimson haired girl walked away, majestic, shouting something defiant behind her. In that moment she was 'my red girl', the regal beauty she had always been, the one that destroyed young men's hearts and ruled my parents' household.

The glowering officer roared at her, ordering her back, the spittle flying from his mouth caught in the truck's headlamps. A pair of foot soldiers raised their weapons. My father cried out her name and Jana turned toward him. She was wearing a smile of reassurance, as if to say it's alright father; I have decided that this is how it should be. Her body flew forward, propelled by the discharge of the rifles fired in unison, collapsing face first; blood seeping through the back of the coat she had pulled over her ragged clothes.

Pushing through the gathering of stunned men, my father and brother struggled toward her. They were clubbed to the ground with rifle butts, the moment they broke free.

The women wailed as one. The soldiers moved to gain the upper hand, forcing us further down the street away from the body.

I stood for a moment, caught up in the blood and the noise, unable to take in what I saw. The crowd surged and the soldiers pushed back. Their mass moved me along, still uncomprehending, as if I was a leaf in a downpour, until we too were battered down by the soldiers; the first line of men and women collapsing just like my father and brother had. Those around me fell back, slamming hard against the redbrick walls. I landed between two buildings and crawled backwards on my hands and knees into the darkness.

In the night, despite being completely sealed, the hut's temperature dropped till the walls and roof were covered in ice and my breath billowed out into a misty cloud. My body shivered with cold while the fever still held me in its grip.

Through my dark, wracking pain came a sunlit place in Warsaw and there I heard, 'Father said we can go to the city, to the museum and the art gallery.' It was my Jana's voice filled with excitement. There she was in all her glory, my flaming sun. Not a voice but a girl - like some young Hollywood starlet.

The tail end of Winter 1939, late February, a street, the old part of town as two children freely walk. She strode ahead, I dawdled inspecting this and that. My sister, the fiery red-headed beauty, was almost sixteen and I was already eight. Our father had given me permission to go with my sister. At first, I was pleased that Jana had included me in her plans, after all she was twice my age. But before long I realised that I was part of her deception and not her excursion. That this was not about museums and libraries but about meeting boys in parks and railway stations. The first of these was Jan who lasted only one weekend. Apparently, he kissed very badly. It was not till boy number four that she was even half-satisfied. By then I had learnt to make myself invisible by wandering off and exploring nearby streets. Because we did not want to lie to our father, we did spend a brief half hour or less in the library each time. Jana would clutch her recently exchanged romance novel as proof of our visit. Unless it rained of course and then we truly would spend all afternoon in the library or a museum. She and her latest infatuation would saunter, hand in hand, in the galleries, while I trailed a long way behind, like a puppy on a very long rope.

As always, while I made myself scarce, I set myself the challenge of naming all the main streets and those that crossed them, until I was able to see in my mind the whole city, for five miles in any direction. Every week I increased my knowledge with bus stops, trams, docks and wharves and even drains and canals.

I drifted in and out of fever. What I saw through hooded eyes, took me to other places between waves of agony and empty vomit that rose and receded, only to come back like a tide.

Once more an image fixed itself within me. My sister, her body face down on the street, her back drenched in blood redder than her hair. I wanted to make it a lie, as if I had not witnessed it. This could not be true! She must not be dead! I need her! All this screamed inside my head as I crawled away into the darkness.

In the alley, on my hands and knees, I felt among the refuse and rubble until I found an opening to a drain; I pulled a grate sideways lowering myself in feet first. As my head disappeared below street level, I saw the last of the men being rounded up and shoved out of sight. Two soldiers looked down the laneway and began to walk its length. I pulled the grate back in place and moved into the deep shadows below ground. One of the soldiers peered into the grate, almost sensing someone was there. From the darkness I looked up seeing his shape against the night sky, divided by the bars of the covering. I pulled back further into the darkness as he crouched above the opening for almost a minute listening for movement. I held my breath for as long as I could. He struck a match but it only lit up the world above. It burned towards his fingers until he threw it away. Only my imagination he decided, I could see that written on his face. The second match also burnt to nothing. Then the other soldier, in a bored tone, said something that must have meant it was time to go. They both walked away. I heard their footsteps echo on the open street then the sound of scraping and the slap of a weight landing in the alleyway. It began to gently rain and still I sat. Should I come up? Would they be waiting for me? The water began to trickle in through the grate, at first clear, then discoloured with dust and grime then finally it turned red. I backed away in horror and knew that I could not come up again and face her body. Instead, I crawled deeper into the stench and safety of the sewers, leaving my dead sister and my family behind. Safe but alone, knowing I must now fend for myself. In the darkness I sat for several hours and now I too was rocking back and forth, not in prayer but in grief.

It had been several days and nights that I had wandered through time and space. Now, at the point of most intense pain I felt a change. There, on the very rim of death as I peered into that black descent, a battle inside me was won. The easing of the pain brought other recollections.

One Saturday afternoon Jana was walking arm in arm with her new boy; I never bothered learning their names because most would be thrown away soon enough. At sixteen, my sister considered herself a young sophisticate, a woman of the world. She was demanding and had the beauty to get what she wanted. She seemed to enjoy her power over these boys. If it was not one, she was going to keep for very long, then she didn't mind me being in their company. I think she liked the way it annoyed the boys having me so close by. I was no longer the puppy following behind. Instead, she had turned the latest suitor into her lap dog and I was a hunting hound snapping at him.

This day, we accidentally wandered into the Jewish section of Warsaw and came across a synagogue. Outside stood one of the 'Hassids' dressed in a fashion that made us gape.

'What is he wearing?' asked the boy, unfamiliar with this place or the strange religion we had tried to avoid.

'Do you think he's from space?' I said.

Draped in a shawl, the man had one whole arm wrapped in a leather strap and on his head, he wore another strap that held a small leather box to his forehead. Jana could barely keep herself from laughing but none-the-less offered an explanation.

'You know how they keep rocking backwards and forwards?'

'Yes,' I said but I could see the boy had no idea of what we were talking about. For at this moment the old 'Hassid' was not praying to his god but merely standing on the steps of the synagogue, enjoying the sunshine.

'Well,' she replied immensely pleased with her wit, 'they rock so hard that some of their brains fall out onto the pillow at night. So, they gather them up and put them in the little box.'

'To do what?' I asked.

'To put it back in when they get a chance.'

'How do they put it back?' *the boy asked, playing along with the game.*

'Through the ears, of course.'

By now we were all giggling and the man on the steps of the synagogue was staring at us.

'And the strap on the arm?' *I asked.*

'Oh, that's to remind them to collect it up. They have very bad memories you know.'

We collapsed together, stumbling away arm in arm, supporting each other through waves of hysterical laughter. As we turned the corner, I looked back to see the Jewish 'moon man' raising his fist and cursing us. His face was red with rage as his eyes met mine. For some reason I felt incredibly guilty, as if I had done something I really should be ashamed of but then he was out of sight and I put him out of my head.

Not all my thoughts in the last of Typhus haze were miserable, there was one that I returned to often. It was only a month old maybe two. One of the last joyous moments before the disease.

The days were closing in, growing colder and darker in the late afternoon. The shadows moved more quickly across the camp and the work details. When *it came,* we all stopped in our tracks. We heard the sound as one and wondered? Someone skeptically suggested it was just thunder but another said no, there were no rainclouds that day. And then we heard it, like timpani in steady repetitive rolls. Artillery fire from the east and for the first time we watched as the guards froze on the spot. The Soviets were coming. You could see the fear flash across the soldiers' faces, passing from one to another. They would come, there was no stopping them and they would cut out these bastards' hearts and shove them up their arses. It gave us all a pleasure to watch our guards, a delight that was deep and satisfying and vengeful. A pleasure we shared secretly and silently with each other; one we'd never known before.

A Russian among us kept saying '1943, 1943 … Stalingrad.' His smile held a savage satisfaction.

'You were not at Stalingrad.' It was Old Frederic, taking the measure of the Russian. 'No Ivan, I have heard the Germans talk about that city. It is rubble. It is full of dead Russians and Germans. Thousands. It was a slaughterhouse.' The Russian grew indignant at the sleight.

'If you fought the Germans in Stalingrad, you must be a walking corpse,' said Old Frederic.

'We are all walking corpses,' said another Pole. The group of men all laughed, myself included. But the Russian was not going to let this lie.

'My name is Brodsky. I speak five languages and I was once a professor in Moscow.' He said it proudly but also with a sense of resentment. We all stopped laughing.

'But I am not a Soviet, I am an anarchist and I do not serve Uncle Joe.' Then he spat on the ground for effect. 'I serve Mother Russia, no-one else.'

Old Frederic smirked, and I thought *hmmm, he still does not believe him.* Brodsky took up the challenge again. 'I was a partisan, not a member of the Red Army, we fought from the forests outside Stalingrad. We blew up supply lines and bridges. We attacked the Germans as they fled. AS THEY FLED IN DEFEAT.'

We all looked around for he had said that much too loudly. Each of us shrank away until we realised that the guards had not heard.

'I do not care if they hear me. We beat them and we shall beat them again.'

'So how did you end up here?' asked one of the others, still looking around nervously.

'We were chasing them out of Russia but they turned and fought a rear-guard action. My unit had got too far ahead and now we were behind their lines. My comrades were accidentally killed by Soviet cannon fire.' He shook his head as he smiled at the irony of that. A sad, half-angry smile.

'Yes, but if the Germans got hold of you, they shoot Russians on the spot,' said one of the oldest men there. We all nodded, knowing this to be true.

'I told you I speak five languages; I convinced them I was not Russian. I convinced them I was someone else.'

We looked at him wanting the rest of his story. He added, 'I speak Norwegian' but gave us nothing more.

The thunder of big guns in the distance rang again, as the Russian anarchist stood and shook his head probably still thinking of what had brought him here. For a minute we stood there in silence hoping to hear the sound again. Why a Norwegian would end up here made no sense and yet it was his explanation; the whole war made no sense, so why would he. He was just one more shadow of a man played by a trick of fate, swept up helplessly like the rest of us.

'What month is it? Is it still 1944?' asked a youth in his twenties, who was probably thinking *I can outlive this now*. I thought the same thing. Some knew, yes it was 1944 but no-one could tell what month it was. It was Old Frederic who finally spoke, determined to have the last word.

'It is November. Late November. Don't be fools, keep your heads down and say nothing. A war moves fast and slow, slower still in Winter. The Germans will be unpredictable now; there is much to fear.'

And with that we all went back to our tasks in silence.

I thought about the Russians coming closer and about the planes that came from the west. The planes were few but the distant pounding of Soviet weapons remained. We all wondered about the English and the French and if they would ever arrive. When I had been in the forest, I heard a rumour that the Americans had landed in Europe but I saw none of them and then I wondered if it was all just wishful thinking. Now I wanted the Americans to be coming like they did in the movies and that they would reach us in time, like the cavalry arriving at some western fort to face off against the Indians. One prisoner who'd arrived recently claimed he had heard the British on the radio all the way from London who said they too were coming. But when? It seemed we had only the Russians?

I hoped there was some truth in it. I spoke very little Russian, though it was similar enough to Polish to understand at least some of it. I'd gone to a grammar school in Warsaw and spoke some English, four years' worth now, although I understood more than I could speak. The teachers made the learning of English incredibly boring: I learnt more from comic books and westerns than I ever did in class. Both Jana and I were in love with Tom Mix and the brand-new cowboy, Hopalong Cassidy that we saw, in serials, at the 'Atlantycki' picture house.

As I lay in the bunk, I knew that the horror was receding and now memories began to occupy my mind that were no longer fever dreams.

In the first year of the war, it seemed we might escape the attention of the Germans. We stayed inside our home and only went out to the market in the early hours and even then, never in a routine way, always irregularly. We sold our furniture and lived on the proceeds. As well, there was money my mother hid inside the wall, from the day Uncle Wilf had left. Money, he had left for her. Money, she told no-one about, not even her husband. She believed her brother even if our father didn't.

'You are the cleverest of all my children!' said my mother as she pulled the panel away behind the stove. 'I want you to know where this money is, if anything should happen to me and your father.' It was not a huge amount but it would keep us fed for a while. She replaced the panel and turned to me. 'You are to tell no-one about this.'

For Jana the occupation was especially hard. She kept the last romance novel she had taken from the library, which was now many months overdue. This she read and reread till she could almost quote it. The cinema also disappeared from our lives. Jana and I contented ourselves by relating the stories of films we had seen, filling in the parts the other forgot. We challenged each other to guess what was going to happen in the next episodes of the cowboy serials that we knew we would never see the end of. We created our own ride into the sunset for our western heroes.

One day my father disappeared, for more than a month we heard nothing from him yet none of us dared even think or say that he might be dead. Then after forty-nine days of waiting, he was back, standing in the doorway, diminished, broken.

'My God, where have you been?' cried my mother as we all helped him to a seat at the kitchen table. For many minutes he could not talk but finally he offered, *'They have me working for them in a chemicals factory. It seems I am valuable, at least for now.' 'As an engineer'* he added, as if this statement would calm our fears.

And then we all blurted out our questions at once but stopped when we saw our father recoil, like a street dog that had been beaten and now cowered before us. My father slowly explained that the commandant had given him permission to come home. He couldn't explain it, something about his father being an engineer. The war was like that sometimes. We all looked at him and felt as puzzled as he was. Perhaps the overseer missed his family and for a moment decided to be generous, an act of kindness as a reminder to them both that there was humanity beneath the demands of the war. It sounded too incredible to be true. He said he could come home to us, when they chose but he would never know when. That he worked every day until he dropped of exhaustion and then would begin again next morning.

'The main thing is that as long as they need me, you will all be safe.'

We looked at each other not knowing what that meant and wondering what price our father was paying.

The following morning, he was gone again.

By now the typhus had done its work, I was the last one left alive in our hut. I dragged each body from its bed and piled them as the others had done by the door; each one of them frail and almost paper thin. Then, with the strength remaining in me, I pulled apart the straw from the bunks and stuffed it inside my clothes.

Winter had come and I could hear the roof creaking under the weight of snow. It turned the inside of the hut into an icebox. I broke off icicles and sucked on them to ease the last of my fever.

Through a break in the wall near the ceiling, no wider than a hand, I watched the others pass by, trudging to their huts. Now that I was surrounded by dead men, I hungered for human company. I talked to Michal though he had become frozen and was beginning to ice over. Unlike Jana there was no reply. And even she was gone. Perhaps she would return now that the pounding in my head had subsided. *Jana, I have survived it*, I cried out in my raspy whisper but my words just hung in the cold and the emptiness. She did not come.

But what did come were the two strangest sounds of my confinement.

'Boy...eh, boy?' Not in German, not in Polish but in English. I was weak and delirious but was I imagining it?

'Boy?'

No, someone outside was whispering up to the gap in the wall. Boy was one of the first words I learnt in class; someone was calling for me...*for me. It had to be Horst. He must have seen my face staring through the break in the wall.*

Oh God. A long shank of beef passed through the hole. It was lean and much of it was cut away but there was meat on it. I scrambled to the hole and took it eagerly with both hands, desperate not to have any meat fall off. I wrapped my mouth around it but I had no strength to chew. I sucked like I'd done with toffee as a small child, till the bone was picked clean. Had I the strength I would have broken it open and eaten the marrow but that effort was too great for me now. I ate slowly over several hours, melting the meat in my mouth, then drifted off to sleep, the work of eating had taken its toll.

Hours later, I woke to the second sound.

It began as a hum from outside. Dark, sometime at night, that much I knew from the gap in the wall. Generators perhaps or machines nearby? No, the hum seemed distant. It rose slowly moving towards us. Two, no three, possibly more hums - like droning wasps. And now, now I was sure of it, above, somewhere in the sky. Louder, distinct, the roar of engines being altered as the sound passed through whirring propellers.

Shouts came from the guards as they met the threatening buzz with single rifle shots. Even from my bed I could imagine them - terrified knowing that the inevitable had come. The first distant bass drums came rolling into the camp, and more timpani overlaid till I was sure of it. Explosions coming from the east. The Soviets were here.

'Bomb us!' I laughed, 'blow us all to hell.'

Did I really want to die now? Perhaps not but maybe yes, if I took our captors with me.

The closest explosion sounded just outside the perimeter fence and was met with curses and machine gun fire. Another came almost immediately, somewhere inside the camp. Total silence followed, for several more minutes. No further planes, no more gunshots in reply, no orders being barked, only silence. I could picture the Germans watching the horizon, wondering would there be more? I looked up at the roof, as if I too could see the sky.

'Finish them, you cowards. Come back.' But no, the planes did not circle round, they had moved on.

'Alright then. Go on, bomb Berlin. Make the bastards burn!' I cried, though the effort exhausted me. It drained my body but also my heart, I was desolate, alone in the world while all hope or even retribution disappeared into the distance.

And then a whistle - low but continuous. They were answering my plea, returning my call, with one of their own. An object falling from a great height, falling above our heads, one last message from the Russian postman - a telegram of death.

The sound was like a force itself. Thrown from my bed by the flash, it shattered wood, steel, and masonry all around. A ringing so loud it muffled all else. I fell away into unconsciousness.

Slowly I came out of the sea of silence that I had been drifting in, as the world came into focus, sight but still no sound. In the morning, the door and half the wall had vaporized. The hut across from ours was completely gone. Was what had happened a fever-vision, was it real - this sight before me? Perhaps some Houdini parlour trick? The world had opened up, the light flooded in and all the bodies that had kept me company, the bodies piled up against the door, even Michal's -had mysteriously vanished - gone or perhaps they were smoldering in the huge crater that now stood outside the hut.

The explosion had deafened me to everything. I clapped, exhaled, scratched, rocked the bed but it all appeared before me like a silent film. Like the ones Jana and I had seen sometimes at the cinema. We always found them strange and dreamlike, without sound. I heard the words inside my head while the world of sound disappeared except for the buzz, ringing continually in my ears. In this new world that the explosion provided, Michal's words repeated in my mind. The strange conversation that made so little sense but clasped itself to my soul.

'I want to die too.'

'No, don't drown!'

'No Bron. We've come too far,' he'd replied.

'I want to be with Jana. With Ryszard. With Mama and Papa,' I heard myself say. These last words ached in me, now I knew for certain they were gone; that my parents must have come to a place like this.

For many minutes Michal said nothing but instead fixed me with his eyes. When finally, he spoke again, his voice was slow and harsh.

'You must not wish this. You must hold on.'

'Why?'

'Because ... because someone is coming to save you.' And then his eyes lost their glaze and instead grew fierce as he said, 'A white horse is coming. A white horse that will save you.'

I looked at him, completely bewildered. What madness was he saying? Was I to believe him? Or was this the Typhus speaking? Was he just delusional? No, he spoke with such a firmness, with such conviction for a man about to die. But what could it mean? What kind of horse would a white horse be, would it be a knight in armour, would it be Pegasus, or maybe my new hero Hopalong Cassidy? No, this had to be my great friend rambling. How could he possibly know this?

'That will save you and take you home.' He said it with reverence as if he really did know. And then he put his head down, finished by all he had forced his body and mind to do. I wanted to ask him more but he was fading. He never spoke to me again. He lay there for several hours breathing slow and shallow and then he

stopped. I looked across at him and I could see that he was gone. I was all alone, alone with his words.

The shattered hut leaned dangerously, the snow weighing down on the roof that now threatened to collapse and crush the entire building. It creaked and groaned above me but I was still too weak to leave. I crawled down to the bottom bunk hoping that it might protect me if the roof did give way and then I fell into a slumber.

My hearing restored, I awoke at dusk to the sound of shots and the crack of bullets ricocheting off hard surfaces. All around in the last light came shouts in German and the return of gunfire. From beyond the furthest fence, rifles found their mark, piercing huts and towers and sentry posts, I could hear the guards scattering in all directions, their yells disappearing away from me. The gun battle that began at sunset continued into the night. Wave after wave of rifle exchanges. I listened to cries and orders from both sides. The distant shouts sounded like they were Polish but they were too far away to really tell. No grenades, no tank fire, no support from artillery. We did not sleep that night, SS or prisoner.

The Germans held the camp and by the following morning their attackers were gone. Was it the Soviet Army? Foolish thought, they would be in greater numbers and would not have moved on.

'When the Red Army comes, they'll have their pound of flesh, blood for blood,' I remember my Russian companion had once said. He was dead now and only I knew his prediction was coming true, it didn't console me. To be so close to liberation then nothing, was crushing. I determined this was not the Red Army. This was a partisan skirmish, nothing more. Was it Jakub and Marek? No, that was just wishful thinking, they were hundreds of kilometres from here. Still, it was partisans, it was Polish; I felt sure but disheartened for they too had abandoned us.

In my guts, I knew that we were unimportant to the war. Killing our jailers achieved nothing except revenge, it would not bring the war to an end. Anyway, who wanted to save a bunch of prisoners who were dead already but hadn't admitted it to themselves? No one is coming for you, you fool. No-one.

'Boy'

Horst climbed into and across the crater, standing at the blown apart entrance to the hut. For a minute I watched him study the structure, deciding if it was sound enough to enter. Behind him another young soldier waited, a look of trepidation on his face, not keen to enter what was once a Typhus hut. He stood on the far side of the crater. Horst came to my bed and whispered, 'Listen, they are moving everyone out. They are going to march the camp back into Germany, ahead of the Russians!' He looked around as if the dead might be listening. 'I do not intend to go. This war is over for me. Do you remember our promise?'

I nodded. Out of his pocket he pulled out a crust of bread, solid as rock and dropped it in my lap.

'I will come for you.' And then he stepped out into the sunlight where the other soldier waited.

'Alle tot.' The other soldier backed away quickly, the idea that all inside the Typhus hut were dead, terrified him.

Memories came back to me as I lay waiting, wondering - *Dunaj Street, Warsaw my home. In the middle of the night a wagon pulled up and a farmer stepped down and helped a figure, draped in a blanket, out of the tray where he had been lying, curled into a ball. The blanket dropped to the ground and my father fell out. I had stood at the upstairs window for seven weeks watching, watching for some sign, willing my father to come home. Now he was here I wanted to run to him but held myself in check. I surveyed the street. The street I no longer played in. No lights were on. I waited till I heard the front door close before I ran down stairs. It seemed that the Germans no longer needed my father. Yet they had not shot him but merely set him out on the road and told him to go home. Another puzzling mystery of the war.*

The throbbing reduced, like the pounding of a drum gradually fading into the distance and with it the jabbing pain, eased to a dull continuous ache. The fever was gone but hunger and cold remained. At last, I began to think clearly. The camp was marching back into Germany and they would push us till we dropped and then shoot us where we lay, just like they had done in the tunnels. Of this I was certain.

But this was idiocy. Where was the German efficiency in this? Why not shoot us here and then flee? Surely, they could move faster without these sick and weary stragglers? For certain Horst could see the stupidity of their actions, is that why he was abandoning his post? They must know they were losing the war; it was only a matter of time. But so much of what the Germans did made no sense to me. I had often tried to fathom their thinking but it all seemed so wrong-headed. I could no more understand why they were doing this than why they had rounded up my family, who had not been Jews for two generations and who loved all things German. Well, all things German before the war, at least. In the end I gave up trying to solve these riddles and set my mind to saving myself. They believed my whole hut was dead but would that be enough? If I stayed in this hut and they searched again, they would find me, forcing me to march till I dropped.

The camp would set out soon, probably within hours, the Germans desperate to be gone before the Russians arrived. I pulled myself from the bunk and crawled across to the splintered door. Part of the floor too had been blown away, offering a space below the hut. I pushed as much bedding as I could into the hole, then slid over the edge and hid beneath the floorboards. If there was another check of the huts, this time it might not be Horst. The effort to hide myself had taken all the energy I had; I collapsed aching and barely conscious. Reaching out, I scooped up some snow, placing it in my mouth making my teeth ache with cold as the snow melted, quenching my thirst. And if *they* returned, they must not find me - the thirst, hunger, and sickness, these I lived with always but the Germans now perhaps I could escape.

Then I faded. And as I drifted between agony and exhaustion, a sound came.

The sound of something approaching from a great distance, as if they were traveling across the great western grasslands of my cowboy films, hoofbeats drumming on the hard land growing louder as they came. Hoofbeats coming toward me. And there in that dream, half wishful desire, half sickness - a fog rolled in long banks, grey and sulphurous like a smokestack, huge, monstrous yet beautiful and out of it she appeared in the mist, her chest pushing through the vapours then disappearing again. I cried out to her and as if she could answer me, she reappeared on command. She looked straight at me and raised herself up kicking her hooves out as if fighting off unseen foes, then turned quickly and was gone.

One vision melded into another, this time- dreams of home. *Through the darkness our kitchen appeared, lit only by a single candle. The war had already been with us four long years and in each of my family I could see how it had taken its toll. Our hair was badly cut, our clothes were frayed at the edges and discoloured yellow from being hand washed with no soap. All my family were now pale, ashen and far skinnier then was healthy.*

Someone had come in the middle of the night and slid it under the door - a letter from America, from Uncle Wilf. We all gathered around as my mother, whose brother it was, read it aloud and as she read she cried, telling us that it was because she missed her brother so much but we all knew better. My older brother Ryszard looked across at Jana, who in turn looked at me. We all remembered the last time Uncle Wilf came, bringing a warning before he fled.

What he said had come to pass, we had been invaded, Poland was the first casualty when the real war began. We watched in horror as they annexed Austria, took the Sudetenland from the Czechs and that should have been enough warning but foolishly we ignored it. We let the months and years go by till with lightning swiftness they swallowed at least half our country, whilst Stalin took the other half soon after. The sad, brave Polish Army on horseback, armed with First World War rifles, could not contain them. The Twentieth Century had eaten up the Nineteenth, as our uncle said it would. Poland had ceased to exist except as a prison, a land without justice, where you never knew when you would be condemned.

But here was a miraculous letter from the world of freedom. Not delivered by post but carried by hand and passed from one trusted Pole to another. A miracle so astonishing that it was almost beyond comprehension - a letter that no-one had opened but had arrived from somewhere untouched. How had it got here? Had it been dropped from an allied plane? Whatever the answer we all knew that this message from the outside world would be the last. The borders, the ports and airfields were all closed long ago; the steel doors of our prison slammed shut across our country. They locked the world out and locked us in.

My father would not meet anyone's eyes, he sat slumped in the corner of our kitchen, as every word our mother read stabbed at his heart. He had tried hard to save us once he had seen the folly of his denials. But now the Germans had used him up and spat him out and our uncle's words condemned him for the fool he had been.

Inside the letter was a second sheet of paper, wrapped tightly around a bundle that Mother pulled out to reveal ten faces of Benjamin Franklin splayed in a fan across the table.

'My God, it's a thousand dollars!' cried Jana.

'American money' I said emphatically.

'Can we buy our escape?' Ryszard wondered aloud. Every one of us thinking the same thing. Was it possible or was it already too late?

Awake now, I pulled myself across the soil below the floor, moving as far away as I could from the crater hole. Beneath the hut, the ground was as hard and cold as iron. My breath, weak as it was, billowed out in the cold air, like some frosty dragon breath. Above I heard boots walking the length of the hut, many pairs. I was right to have hidden; the Germans in their thoroughness were searching the huts one last time.

They departed and as the hours passed, I began to feel that yes, they had truly gone. Marching away, taking the much depleted, ragged army of ghosts with them. The Germans marching themselves to their hoped-for safety, taking the last of the Poles, the Russian P.O.W.s, and all who had defied them, grinding their bodies into blood and bone and finally dust - somewhere on the road to Germany

I lay beneath the hut for a night and a day in the twilight on my frozen ground, I watched the light beyond change within the camp, not daring to move. The place was now deathly still and yet I could not help feeling that I was not alone here in the camp. But I saw no sign of Horst. He must have changed his mind, having decided to take his chances with his own kind, rifle in hand. It was an insane idea, why would a German stay behind in a camp, waiting for the Russians? *'I will come for you.',* said Horst. No, I was certain now, he had changed his mind and fled with the others.

My weakness mixed with an overpowering fear kept me paralyzed. I had tried so hard to survive, to be one step ahead but there was this feeling inside me, that my luck had run out. Michal was dead, Jana was gone. What did I have? No, death was the only thing coming for me, all I had to do was wait.

On the second day I heard the distant churning sound of diesel engines. Not bikes, not even trucks but engines pushing great weight, their pistons and turning parts complaining bitterly with a high tensile groan. It was the sound of tanks, more than one, and as I listened, I was sure the sound was coming my way. By late afternoon it had reached the outer gates and behind the tanks the marching of soldiers' feet. It was the Russians, at last.

My brother Ryszard came back to the house and gathered us altogether. The kitchen had always been the centre of our house; it was larger than most kitchens. In the middle once stood a long wooden table, able to fit twelve or more people. It was gone, sold to feed us and yet we gathered where it once stood. Everyone feeling his excitement, as he tried to keep himself from dancing around the room. Jana was almost angry with his posturing and his need for theatrics. Yes, Jana the theatrics that usually belonged to you, I smiled. But one by one he sat us all down and began his little show.

'You must bring one suitcase, only what you need. Wear as many clothes as you can, so that you don't need to put them in your case. Bring tinned food, money, and valuables and what else was it the black marketeer said? Oh yes, bring perfume and soap, because we will all smell, by the end of the journey.' We all laughed at the ridiculousness of that, the mention of two things that had disappeared from life long ago. We had clothes, those we could not sell and yes, we had some tinned food but soap and perfume? What an idea!

'You found a way out?' asked Jana, sounding incredulous but wanting to believe it was true. My mother began to cry and my father sat doubled over, silently in the background with his arms folded. We knew that we must take this chance. Our father now needed medical attention that only escape might bring him. It was sometime after two in the morning, when we walked toward the small park that sat at the edge of the old town. We were each carrying a single suitcase as we had been instructed, although both Mother and Jana looked like theirs were more heavily laden. Father and Ryszard led the way. My father, despite his damaged body, made a superhuman effort to be the leader he had once been for our family. As we approached the park, we could see several other families looking bulky in too many clothes standing next to suitcases.

'Let's just wait here a moment' said my father cautiously.

My brother gave him a quizzical look but did not argue. Instead, we all slipped back into the lane where we could see the park and the other families, four separate groups eyeing each other.

Jana asked, 'Is something wrong?'

'*Maybe, maybe not. Let's see what happens. We are close enough; we can join them if it is as Ryszard says.*'

My brother was hurt by this but my father was right. It would do no harm to watch and see who turned up. The early hours of the morning brought with them a chill as we stamped our feet and rubbed our hands to keep warm. The appointed time came and went and the four families in the distance shuffled about and looked up and down the road.

Finally, a truck rolled into the street with its headlights off. As it got closer the driver switched on his headlamps, illuminating the terrified families as a dozen troops leapt from the rear. Three families stood with their hands above their heads but the father of the fourth ordered his wife and children to run. They abandoned their cases and fled down the road, making no more than five or six metres, almost to the corner before the soldiers opened fire. All fell to the ground as one.

We pulled back into the shadows and ran. Behind us the remaining families cried out. If the Germans had investigated, they would have seen five suitcases, just around the corner, sitting unattended on the footpath. A testament to our folly and lost chances.

We sat against the walls of our empty kitchen but my brother, defeated, faced away from the rest of us, deeply hurt. He had been our hero and now he was the dupe who had lost all Uncle Wilf's money, who had been tricked by criminals, who had lost our last chance of escape. I could see it all in his face even though he would not look at anyone.

Jana put her arm on his shoulder but he flinched and pulled away.

'Do not blame yourself, it's not your fault.' Jana's body went rigid with anger.

'If anyone's to blame-'

'NO JANA NO!' my mother shouted.

Shocked, the whole family was on their feet except our father, as my sister stared defiantly back. Finally, she could stand it no longer; she burst into tears and fled from the room

We received no more letters after the one from Uncle Wilf but one day my father came into the kitchen holding an official notice. It had been many months since he had worked for the Germans as an engineer. It was clear he would not be called back; something had changed. Our world was now much more uncertain. Father's hands were shaking as he handed the letter with the eagle crest to my mother. We were to pack and leave within four hours. This time the truck would be outside to take us to the Jewish Ghetto. They had tracked down our ancestry and now we would all live to regret not going to America. My mother cried, my brother held me. Jana took an empty pitcher that had carried water from the town square, hurling it against the wall and collapsing into a corner. From that time on she kept her own counsel and spoke to no-one, not even me. This hurt me deeply and I worried about what was happening inside her head. Our father and Jana passed each other from that day on without making eye contact.

I wanted to go to them, to the Russians at the gates, to finally be rescued. Did I want to eat? Yes. Did I want to sleep in a real bed? Yes. Most of all I wanted to bathe. I needed to feel clean, to remove the hundreds of mites that bit me in every fold of my skin, that ate my flesh, that made me feel like something rotting, something decomposing.

And yes, I needed to see a friendly face. But how would they find me? How to reach them? I tried to pull myself out from under the hut but after I had moved a few feet, my body ached and I fell into semi-consciousness. Sometime later, I do not know how long, I came to; all I knew was that the light had changed drastically.

I heard a single pair of feet moving about above. Feet not in boots but instead the soft pad of bare feet. Was it a prisoner? One they had not taken? I tried to call out but it was barely possible to whisper when your throat was parched because you had only what you gathered from the snow.

A single word, someone calling desperately. Was it English, it sounded like it but it was hard to tell through the floor, it was too indistinct. Another word but this time even more muffled, as if he was whispering, afraid to be heard but again it was impossible to tell what was said. I cried out but nothing came from my throat. The soft patter moved away and then whoever it was climbed out through the entrance, off the broken floorboards, stepping into the crater that stretched all the way down, where the wall had been blown apart. From my position I could see his legs and then his torso. He was dressed in tattered striped pants. It was a prisoner.

'Aaaaaaargh!' came out of me like a wild animal, snarling in a trap.

He dropped down, peering into the darkness and then his eyes met mine. His face and hair, his neck, hands and feet were all caked in dirt and ash but even through all that camouflage, that

masquerade, I recognised him. 'Zundapp', my motorcycle soldier but not in uniform. He was dressed in rags just like me. He no longer wore his boots but instead his feet were wrapped in torn pieces of cloth. Crouching down was a full-bodied German, a lean one true but still well fed, hoping to pass as a starving prisoner of war. Hoping to pass through the gates and escape to the west, under the gaze of the Russians. Even through the grime, his face had the haunted look of a cornered animal. Was death still coming for me? Perhaps. But was it also coming for Horst?

Horst picked me up and carried me away from the hut; I could see it was no effort for him; I weighed no more than a parcel. Through his camp clothes I could feel him shivering, perhaps with cold but I felt sure it was terror. I needed to talk but the effort to get his attention had torn my throat apart. As we moved through the grounds, his body stiff and rigid, he walked slowly clutching me to his chest. Was I meant to be his good luck talisman? The fear was obvious to me. Would it be obvious to our liberators?

'Water!'

He met my word with subdued panic, and then I saw him relax to some small degree as he realised I hadn't spoken German that might give him away, I spoke English. Not 'Wasser' but 'Water'.

As we walked from the huts to the final fence, a tank pushed through the locked gates bursting them from their hinges. They came away like some papier-mâché theatre prop. The soldiers who were milling around either side, staring into the compound, all gave a defiant cheer, as if they were breaking open the prison that was Europe.

On either side of us, like creatures from a horror story, more terrifying than anything from the Edgar Allan Poe tales that my sister had read me, came tottering skeletons, emerging from their hiding places, dragging themselves from their death beds shuffling toward our Soviet liberators.

Some were solitary figures with hollowed out eyes and arms as thin as down pipes, others staggered together, leaning on each other for support. How had the Germans missed so many in their rush to escape? Where had these creatures hid themselves? Or did they gather up some and just run out of time? Would our liberators notice that the one who carried me, was not truly like the others. So many unanswered questions but this war had always been like that for me.

The ghastly spectacle frightened the Russians, some stepped back, some looked away, others grew angry, cursing the Germans. All their faces seemed to ask the same questions - who were these people, the victims and what kind of people were their jailers? But of course, the Russians knew what kind of monsters they were. The Russians felt that cruelty all the way to Moscow and now the Germans would be repaid in kind all the way to Berlin

The Soviets laid out the survivors in rows; I watched them from Horst's arms as we sat in the lee of a large Red Army truck. When the soldiers and their medical officers came for me, gesturing that they wanted to treat me, he shook his head but said nothing. Instead, he held me closer to him, as if I was the children's toy he did not want to share. They looked at each other and moved on. It was then that it struck me what a bizarre escape this was. Horst was going to hide in full sight of his enemies, enemies that would execute him if they knew. Hiding, in the hope he would make it to the Allies. He had once said he was a lucky at cards when he returned my pewter horse. This time he was playing the greatest game of his life. It was mad but maybe it was possible.

I lay curled into his chest like a babe in arms. His body warmth was comforting against the winter, a winter that had been with us for such a long time; I imagined it must be coming to an end soon. By the evening, they had offered us water and a blanket, which we both accepted gratefully.

I looked up into his face like a baby might look up at his mother and made a great effort to speak to him.

'Do not speak. Shake your head yes and no only. No matter what they ask you. Understand?' He nodded. I was sure he did understand, his English was as good as mine.

In his arms, I began to feel that his body heat was almost as nourishing as food or water. For cold had been with me as long as hunger or thirst. And with that warmth came dreams again, soft and gentle.

And all at once I was with my grandfather on our summer farm, so many years ago when I was just a small boy. He took me by the hand pulling me, anxious that I came quickly. He picked me up as we entered the old barn and made his way to the far end.

'You must see' he whispered, his voice full of wonder and pleasure. Inside the barn, he carried me to the last stall where a large dark shape was visible, a beautiful mare giving birth to a foal. My grandfather smiled triumphantly for we had arrived in time. It was bloody and a little frightening as the mare cried out a number of times. But then the foal slid out as effortlessly as you might spit a watermelon seed. The whole barn seemed to glow with the warmth of life renewed, as if it was declaring that all was as one in the world.

That night the soldiers, full of alcohol having discovered the officers' wine cellar, now sat around campfires, talking and laughing. Fueled with wood from inside the grounds, the fires lifted their spirits, so they sang Russian songs. Some were folk songs that had the same melodies as Polish ones I had learnt at school. One had the same melody as an English song I had learnt and one, judging from Horst's reaction, he must have known in German.

As the evening rolled on, they sang with passion what must have been Soviet songs, songs about the revolution and their glorious fatherland, about a future bright with promise for every working man. By the end of the night their revolutionary fervour gave way to songs with much more physical lyrics. One soldier who led most of the choruses, the 'class clown' made lots of rude gestures that had the others rolling in laughter. Women with huge breasts, men with huge members, lots of pumping and thrusting and one song that seemed to have a chorus with the hee-hawing of a donkey. This one they liked so much they did it twice in a row then sang another song and came back to it a third time.

A drunken soldier, full of generosity, came over offering us not German wine but a rough smelling drink, probably vodka but badly distilled. It smelt nothing like the British Gin my father drank each evening at sunset. We both shook our heads. In his drunken state he studied us, as if we were street dogs. We intrigued him. Was he wondering what we had been through or what we had done to survive? Was he suspicious of the well-fed man who held me? He looked at the young German and asked him something in Russian. Horst gripped me tighter and simply shook his head. The cheery soldier was not satisfied and asked the question again. This time much slower, stretching the words with large spaces between them as if this might make it easier to understand.

Russian and Polish are similar, having many words in common. I knew what the over friendly soldier was asking. I had to give him something to send him on his way.

'Glupi.'

He looked at me then looked oddly at the young man in prison rags, then I added, 'Prostak.'

His face grew sad, like he was about to cry but he merely patted Horst's head and stumbled away. Stupid and simpleton were the same in both languages; my friends and I had often used them to insult each other in the schoolyard.

Horst looked down at me not quite knowing what had taken place but I thought he had a reasonable idea. He swiveled around to see if anyone was near and then with hesitation he spoke. It was clear he did not have the right words in English so he quickly spat out 'Angeboren idiot!' and pulled a face that looked comic but mentally deficient. I nodded as best I could and he smiled. His face said it all, he was pleased with the idea and yes, *yes that just might work.*

In the morning the medical soldiers stopped at each body along the rows, taking the measure of the night and the survivors. Almost half of the prisoners had died. I thought that this was what many had been waiting for - their moment of freedom. A moment when they could at last give up this life and leave behind the hunger and pain, on their own terms, that they alone had made the choice, in defiance of their captors.

The commanding officer stood leaning against the engine of the first truck smoking, as the army doctors came to him shaking their heads. I looked up at them from where I lay in Horst's arms by the rear wheel. Much of the Russian they spoke was too fast for me to understand but certain words or phrases made enough sense. I could piece together the situation, the doctors wanted to treat us and the commander nodded solemnly, as if he agreed. It was his second in command who seemed most worried. Again, they began to discuss the situation fast and furiously. His adjutant was arguing to move on. I heard him say 'Comrade Stalin' several times and each time he mentioned Berlin there was a great urgency in his voice. The leader threw the argument back at the doctors. *What to do with these rags and bones?* The doctors insisted that to move us in the trucks would kill us all. But where would they take us? The cold of the night had done what the Germans had intended; leaving us here was no answer. Many of his soldiers had seen the signs painted on various huts and were not keen to re-enter the camp itself. So, taking us back inside the camp was not an answer either. After pushing the Germans out of Russia, and marching halfway across Europe, the last thing they wanted was to die from some invisible disease. Finally, the commander brought an end to the discussion by reminding them that some of these skeleton men were Russians and deserved better than to die in the cold. This seemed to silence them all. He took the second in command aside and talked softly to him. Then the young man nodded and hopped into a jeep and drove away into the darkness.

I wished I could explain it to Horst but we were still sitting up against the back wheel and much too close to the doctors and the captain to have any conversation. I remained silent; Horst would have to content himself with playing an imbecile for now.

The Soviets did not have enough food to feed us all. I watched them move from one body to the next, some they raised from their lethargy and others, they must have decided were beyond saving. One soldier brought us a tin pannier containing a clear broth. Horst took the dish and we both smelt it, breathing it in deeply. Even in its watery state you could smell potato and turnip. Floating in the liquid was one crust and what appeared to be a piece of dried meat. Horst took the piece of meat and began to chew it for several minutes. Then he opened his hand and spat the mashed pulp into it. Slowly he placed one small portion after another on my tongue and I let it melt and turn to liquid then I swallowed. For a few minutes the Russian watched us and smiled. We were like some mother bird feeding its young. It took us almost an hour to finish that meagre meal.

The sun had been up two hours when two soldiers arrived in a jeep, the driver was the young soldier from yesterday's heated discussion, the second was a senior officer who stepped out as the captain saluted him. He pointed back from where he had come. The captain smiled and seeing this both Horst and I looked down the road and wondered what it was that was coming?

It was another hour before the parade of peasants arrived in the distance. Local farmers had been ordered by the Soviets to the camp. They came up the road in drays, wagons, and small carts, one after another, each one filled with straw, clip-clopping in the cold winter sun. An old man held the reins of the first wagon, his warm breath turning into mist in the cold air. I reached inside my shirt and pulled out my pewter cavalry horse and once again held it tightly in my hand.

I watched the scene unfold, with *Michal's words* ringing in my ears. The first of the horse drawn drays was pulled by a magnificent draught horse that stood what must have been seventeen hands high. Here before me was my Pegasus, my frontier companion, my saviour. She snorted and complained of the cold but pulled the wagon effortlessly, bristling with harnessed strength. She was beautiful and strong, her huge chest and flanks glistening with sweat. And from her mane to her tail, she was white all over.

We were carried to the nearby town and the local people were ordered to look after us and after a few weeks of convalescence an army supply truck took us, we were on the move again. I travelled all the way into Germany, in Horst's arms, till we met Allied troops. Perhaps it was my condition and my possessive mute minder's determination to not let me go, that drew their attention but somehow, we seemed to receive special clearance. The American Red Cross placed us in a transport and as we drove away, I spoke quietly to Horst.

'Hospital.'

He nodded and smiled, but still that was not enough; still, he would not release me.

Horst obviously had a clear idea of what he was looking for. He was observant and cunning, determined to make the best of any situation; attributes I recognised well. And I was too tired to even think of fighting him. But then why should I, this was working to my advantage too, just as long as I got proper medical help before it was too late. I wasn't so weak that I didn't know what condition I was in. Sometimes I thought I had made the devil's deal.

Wondering why this strange arrangement existed, why these *'Siamese twins'* clung to each other, army officers made attempts to separate us. Horst would then go into action, behaving in the most obsessed, possessive manner - playing the part of the disturbed man-child to perfection, never overplaying his hand. He was frightening to behold. Soft whimpering or hysterical screaming came first. Then he would snarl and glare at whoever came near. He made them all regret they had bothered with us. They would stop us on the road or at our mutual bedside in the truck, then quickly back away.

"What the hell is wrong with him? asked a continuous roster of military doctors or army officers to which I replied, 'He's my mute brother,' adding the universal corkscrew finger sign for

"not quite right in the head." Whoever we met let us travel on, getting on with their own lives. The war was so full of immense tragedy, that this minor one barely registered.

As I lay in the back of the truck, on a makeshift mattress, travelling through the devastation that was Germany, I began to think of all those I had come across. Tobiaz and Agneta and my great protector Michal - Christians with a sense of right and observance, even if it might cost them their lives to defy the Germans. Jakub and Marek the determined communists, loyal to an ideal of a workers' paradise, even if they didn't live to see it come to pass. And finally, Horst, a man who with the complicity of his superiors had put thousands to death. A man who believed in a something I could barely fathom. What made them tick? What made them who they were? The power of belief and conviction and yet all had differing views of the world as it was and the world they wished to create. I felt as if these were the questions I would grapple with, for the rest of my life.

Horst and I watched, saying nothing, staring from our bed, out through the back of the truck that traveled in a convoy. All along the sides of the road were people, farm folk, town dwellers, and some dressed in clothes that marked them as having come from big cities. They hugged the sides of the autobahn, much of it pummeled by allied bombing, standing ankle deep in mud as we passed by. Some reached up begging for food. Others looked into the distance and shrunk away from the victors. Once a G.I. tossed an apple to a small boy but a grown man snatched it away. I wondered why they were all looking like they had nowhere to go, even the suited man and his wife in the fur coat.

And then we smelt it, long before we arrived. A strange combination of odours - brick dust and smoke, the sickly-sweet smell of rotting flesh, the stench of sewerage seeping from broken pipes. I knew every one of these smells all too well. The outskirts of the city gave us our answers as we looked out on masonry rubble, half buildings standing with three walls but no roof, a church spire held up by only the rubble that lay behind it and a strange absence of animals - no dogs or cats, no horses, and no birds in the air or on the ground. Everywhere was silence apart from fires still burning away the wooden frameworks of what once were houses. We never seemed to get to the centre of the town or if we did it was unrecognisable. Somehow the war had turned all these Germans into exactly what I and my family had become. The ghetto in Warsaw they created for us had become their own existence now and it seemed it stretched all the way into Germany. Did it go as far as Berlin, I wondered?

* * *

'Here luvvie, one for each of you,' said the young nurse patting the white sheets, as if it were a friendly dog. She smiled expectantly.

There, in the brightly painted halls of what once was a school, were two beds, placed side by side for Horst and myself. The others were already filled with the wounded. We had finally arrived in a large, make-shift hospital, deep inside Allied territory. I looked at Horst and I could read his face. I knew it. It was my face. It said, *can I stop now? Can I please, please stop running?* Horst loosened his grip, allowing the nurse to take me from his arms. As she laid me down, I looked at him again. It was not just the last few days and weeks that Horst had been running. Like me, but for different reasons, he had been running for most of the war, at least since defeat had replaced victory and he could no longer believe his leaders. His was a face of defeat, bewilderment, and steely determination to survive. I wondered if there was more. Guilt perhaps? Or shame?

Within days of arriving he was on his feet, ministering to me, my own private nurse, still silent but attentive. The exhausted hospital staff didn't mind; perhaps they were grateful that here was one less body to wash or spoon feed.

The constant talk, between the doctors and nurses concerned the war's end, the final push of the Allies and the Soviets, the fall of one German city after another, the liberation of vast areas of

Europe, the arrest of high-ranking Nazis. This new word - Nazis was one that came from the free world - the British, the Americans. It was a word I had never heard before neither at home, the forest or the labour camp. I turned it over in my head - it was strange and sinister sounding but somehow it seemed to fit.

The crimes the staff described were told with a mixture of horror and disbelief. Crimes I knew first hand, that no longer surprised me, crimes burnt into my soul - part of my memories and probably my nightmares for the rest of my life. None of Germany's defeat filled me with pleasure, I was exhausted by it all, weary of the blood and the bodies.

I wanted some quiet place where I could simply disappear from this world. To do what, I didn't know? I wanted something unknown; some place so different that nothing there reminded me of this life. For now, that I had survived, I realised I undeniably had nothing, in a way that I only thought I had come to terms with before. I was adrift in a wounded world that was struggling to create a sense of order - a world of parents who no longer had children, of children who no longer had families, of an entire generation or what was left of it who had neither shelter, community, or direction. I had lost as much as any of the survivors, I had lost all of my past, ever since my family disappeared, but now I realised I had no idea of where I would go in the future.

Three days after we arrived a young woman from the Red Cross came to our bedsides. The nursing staff told her all they knew of us and she nodded enthusiastically. Finally, clipboard in hand, she pulled her pencil from behind her ear and tapping it on the board, she came to my side.

'I hear you speak some English?' she said with what sounded something like an American accent but wasn't. I nodded.

'Can you tell me your name?' asked the girl with the beautiful blue eyes and the sun blond hair.

'Bronek, sometimes Bron for short'

'And your brother, his name?'

'Richard.' I said my brother's name the way that English speakers would. But then I realised she was talking about Horst, the man in the next bed.

'Do you and your brother have other family that might still be alive?'

I froze. Would I go on with the elaborate charade? I decided for now I would and reached for her clipboard. I wrote my father's name in full and my mother's including her maiden name. I put the city I came from on the form, along with my age and my father's occupation.

'My mother had a Jewish mother. But we weren't raised that way. I don't know if that helps.'

'Perhaps, we can find them for you? For you and your brother. But it could take some time.'

She turned to walk away and I knew I must say something, because if Richard was in the next bed, they wouldn't look for my real brother.

'You have to look for Richard too.'

The young woman looked at me sharply, 'But I thought…. Who?'

She turned to the next bed, where Horst was looking directly at me with pleading eyes. It was then I saw him look down, crumpled in on himself, feeling he had run out of luck, that his crimes had caught up with him.

I hesitated then said, 'No this is my cousin Marek, All his family is dead. He is my Uncle Wilfred's boy.' Horst's eyes began to fill with tears and then he turned away and buried his head in his pillow.

The beautiful young woman with the strange accent took down the new details- the name and family of someone who didn't exist till now.

'It's a mess out there, so many people without homes and families. Already some are going to other parts of the world. You and your cousin need to come to the Red Cross when you are well enough to leave. We will try to find your loved ones.'

Horst groaned into his pillow; something was going on for him. I had never seen him like this.

She turned to go.

'Excuse me. What part of the world are you from?'

She turned back and smiled her expansive smile, 'Why I'm from Australia.'

For the rest of that day and into the night Horst would not meet my eyes but I watched him. He was struggling with something as I was. The same question kept resonating repeatedly in my head. Why didn't I denounce him. He was German, he was SS, he was a camp guard and had as much blood on his hands as any of the others that were being rounded up, jailed or executed. I'd had numerous opportunities to have him arrested, to expose him. But I did not. It puzzled me. It disturbed me. I should hate this man and every one of his kind. I had no way of explaining to myself what was happening here.

The clock on the wall said it was midnight but I found no sleep whilst I wrestled with all these questions. My feelings and my logic were not the same, I knew what I could do, perhaps should do and yet I could not bring myself to expose this man. I watched Horst who all day had his back to me. I wasn't sure but I felt he was weeping softly. Still the questions wouldn't go away. *Why am I behaving like this. I could reveal this man right now*. I had the power of life or death over him and yet I didn't take it. *Why didn't I?*

Two days later, an American four-star General with a delegation of lesser officers, doctors and reporters, armed with cameras and notebooks, made the rounds of the ward. Flashbulbs popped and everyone talked at once. The General gestured for silence and standing beside the first bed in the ward, began to discourse, as if we were his exhibits.

'Gentlemen, what you see here are the victims of Hitler's madness. The sickness that was the Third Reich. A disease that the U.S. and its allies have ended.' He puffed out his chest as if he alone was responsible.

Reporters all furiously scribbled notes in their books, still more flashbulbs, more questions, more exclamations and nodding of heads. The whole scene reminded me of a teacher with her excited children, at the zoo. I was amused, but I could see it put Horst on edge.

When they came to the line of beds closest to us, but still three beds away, Horst froze. I saw him look down and alter physically into the strange simple man that had saved us both. Arriving at our side the General and his entourage smiled down at me, whilst Horst stared off into the distance, as if strange voices were talking to him. Now was the moment, if I chose, to reveal his identity, to punish him for all the crimes committed against me, my family, my brother, my sister.

Don't do it.

I went rigid, my mouth agape. Then I too looked around for the unseen voice. The head doctor, I think, fearing that I was about to turn into an imbecile as well, moved the General along.

'Aaaargh!' I cried. Jana was back ... back inside my head.

The delegation who, by now were two beds further down, looked back at me with concern. I turned away and they returned to their duties, probably convinced I was having a violent daydream - that I was reliving the war.

You're here, where have you been? Why shouldn't I do it? How can you say that, they murdered you? These questions all crying out in pain and anger and loneliness. *Damn you, where have you been?*

You are alright now, Bron. You are going to make it. And me, I want to rest. But I have to know that you understand, that you are ready to heal. I have to know this before I can leave. I am so very tired, Bron. Please tell me you understand.

'What is there to understand?' I cried out, realising that I had spoken these words, not simply thought them and now everyone in the room was looking at me. Did I say them in Polish or English? I couldn't tell?

A nurse came back, smiling down at me, with a look of enormous pity.

'What's the matter, Hon?' she said in some American drawl that reminded me of the 'Talkies' back in Warsaw, with my sister.

'Can I get you anything, Hon?' And there it was again, for a moment I thought she was saying my name but no, it was Hon she said not Bron.

'No,' I said burying my head in my pillow. She placed her hand on the back of my head, stroking softly. For almost a minute she comforted me, by which time, the others were leaving so she rejoined them.

I am going Bron... soon. I cannot stay much longer. The war is over and you are safe. Yes, it will take time for you to heal but I must leave soon. Are you healing, Bron?

I thought about it for a long while Jana waited silently.

'I still have to live in this world; it will take some ...'

Before I could finish answering, another nurse arrived with a trolley of bowls and began to distribute them to those who were able to feed themselves. I looked across at Horst. The General had gone but Horst was still shaking.

'Here,' said the nurse handing him a bowl of broth. He fumbled it, sending the soup sloshing across the bedsheets. Trying to regain a hold he dropped the bowl completely. It shattered and spun across the floor landing under the next bed.

'Scheisse!' he exclaimed, then he looked at me, horrified.

The nurse disappeared under the next bed but when she rose with the two halves of the bowl she stared at Horst, who would not meet her eyes. Then she looked at me. I had been staring at Horst, as if the whole world knew our secret; now I too looked away.

Half an hour later the nurse returned with a bucket and mop. With her was the nursing sister they all feared, the one they all called 'Brunhilda' behind her back. She was Dutch-American, fierce, demanding and three times as broad as the young nurse was slight. The girl took her time cleaning up, while the Sister studied the patient that only minutes ago had been a Polish mute. Horst never once looked her way. They left, talking conspiratorially to each other, as they went. No-one came near our beds for the rest of the day but later that afternoon I noticed that there was now a guard standing outside our room.

Jana too remained silent, no longer demanding answers from me.

It was sometime before dawn when they came. At first, I heard them from deep inside my dream and as the dialogue continued, it dragged me into the waking world.

'Time to get up now son.' It was an American voice - soft, warm but commanding. Through half-opened eyes I saw a sergeant, tall, stocky, well fed with that shine that American soldiers had, like they'd spent their lives in the sunshine eating apples. Behind him stood two military police, their armbands black against the khaki. Both had rifles slung across their shoulders and the closer of the two had the clasp on his holster open and his hand resting on his pistol.

Horst got up without saying a word, put on pants and shoes, pulled open the steel drawer of the hospital cabinet and removed the shirt and jumper that some American charity had given him. It was all he had in the world. He smiled at me once and ran his hand across my head ruffling my hair, then went with them.

I don't think the soldiers knew I was awake but I was almost certain that Horst did. As the door closed, I began to cry and realised that no, I would not have betrayed him. I buried my head in the pillow and wept until I was aware that someone was watching me. I stopped and looked up but the room was empty.

Goodbye!

It was Jana. I sat up in bed and I knew that she was finally going. Through my tears I looked around, as if I would see her walking out the door.

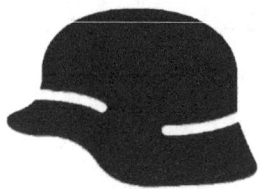

LUNEBURG SPRING 1945

20

The barracks, outside the town of Luneburg, was now an internment camp for German soldiers. It was far better than Horst expected. The British flag flew from the flagpole and Military Police stood at the sentry post while regular soldiers patrolled the perimeter. Both German infantrymen and officers were held, but each in different huts. There were bunk beds and blankets enough for all. A head count took place on the parade ground each morning but there were no summary executions, no starvation rations, all regardless of rank were fed and treated well. Horst looked around the compound and it struck him that sanity had returned to the world. Not kindness, not forgiveness but clear reasons for behaviour and an order where you knew where you stood.

Each day they went out in trucks to clear bombed buildings both officers and foot soldiers alike, stacking bricks in neat rows beside the road and removing bodies from the rubble. A necessary thing to do to prevent cholera he told himself. At the end of the day they were often told they'd done a good day's work and driven back to camp. The guards spoke to them in a disciplined way but not harshly.

Many of the soldiers were surprised by this, assuming they would be paid back in kind - beaten, abused perhaps even shot. But soon after arriving most talked, wondered, hoped that they would eventually be freed and sent home. Even Horst.

The processing team were unaware he had been an SS guard. The *other Horst* from his own home town had died, early in the war, allowing him to adopt his identity. The one he'd been holding in his memory, for the last two years. *Just in case,* he said to himself, *just in case.* The interview room was bare, a desk in the middle of the room directly below a bare bulb and enough chairs for four people.

'Why the prisoner's clothes?' asked a hard-faced British sergeant, as a private beside him took notes.

'I've been in disguise because I wanted to turn myself in to the Allies and not the Russians.'

The officer and the clerk exchanged looks, Horst was almost certain that meant he was believed; as the Russians were committing atrocities all over Germany, the Brits had some reason to take his word. From that point on he filled the interview with a mixture of his own life and family and that of his compatriot, coupled with a life as a common infantryman, far from his own crimes.

Back in barracks, Horst kept to himself, quietly listening to stories from both sides. "The Tommys," as his fellow prisoners called the British, seemed an easy-going lot and would even share their cigarettes with those who a few months before were shooting at them. The Military Police were less friendly but the regulars were quick to start up a conversation. It all felt as if some dark storm had passed and sunlight was breaking through. As if some terrible dream was finally over.

Both sides had tales of where they came from and what campaigns they fought, of losing comrades and narrowly escaping death. Reliving the horrors they had survived helped the long nights pass for some. Others could not bear it when talk turned to their war exploits, disappearing outside to smoke, till it was all over. The British guards would often demand that the English-speaking Germans retell their stories for them. For most, the hardest stories to tell or to hear told were of the Russian campaign.

'Thank God we weren't captured by the Russkies!' one said and all nodded in fervent agreement. The days were filled with physical work that restored much of the prisoners of war's dignity and the nights drifted by with reminiscences, battle tales and card games, there was little to do but wait till they were all cleared and de-mobbed.

Out of earshot of the Tommys, one of the young soldiers asked, 'These camps they say they've found, do you believe the stories?' Horst watched from the edge of the group.

'No!' came an adamant reply.

'It's propaganda,' offered another.

'They won, they don't need propaganda,' said the eldest in the circle - a sergeant.

'It's true! They have thousands, maybe more, in these places. Do you really think that Hitler wasn't going to follow through? You remember what he said before the war,' added another older soldier. Horst remained silent but couldn't help wondering if others among them were also hiding what they knew, what they had done?

Encouraged by the frankness, the sergeant added, 'We don't have to be patriotic Germans now. We lost. I hear the Fuhrer is dead. We can speak our minds.'

'That's the kind of talk that lost us the war,' spat one of the youngest of them all.

'We lost the war the moment we marched on Moscow, you fool,' said the sergeant. 'And if you can't see that you're as stupid as the generals who forgot about the Russian Winter.'

'Napoleon!' said another with heavy emphasis.

'1812,' said another. Those with a knowledge of history nodded their understanding.

The sergeant and the young man glared at each other, as the threat of real violence hung in the air. To which the older soldier added, 'And when the Americans joined, we were truly fucked.'

With this they all laughed, even the patriots.

The fact that Horst had no identifying papers interested his captors; they were suspicious but had nothing more to go on. Periodically during his second interrogation the officers would pause then huddle together discussing what information he gave. Horst gave them his own version of the infantry battles he'd heard the others talk of, at night. He peppered the tales with details that he knew were true, placing himself in campaigns far from the great crimes the Nazis were being made to account for.

The chaos of the war helped his situation, for many soldiers no longer had papers. He and *'the Horst'* he was impersonating both came from the suburbs of Dresden. That fact also helped his position.

'Dresden is gone. Nothing left!' the interrogating officer told him. 'The whole city was burnt to the ground,' he added. There was a triumphant note to the way he said it, as if to say, 'you bastards had it coming to you.'

Horst found it hard to believe. Something so big, so beautiful, so old was nothing but ash. He had no family, had grown up without sisters or brothers, his parents were both dead long before the war. But to think that the street on which he lived, his house, his school, the people he knew, the city squares, the castle, the cathedrals, the parks, the cinemas, and dance halls - were all gone. Gone was the barman at his local haunt, his barber, the baker who sold him bread, when he rolled back to his room drunk, at four in the morning. Gone was the cheeky boy who sold him *'The Anzeiger,'* the daily newspaper, when he wandered out hungover, mid-afternoon. It ripped at his heart, hurting him in a way that he didn't see coming.

Unlike the things he had done, the things he'd steeled himself to do, he hadn't protected himself against this savage truth. This new knowledge ate away at him. A whole city, a whole way of life all gone.

But is it any different to what you have done? You've destroyed a city's worth of people. Haven't you? the voice inside himself argued. It was a voice that he'd held in a prison in his mind, for the last six years. A voice he'd justified when he thought of the humiliation his father and the other soldiers faced after their defeat in the Great War. A father who had suffered mustard gas attacks and had never breathed properly from the day he staggered home to a defeated country, a hero unsung, till the day he died, drowning in his own lungs. A father who called out for justice from the victors and from the government that had betrayed him. Still the voices Horst had silenced called out to him too. Now they were combined as one; a single voice, that was so much more – families, generations echoing, that grew more insistent each day. The demands, the accusations, the condemnations would have to be met, one day soon. *But let's just get through this day*, he told himself. He struggled to push them aside, for now.

* * *

'Faith is superior to intellect. I believe in the future of our country,' *the other Horst* offered up one evening, with all the enthusiasm of youth. 'National Socialism is the future!' he added and the two of them embraced each other. Brothers in arms for a noble cause, they told each other.

At the start of the war they made a pact, over drinks in their favourite Dresden bar. The only one they hadn't been thrown out of - a pact imbued with their notions of honour and right.

'We will fight valiantly for the justice the Germans have been denied,' Horst offered, feeling overcome with a sense of destiny and alcohol.

'We will lay down our lives, if that is what is demanded,' added the other Horst. They enlisted together, certain that only blood and sweat would lead to glory. And then they made a deeper, more personal pact, memorising his childhood friend's identification, his friend doing the same, they told each other that they would keep the other alive in their minds, no matter what. And return home with news of the other's death, if that was how fate turned.

'All I have is a distant aunt and uncle you could tell,' Horst laughed to his 'new brother.' Despite having no family of his own, he took the promise seriously. His friend was sent to Greece to fight, only lasting a few weeks into the Greek campaign. Horst joined the SS; it was he felt, the true brotherhood, a feeling of belonging he had never had.

It was almost three years before he found out that Greek partisans had ambushed his blood brother's troop on some remote island. His death made Horst ache but then it also strengthened his resolve, still believing in righting the wrongs that had been perpetrated against his country.

Now Dresden had been bombed, burnt beyond recognition, now there was no-one to return home to, nowhere to take word of a lost son and give to a grieving mother.

The last year had changed everything. The Soviets were coming, polluting his world so that everything the brothers stood for would be lost. But another invasion had already taken place inside him, consuming him, growing stronger by the day as the war turned against them. He began to doubt his leaders, began to believe that Germany was finished, that the cost was too great and worse, that what the French had wanted at Versailles would be realized - that they would be ground down and forever be in bondage to their enemies. He was glad his friend was not here to see this, that there was nothing left but to survive, leaving all these broken dreams behind. Bitter as it was, survival was all that mattered.

As the war continued, his friend's death began to alter in meaning. The rallies all seemed like just some intoxicating moment in his youth. He had expected the 'blood and sweat' of battle but the mindless mediocrity of what he ended up doing left a taste in his mouth that he could not get rid of. and a voice remained, a voice that was also multitudes in his head that clawed at his guts, when he lay awake at night. What had he done? So much blood.

'H' SPRING 1945

21

The two men shared a cigarette on the parade ground, Horst and the corporal he'd come to know simply as Jones, a friendly country boy, with an outgoing personality. They both knew, this kind of familiarity would not have gone down well with the officers but they were both lonely and Horst was one of the few who spoke reasonably fluent English. They talked weather, for it was the warmest day for many weeks and they both wished that summer was finally here. Still the cold had clung to the world for too long and had refused to give way to the season. But most often they talked motorcycles, arguing whether British or German bikes were superior - it was combative but good-natured.

Out of the darkness came yelling from the closest barracks, as a German private, gesturing wildly, ran towards them, shouting in a mixture of both languages.

'Er! Das ist er! … Him! Him!'

Horst looked at the boy, trying to get the measure of what he was saying. The guard, sensing the urgency, removed his rifle from his shoulder.

'What does he want?' asked Jones.

Horst calmed the young soldier and in German told him to, 'Tell your story slowly.'

The boy took two deep breaths and began again. There was a soldier dressed in a Wehrmacht uniform, a sergeant who was ordering everyone about in their' hut.

'But I know who he is! I need to tell someone!'

Horst looked at the soldier, he was not like the patriotic ones from the previous day. The hatred radiated from him, Horst could feel it.

'Himmler! Himmler! Reichsfuhrer Himmler!'

This piece of information needed no translation. The corporal ran to the officers' rooms and returned with a captain, walking quickly to the barracks, the young boy just ahead, the two British soldiers following, with Horst slightly behind. The first three entered but Horst stopped at the door of the hut and watched. The captain stood before the small gesticulating sergeant, who ignoring him, continued to bark orders at the hapless soldiers, some of whom obeyed.

Was it Himmler, Horst thought? The moustache was gone but the glasses were still there. Weirdly, one glass of his spectacles was covered by an eyepatch. Was that some kind of disguise? Perhaps, but it wasn't his features that gave the SS leader away, it was his manner. He seemed unable to be anything other than what he was - a tyrant.

'I have reason to believe that you are a high-ranking German officer,' said the captain.

The masquerading sergeant turned and smiled a condescending smile.

'I believe you are Heinrich Himmler.'

'And you, my boy, are just a captain, I wish to talk to a superior officer.'

The captain and the young corporal moved toward the prisoner but before they could lay a hand on him, he reached up into his mouth and appeared to dislodge something. Do not fall into the hands of the enemy; it was what SS officers held to - rather than face humiliation and a firing squad. It was the creed of death before dishonour.

Even from the door, a distance of ten metres, Horst could see the look of defiance on the man's face and that brief grimace, that Horst was certain was Himmler biting down hard. It took only seconds for the poison to take hold. He collapsed onto the end of the bed, his body going rigid, then wracked with a violent spasm, he kicked out twice and fell to the floor dead.

For a long time, no-one in the room moved, each one staring at the inert body. Even in death, he seemed to hold them all in a kind of suspended animation - a commanding spell. Finally, the boy who had raised the alarm, walked across the room and kicked him hard. No-one else moved. Then another soldier, an older one, came over and spat on him. The captain shaken out of his stupor, looked up at the stunned soldiers.

'Enough!'

Shaking his head, he ordered Jones to stand guard over the body. He left the hut passing by the reticent Horst, grimacing as he went, returning two minutes later, with two higher-ranking British officers. Looking puzzled, they too stood around the body, wondering what to do next?

Horst, by now, had stepped away from the hut and was watching all of this from a distance; he knew enough to remain invisible. Never get noticed by your superiors, if you want to stay alive, this was his creed now.

Eventually high-ranking German officers were brought to identify the body. As they left a few minutes later, they no longer walked erect, the enormity of Himmler's death hitting them hard, their faces were ashen. Here, Horst thought, was the final evidence that Germany had lost the war. The guards were already doubled outside their barracks. From the window of his own hut, Horst watched as British officers came and went for most of the night.

Sometime after midnight, a military truck pulled up and Horst watched the body being carried into the back. The Wehrmacht uniform had been removed. *And so it goes*, Horst couldn't help but laugh to himself. They were going to get rid of the body, so that stupid, young soldiers didn't worship him.

Horst was laughing in full stride now, great bellowing laughter releasing from deep inside him. All those promises, the noble brotherhood he had joined, the quest to restore Germany's honour, the glory that would last a thousand years when Germany ruled a united Europe, all gone. It had all been for nothing, a tragic folly so absurd and painful it was funny and this was the greatest joke of all. The great Reichsfuhrer, the second most powerful man in Germany, the self-styled leader of the order of Teutonic Knights - the SS, was being taken away to be buried secretly, *in his underwear*.

Horst's city lay in ruins and for all he knew every other city across the country. They had all turned out to be liars and fools, making him into a fool also, a fool with so much blood on his hands. A fool now cast adrift, where he too, if he lived, would be a refugee walking the roads, flung to some far distant part of the world. And in that moment, he thought of the only person he knew on that road- the boy Bronek and wondered where *he* would go? The boy who, like him, could fix motorbikes, who helped him escape, who never betrayed him when he had every right to. How was it that this Jewish kid was the only one who was true? That truth hurt him more than any other

BOOK THREE

'TRELLEBORG'

'Tread softly upon the clouds, child

There laid out before you

A gift to lost innocence

Soon to restore you

Whisper to the heavens child

For much is uncertain

But much is given in gratitude

From a father unspoken'

OLD WORLD 21ST CENTURY

22

THE FIRST MONDAY

'Ah, you must be Tara,' he said with a warm smile and a hand that clasped hers, catching Tara unawares. He shook it vigorously, in a pantomime of mock formality and playfulness.

'I am Dr Wozniak.' Tara took a step back attempting to fully take in this large personality.

'And you are Kate.' Her mother nodded, she too was taken aback by his mix of the blunt, the jovial and the commanding.

Looking at Tara he said, 'I call your mother Kate because I have no time for formalities. I've seen too much in my life for that kind of nonsense.'

Tara smiled back up at him, feeling that perhaps she had been concerned for nothing. That all her misgivings about coming to the doctor, were just more of her powerful imagination, nothing more.

She was however, shocked by his appearance, although he was handsomely dressed in a tweed coat and trousers held up with old fashioned suspenders, he was surely the oldest doctor she had ever seen. I didn't think they let doctors that old practise, he must be at least ninety, maybe a hundred, Tara thought. He was long and skinny and yet smaller than her, this puzzled Tara. For he was no bigger than some of her school friends and yet he carried himself as if he was tall. As if he was once taller but had shrunk with age. As he walked toward them, he did not stoop or shuffle, though he would pause to catch his breath before he talked. His arms were covered in spots and wrinkles and his face was the same and yet he had the energy of a younger man. He glowed with a love of life; his presence filled the room, with his fast mind and an even faster tongue, cheeky and charming. For a few moments Dr Wozniak stood near the door talking quietly to Kate as Tara moved about taking in the magnificence of the stately old room.

She sat briefly in the large leather chair that swallowed her up and surveyed the room. It was a modern building but as soon as they walked into the doctor's rooms it took on an old-world feel. The walls were paneled in varnished timber - maple or rosewood and the drapes were a rich dark green with fine embroidered gold stitching. The air was filled with an aroma she thought to be a mixture of lavender and pipe tobacco. Tara picked up his pipe of carved brown wood that lay on the edge of his desk. Yes, that was the smell.

Dr Wozniak turned from his conversation with her mother and shook his head.

'Yes, disgusting habit. You'd think as a doctor I would know better. But alas, old habits.' He shook his head again in mock disgust. 'Now don't you start smoking Tara. You would look ridiculous with a pipe, I think.'

Tara laughed and decided she rather liked this joker. Throughout the conversation the doctor kept one eye on Tara as she studied the room.

'I will be with you in a few moments, have a look around while I finish up with your mother.' They continued to talk in hushed tones but it was all too obvious the subject was Tara.

Tara wandered across to a large glass cabinet, scanning the objects and pictures of another era – Eastern Europe and America and some from Australia. "Old World" family photos in faded browns and yellows, some coloured photos that looked like the colours had been painted on with a brush. The world within them looking not so much real as a fantasied realness. like a comic book, she thought. Citations in Hebrew stood beside photos of old Hassidic men of reverence with curls that fell down the sides of their faces, from what was, she suspected, even earlier times. These had no dates but Tara placed them in the early twentieth century or maybe even before. They were the kind of photos where people had to stand still for a very long time. Some of the photos, particularly the ones of towns and cities, looked like the ones Katya had borrowed from her grandparents for their project.

Then there was a more modern studio shot of a man in his fifties holding a small American flag, smiling broadly out of the photo, his arm around his wife, his three children dressed stiffly in formal attire; they were all well fed and standing in new clothes. If it wasn't for the flag, Tara might have mistaken them for Australians. A Military Cross, set in a small leather case, was clearly from the First World War, a lock of a woman's hair draped around the edges of another studio photo of a girl in her early twenties, dressed in a short skirt, in almost modern clothes, perhaps from the 1960s, Tara thought. Next came a picture of the doctor with his arm around a boy who was holding a fish he had just caught and was beaming at the camera. The doctor was much younger and was smiling down at the boy; father and son Tara concluded. And finally, a faded newspaper clipping of a man in a suit, cutting the ribbon at a bridge opening, watched on by dignitaries in top hats. The captions and the article were written in a somewhat familiar language. It always puzzled her how to read words that seemed to muddle up where you put the letters, or that left letters out. She was sure Katya would know how to read it. Tara looked hard at the headline and wondered how you would even try to pronounce words that complicated.

'You like the photos?'

Tara half smiled a yes and nodded. He opened the glass doors and ran his finger along the frames of each photo. His eyes turned watery, brimming almost ready to spill, as he spoke with a deep sense of affection.

'I came to this country with nothing. Well almost nothing.' He took from his coat pocket a pewter cavalry man and horse, placing the toy on top of the glass cabinet. And then he looked for a long time at the flag waving photo, before he put it down and returned to the real world. Tara watched fascinated.

'Come and sit down. I have some things I want to ask you.'

'Where do they come from, the medals and stuff?'

'Some are my photos.... from after I arrived. Most of this came from my uncle in America. He's gone now but to him I owe a great deal. This is my family history, he kept it safe when I couldn't. He took it away with him, when he left from Poland, you know where that is?'

Tara beamed, 'Yes, I know lots about Poland, especially Warsaw'

'Tara did a project,' offered Kate from across the room.

'Hmm, my home town, I see. I bet you have a great memory. I bet you remember lots of things.'

'Yes,' she nodded enthusiastically.

'Lots of facts and figures I'm betting. Lots of important things. Aah but I wonder can you remember your dreams, Tara?'

Tara's smile faded, as she shifted awkwardly in her chair. Ambushed, she had trapped herself as all the reasons she hadn't wanted to come in the first place came rushing back to her. Her parents had tricked her. She looked across to her mother who sat with her hands folded in her lap, looking concerned but innocent then back to the doctor who smiled at her.

He didn't wait for her to answer, instead he said very softly, 'Well, how about you tell me one?'

Squirming, she looked sideways at her mother again, unsure of where this would go. Why couldn't she stay in the "Old World", let the Doctor tell her his stories of that time? Why did she have to come back to this time? A minute ago, he sounded like her old joking uncle, but now the playfulness had disappeared, now they had returned to her world of imaginings, that were real only to her and yet filled her with dread.

'Which one?' she asked hesitantly.

'Any will do.'

She baulked at the proposal for she kept her dreams to herself, even the terrifying ones. She did not want to share them with her mother, did not want her mother to ask her questions. And this old man he too would ask questions, perhaps worse questions, more prying; yes, that's what child psychologists are supposed to do, she thought. He was waiting, she would have to give him something. Great silence filled the room but not inside her head.

Be free of these terrors her thoughts demanded of her; *go to bed without fearing the nighttime* but, now that Tara was here, the prospect of going deeply into them frightened her also. It all seemed too hard.

She gathered up her strength and looking at the floor said, 'There is one I had a few times. It's about Cory. He gets trapped underground.' The doctor referred to his notes. 'Cory is your brother.' Kate put her hand to her mouth but said nothing.

'He climbed down a drain and couldn't get out. It's the big one at the end of our street, just where the bush starts. I think it's called a convert.'

'Culvert,' offered Kate but quickly retreated when the doctor's look said do not intrude.

'I'm on my knees, crying. I can hear him and he can hear me. I tell him I'll run for help but he doesn't want to be left alone. I call out for Mum and Dad but no-one comes.'

'Oh God,' Kate let slip and Dr Wozniak again gestured with his eyes and a stern grimace, making it clear he needed her to be quiet and just listen. Tara absorbed in the retelling, noticed none of this.

'Then Cory says that he can hear a rumbling. I can't hear it but he says it's coming. He's yelling now, really loudly. And then I can hear it, it's like the ocean. I start screaming but Cory doesn't answer. I scream his name lots of times but he still doesn't answer. Then the water comes up through the grate and onto the street. Then I wake up.'

Tara watched the doctor make a number of handwritten notes, shaking his head at Kate, who by now was struggling to hold in her emotions. Tara's body lifted up just a little, her shoulders rose, the weight not quite as much now. She studied the doctor's intense concentration on his notebook.

He held a beautiful gold fountain pen, that caught the light of the desk lamp. Though she could not read it, Tara could see that he was writing in a very artistic style. It came out on the page effortlessly; even being upside down it was beautiful, like artwork from another time. She had struggled with the same look in her project. The writing she felt was like him, beautiful, old, delicate, all done with great care; it was "Copperplate," something Katya and Tara had tried to do to all the headings in their project but never as artfully as his.

The room was so quiet that Tara found herself looking across at her mother who looked away, forcing herself to stifle the sound of her crying by keeping her hand over her mouth. Why was she so upset; had the dream frightened her mother in the same way it had terrified her, she wondered? Or was this something else, maybe what was happening between her mother and her father? All these emotions and nightmares seemed to be wrapped in each other.

Dr Wozniak finished his writings and looking up, silently studied Tara for a while, his pen between his teeth. She felt he was on the edge of saying something but did not. He seemed satisfied with what he had learned but Tara could not see why. For the rest of the session, she answered questions about her room, her house, her school, her brother and finally how she saw the world. This was the hardest question of all.

'What do you mean, how do I see the world?'

Kate leaned in as Tara mulled this over.

'I mean is the world a good place? A kind place? Do you trust that the world will give you good things? Do you wake in the morning excited by its possibilities?'

It was a strange question and yet she thought she ought to have an answer for it, but then maybe this was too big to find an answer straight away. After what seemed to her a long time Tara shook her head.

'I don't know. Should I know?'

'Perhaps. Maybe not today. Eventually, everyone must know how they feel about the world around them, don't you think?'

Tara didn't know what to think. She knew she was being asked larger questions than she had ever been asked before. It puzzled and challenged her at the same time.

'Never mind, we will talk some more on this one when next we meet.'

Tara sat up in the large leather chair and raising herself to her full height, queried why there were so many questions? He answered with a wicked grin and a familiar line.

'All the better to know you with!' Tara recognised 'Little Red Riding Hood' and laughed. As did her mother.

'I think that is enough for today. I will see you again in…' he double-checked his diary. 'In two days and I think when you come again, we will talk alone, yes? No more tears!' As he said the last sentence he looked solidly at Kate.

He made another note. 'I want you to think about your dreams, not at night…no, at night I want you to sleep. In the day, I want you to think about what they mean. But you need to control them, not them control you. Do you understand?'

Tara nodded earnestly but wondered how do you control dreams?

He turned to Kate while still talking to Tara. 'Now I am going to give your mother something to help her sleep. Oops, sorry to help you sleep.' Tara giggled, then gave an unsure half smile to him and knowing she had been dismissed moved to the door, taking one last look at the "Old World" photos as she went.

'And when we meet next time, we will get to the bottom of this dark well, yes?'

Tara looked back at him, a mixture of relief and uncertainty. Did she want to get to the bottom of the dark well? This too she didn't know.

JOURNAL 21ST CENTURY

23

THE SECOND MONDAY MORNING

Tara pulled the slim, black book from her desk drawer and smelt its binding. It had that old world feel; it was a strange thing for a doctor to do - to give her something so old, something from another time.

'And this is for you', Dr Wozniak had said at the end of their Wednesday appointment, 'We have been to see each other twice now and still you keep dancing around the subject. Still, you keep your secrets young Tara. This second session has been nothing but mumbles. It is all well and good to tell me about your brother and the house and the room you love but we are dancing around the real issues.' He had looked at her with a mixture of concern and slightly comic disapproval.

'So, I want you to write your next dream and anything you want to say about it in this book. You don't have to tell me but you must at least share it with the book. Bring it when you come. Then the book can tell me what you will not.'

Did he do that for all his patients, she doubted it? She placed the book next to her and Katya's project. Along with the two dioramas, they had completed a scrapbook of photos of beautiful European cities full of vintage cars and horse drawn carriages. It didn't have the strange scent of old paper and glue like the journal but together the two objects drew her into a lost time. That smell wafted through the room as she slowly turned the scrapbook's pages. There were the capitals of distant nations, before the Second World War - grand buildings and wide streets, people clothed in elegant dresses and fine suits taking their children on Sunday walks, in the parks. There were the photos of the same cities at the end of the war, when only every tenth house stood, hollowed out and bare. She smelt the book again. *This came from there before the bombs, she felt sure. This is from that other world. But he had come to Australia with almost nothing, he had told her that. Where did this book come from? It was one more puzzle Tara associated with him.*

It was early morning as the light began to make the objects in her room move from soft focus to distinct and present. The book lay open beside her and was illuminated enough to be workable. Although she was tempted to go back to sleep, Tara felt an urgent need to get the previous night's dream down, while it was still in her memory, before the events of the day took hold.

Dear Diary   Monday morning   6 :11 A.M.

I want to tell you about my dream.

I am sitting at my desk in class. Everyone else is working hard, no-one looks up. I am looking out the window, I do that a lot. It gets me into trouble. There is music playing, I can hear it but nobody else seems to notice it. It is old music, like in old movies, you know those black and white ones from a hundred years ago or whenever - old violins and concertinas and stuff. It's really nice though a little sad sometimes but then it changes. Now it's marching feet, hundreds of them and then there is the sound of steel smashing against steel. It's really loud and scary.

I turn to warn everybody that something dangerous is coming but the classroom is empty. I didn't notice anybody leave, that's even scarier. Where did everyone go? When I look out the window they are all in the playground but I didn't hear the bell ring. The whole class is playing netball, even the boys which is weird because they hate it. I guess Miss Cork made them.

They're all passing the ball and no matter where I go no-one passes the ball to me. They all run around me.

Then my brother comes up and says, 'Excuse me, Miss Cork, is Tara here?'

And even though she is looking right at me she says, 'No, she didn't come to school today.'

I start shouting 'I'm here. I'm here.' But it's like I'm not there at all, like a ghost or something. Cory walks away, I yell but he can't hear me. I begin to cry.

Then I start to run home but it's not daytime anymore. Well, it is but it's earlier, it's sunrise and everybody is putting stuff in the car, you know holiday stuff – boogie boards and towels and things.

Then they all get in. They even take the dog, which is kind of cool cause we don't own one. And they're all happy. Cory is shouting 'Holidays! Holidays!' and this dog that we don't own is barking. And then they pull out of the driveway, just as the sun is coming up. But they leave me behind. STANDING THERE IN THE DRIVEWAY.

Tuesday – After School 4PM or close to

P.S.   Dr Woz, I don't know how to spell your name properly. But I have thought and thought and I don't understand what I wrote, what it means. I've read it two times more but I still don't know.

P.P.S   I guess I should write this too. After the dream I went downstairs and opened up the family album. I don't know why but I really felt like I needed to do that. I sat up for an hour just going through the pictures. It was about one in the morning, I think. For a while Cory came down and sat beside me, I guess he couldn't sleep properly either so we looked at the pictures together. Just regular pictures, our beach holidays, some birthdays, Cory winning a soccer pennant. It made both of us a bit sad. Then we both got sleepy and went back to bed. Mum and Dad didn't know we were there.

Bye Diary – talk again tomorrow. I really like doing this, it's like telling stories only they're real. Bye again.

    Tara closed the book and once again smelt the binding, it was rich and leathery, like the library at the University in Liverpool her father had taken her to once, when he was visiting his own father, her grandfather -the teacher. Perhaps all old men had books like this.

    The doctor offered," If you tell me your big secret, I will tell you mine." Would the telling of some of her dreams be enough to hear his? She was still holding back on the ones where the Dark King had invaded her nightmares.

    She felt certain that the doctor's secret would be powerful, like the pictures in his glass display case. It was hard to explain but something inside made her feel that she was doing something important, that she was moving now in the world of adults. Though at times it troubled her the idea of giving up her own inner world, this seemed greater than anything she had done before, that now she would find an even larger world to make her own.

She placed the journal under her pillow, promising herself that she would read it again before she went to sleep, the following evening, just to make sure that she had everything she wanted to say written down.

*   *   *

The family garage smelt of oil and grease, of plastic and wood, of years of accumulated dust, everything stacked in PVC coloured boxes, with marker pen labelling. Tara looked around, deciding this is the place where things go when there is nowhere else to put them. She liked the randomness of the varied objects and the order of the boxes that tried to contain them. The walls were covered in pictures of surfers barreling down the crests of waves. Several of them Tara knew, were female world champions; she stopped in front of each admiring their strength and agility, in their wetsuits they almost looked like costumed super heroes. In the corner sat a big Malibu board and a smaller lightweight twin fin. She ran her fingers along the smaller one, her board, remembering how her father had taken her out the back, into deep waters and taught her how to read the waves. How to know what was coming and which one promised the lift and grab that she could ride all the way in. That was three summers ago, the holidays so rarely meant going away now, now her parents were too busy, too poor. 'We cannot afford holidays at the moment,' said her mother. But Tara felt that was only half the reason.

Her father was in here somewhere; she heard him grunting but the place seemed empty. Then he slid out from under the car, on a flatbed dolly, his hands covered in grease.

'Got to do this myself, can't afford to send it for servicing,' he said as he stood, wiping himself down. He opened the hood, careful not to get any muck on the duco. Tara stepped up beside him and looked in.

'Mum says, dinner is in half an hour.'

Her father nodded then returned to studying the car. 'Talk to me Jack, what's the matter with you?'

Tara smiled, her father had always given his cars names and he always talked to them, as if they could talk back. In that accent, the 'Scouse' accent as he called it, that all the years in Australia had not taken away. Without looking sideways, he asked, 'How's school?'

'Okay…Dad, how come you don't go surfing anymore?'

'Haven't got time anymore.'

'Why?'

'It's just what happens to people's lives, honey. They get busy.'

'You should find time.' Tara said it with some authority. She knew her father had left England behind, telling everyone he was going to Australia to surf and be with the girl he loved. It was another of the stories Tara always wanted her father to tell.

'YOU SHOULD DO IT, YOU LOVE SURFING,' she said more stridently, hoping that he would address her concerns. No answer, just a small nod from her father, who didn't give any indication that Tara had said this twice. Instead, he systematically traced the connections, checking various parts, going through the engine in his mind, determined to find why it was not running well. Tara studied her father's face, as intently as he studied the engine. As she watched she gathered up courage and asked.

'Dad, is Mum going to leave us?'

Ray flinched but again did not look her way. He replied, while keeping his eye on the job ahead, 'No, Taz, we are going to try to figure it out. If anyone must leave, it will probably be me.'

Tara gave a sharp intake of breath. He stopped for a moment, gave her a half smile then returned to the task. But it had already done its damage. The thought of her father leaving almost brought Tara to tears. She held it in check.

'Oh,' was all Tara gave. But it was enough to make her father ache and turn to his daughter to give her his full attention.

'We are working on that,' he said, though Tara knew it wasn't really true. The lie told, he returned to the job at hand.

'Pass me the socket spanner.'

'Imperial or metric?'

'Metric…Japanese parts.' A few moments later he said, 'Hold your hands open.'

Ray dropped four nuts into her waiting hands. Tara stood in silence watching her father puzzle over the engine. She shifted uneasily, gathering up the courage to ask the real question she had been skirting around.

'Dad, would it help if I asked Mum to let you stay?'

'No!' he said emphatically. A few minutes later he took the nuts from her and replaced the part. Hands on hips he stood back admiring his work. 'There it's done. 'Tara waited for a greater explanation than no, but there was none.

'You forgot that hose, it's not tightened.'

He looked to where she was pointing, 'Yes, yes well spotted. Thank heavens I have you here to help me.' Ray smiled proudly and held her to him with his arms in a heartfelt but awkward embrace, his hands splayed outwards, still covered in grease. 'My little mechanic!'

SECRETS 21ST CENTURY

24

'Come no further, it is forbidden!' said the Falcon Wielder, surrounded but unarmed.
Tara took the branch and struck it hard against the trunk of the scribbly bark gum. Cory did the same with his stick but it broke in two. For a second he looked bewildered and then inspiration seized him.
'You cannot prevent me. I will forge another.'
Tara looked at her younger brother, pleased that he was able to continue the story. She strode up the hill while soldiers dressed in fine livery, gathered in their thousands. She raised one arm over her head and then crouched down. The army ahead gave no sign that they would yield.
Cory came up beside her and spoke in a soft whisper, 'What is it Falcon Wielder?' It was a story they had been building over the last few months, each time they came, they began from where they left off. Now that their home life was in turmoil, they spent

more time in the bush and the quarry, keeping their troubles at bay making their story stronger, more compelling.

'There in the distance, it is riders of the Broken Shield. We must make our peace with them and seek their aid. But be careful, they only make deals so long as it suits them. They have already stood by and allowed the Dark Army through.' Her second in command nodded. Negotiations to travel in other armies' lands was a delicate matter, even a ten-year-old lieutenant knew that.

Cory picked up a more promising branch and tested it with a huge swing. He ran ahead, whooping and yelling, taking the adventure in an altogether different direction than Tara had planned. She looked exasperated, then gave in to his enthusiasm and ran up beside him. This time there would be no parlay. Together they swung in every direction against their invisible foe. For five minutes they ran up and down the hill, bringing down all those who stood in their way. Warriors of the Broken Shield lay bleeding all around them, their leaders having fled, knowing that they must live to fight another day.

'Now they will think twice about siding against us,' she thought to herself, remembering the last time the Broken Shield had betrayed them to the Dark Army and its leader, the unforgiving and treacherous Dark King. '

Finally, Cory sat down and leaned against a fallen tree, its roots still intact, twisting and turning as if they were branches. At the base was the hole it had left when a huge wind had toppled it the previous winter. Tara sat beside him, sweating and panting.

'What time is it?' he asked, falling out of character as he did.

'Five thirty. Mum and Dad won't need us back for another hour.'

'I have to feed the guinea pigs.'

'They can wait.'

'No, Mum said I've got to clean out their hutch,' he said as he walked down the hill toward home.

Tara reluctantly got up and began to follow. She knew that Cory would only play her game for as long as it suited him. Certain things must be done after school and before their parents came home.

'You have to put them in a box. I'm not going to chase them like last time.'

'That was funny.'

'No, it wasn't. Guinea pigs don't like to be chased. Remember Little Pete?'

'Oh yeah,' replied Cory thinking back on the one that died of fright.

'I'll help you, ok.' And with that Cory put his hand in his older sister's and together they left the battlefield and walked towards 'Madame,' towards home.

TUESDAY   THE THIRD VISIT

It was unseasonably cold for November and Kate made sure that Tara wore her padded jacket to the doctor. The dark sky that morning matched Tara's mood. Once more she would sit before the ancient man with the probing questions. She held the old book tucked into her arm. Perhaps he would simply read her writings and that would be all.

From behind Tara heard her mother say 'Just answer what he asks this time alright; this is costing a lot of money Tara. I'll be waiting out here.' Tara smiled wanly and walked into the doctor's rooms like she was going to have her teeth pulled.

Doctor Wozniak opened Tara's diary and quickly scanned it. He seemed pleased with what he saw and Tara felt she had accomplished what was asked of her. But she had mixed feelings about the book and its purpose. Yes, her dreams puzzled her and maybe the old doctor could tell her what was going on, what her dreams were saying, what power and fascination they held. On the other hand, she wanted nothing to do with the nightmares; they confused and frightened her. How could you hold onto what you hated and both want to be rid of them and yet hide them from others?

The large leather chair she sat in could not contain the mixed emotions she had about being there. She wanted to know what he thought of her journal, wanted his approval, but it came at the cost of her privacy. Before he began to read it more deeply, he closed the book and looked straight at her.

'Thank you for this Tara. So today, are we going to keep our secrets or are we going to share … hmmm?'

Tara shifted uncomfortably and looked down at the floor. Gone was her sense of fulfilment, he wanted more than the diary; he was going to ask her prying questions again. Of course, she knew that he would want more, to think otherwise was foolish, but she hoped that writing the diary might put off the inevitable. Instead, he would read it and then ask her about it.

'I promised you last time we spoke, well *I spoke* … you barely said anything.' He was having his joke but Tara felt him criticizing her too. He smiled at her and then sighed deeply.

'Last Wednesday I said I would tell you one of my secrets … but I am not going to do that. I am going to tell you *two secrets*. One I have never told a soul.'

Tara leaned forward, eager, fearful, entranced. So many mixed feelings he conjured in her; she decided that he was some kind of wizard.

'My name is not Wozniak, that is a name I took for myself when I had no other. It is the name of a man who became my father when I most needed one. My family name, my real father's name was Nowak, though here we would say Novak. A good Polish name. But my mother's family name was Kline and that was our undoing, all of us. So, I have three names. No wonder I am such a confused old man.'

They laughed together.

'You have seen the pictures on display, yes?'

Tara nodded.

'Well, I have American cousins who still carry my old family name but in my European family I am the last of them. I am the last of the Novaks and the Klines too. But not the last of the Wozniaks. Now I see you could not spell Wozniak, so what about Novak or Kline?'

Tara nodded again.

'Call me anything you like ... except late for dinner.'

Just tell jokes please, she thought, don't ask questions.

'And *the second secret* is that you are my last patient. Yes, don't look so shocked my dear Tara. There will be no more after you ... I am a very old man now and it is time. I saw the way you looked at me when we first met. You think I am very old too, I know. So, I would like to go with a good batting average as the Australians say. Will you help me?'

Without waiting for her reply, he returned to the diary and read through all she had written over several days. Tara wondered what he meant when he said that it was time. She watched as he periodically went hmm, the more he noted passages the more she fought with herself. She had been too honest and now he would ask the right ... *the wrong* questions. She had begun something now that would not be stopped, as she knew just where he was focusing in her journal and what he would ask. *Will I tell him?*

Finally, he put down the book, gripped the arms of his chair and rocked back. Here it comes, she thought.

'I am intrigued by a line on your third page Tara. How did you put it *"it is punishment"* ... What is? What is punishment?'

She held her breath; he had found it.

'Hmm?'

Without a pause Tara's answer came quickly but not easily, 'It's my fault. It's all my fault ... that's ... that is ... why ... why I have bad dreams!' The moment she said it she felt relieved. The air in the room seemed to crackle with an emotional release that lifted her.

'I see. And what is the terrible thing that you have done?' He said it in such a way that Tara could hear how important he felt was the question and still had the slightly mocking tone that said nothing is all that important.

Now Tara stopped and gathered herself, trying to collect the thoughts that would best help explain her diary. She had gone over her faults so many times but to air them now was difficult.

'This is my final year before I go to High School.

She stopped and for a moment hesitated then took one deep breath and gripped the arms of the leather chair. The doctor waited a look of reassurance on his face.

'But Daddy, my father ... well, he has a business and it's not going very well. So, my Dad wanted to sell up and move us all. He said it would be good for us ... for everyone. But I think he really meant him and my Mum.' Now that Tara had started, she knew she would not stop, she wanted to spit this poison out of her system.

'Things are not good then?' Realising that Tara did not quite follow, he added, 'between your parents.'

'Yes, Mum refused. She said it would be wrong to move me just before High School. And that was it. Except it wasn't because they started arguing almost every day. It's Grandpa's money that she lent Dad and she feels responsible. They think we don't understand that Dad's business is in trouble. It's complicated. They tried to hide it from us but me and Cory, we know.'

'And so, the nightmares as punishment, yes?'

Tara nodded, falling back into herself, the lightness gone now; the weight of her judgement bearing down upon herself.

Dr Wozniak leant forward and picked up his pipe. Although he never lit it, he held it in his hands. Tara thought he might be connecting to some distant past - that "The Old World" might give him some kind of wisdom. The kind of wisdom a doctor would need to deal with a child's nightmares.

'Mmm. Let's see, you have terrible nightmares because you need to be punished, yes?'

Tara said nothing, nor did she make eye contact with him.

'Tara is it possible that your mother had her own reasons for not selling up? For not moving? ... Well?'

Tara looked up. At that moment the thought entered her and took a tenuous foothold.

'It is altogether likely that she used your reasons, instead of her own'

'But why?'

'Because your father would listen to reasons about you and perhaps, he would not have listened to hers. As you said it's complicated.'

This idea was now growing inside Tara, but she was not fully convinced. She watched him study her and felt he had the measure of her. She shook her head.

'You don't believe me, do you? '... For a moment he hesitated. Tara could see that the doctor was debating something inside himself. Would this be another secret, she wondered?

'I knew a boy who blamed himself for all the terrible things that happened to his family. And these were truly terrible things that happened. He spent his life running, until one day in a very frightening place he began to think about why this had happened to all those he loved and finally to himself. And there, when he needed to hold onto life the most, there he decided that he was the reason. And so, he fell into a very dark hole. A hole in which he wanted to die. Which was all his jailers wanted anyway. Then something unexpected happened to him. He was given the gift of life by the man who lay in the next bed, his friend who was dying. He was given a story that would eventually set him free'

Tara watched the old man tell the story and as he did, he seemed to change, to grow larger, younger, stronger. It seemed the old man shone with light.

Three quarters of an hour later Tara bounced out of Doctor Wozniak's timber paneled rooms with a lightness of being that her mother could plainly see. Kate watched as Tara skipped past her and down the corridor to the lift. Even for her doubting mother the moment was electric.

Dr Wozniak smiled. Kate smiled back and then opened her mouth to ask a question but at that moment he turned and went back into his rooms. She stepped forward to follow him then thought better of it.

On the street as if to match her mood the sun had come out so Tara stripped off her padded winter jacket, almost dancing on the footpath. Waiting for her mother to arrive, she stood by the car, holding herself with such a deep look of assurance. Kate stared at her daughter quizzically; some kind of transformative alchemy had taken place. The defeated look she had carried for the previous month or more had evaporated. The Tara that had been missing for so long, now was back. It confused and elated Kate.

'What did the doctor say?'

'Oh, just things.'

'What sort of things?' asked Kate as she snapped the car open with the remote.

'Oh, he just told stories that's all.'

Tara pulled the door open with a theatrical gesture and jumped into the back seat. Kate stood by the driver's side and looked at her daughter sitting in the back as Tara looked back out at her puzzled mother. *Ask all the questions you like, I will tell you nothing,* but the thought was not hostile. Instead, it was full of power, it was full of promise.

They pulled into their driveway and Tara leapt from the car, running at full speed toward the house. For a moment she stopped and smiled. 'Madame' was there to greet her and as she looked up at its beautiful tattered facade, she knew that the house understood.

She mounted the veranda steps two at a time, stamping on the stairs as she went. The underneath boomed out like a bass drum as she ascended. At the top of the stairs Tara turned around to see her mother staring, seemingly puzzled, unsure of the magic that had just transpired for her daughter. Yes mother, look as bewildered as you like, that's just how it should be, she thought

* * *

Tara lay in bed, too excited now to put herself to sleep; at last, she had an answer. Tonight, she knew that when she slept, she would do so without being haunted. Lying there in the dark she made a note of all the things that would be needed. Now, there was a way ahead even if she had to wait till the weekend. She drifted from one implement in her list to another, until sleep, without nightmares, eventually overtook her.

SATURDAY AFTERNOON

The hammer and chisel she borrowed from her father's garage plus a large art book that came from his den, lay inside a canvas duffle bag. She pushed the bag ahead of her and then climbed through the break in the wire mesh fence. The long shadows of the late afternoon cast her up the steep incline, like a shadow puppet. At the top of the hill the rise stopped abruptly at the rim, as if some giant hand had swept out of the sky and sliced the other half of the hill away. Deep below in the quarry, the excavators and earth-movers lay idle. The rock catching the afternoon light, stretched in layers of various colours and textures. At the top of the quarry sat the strata of sandstone and below that the harder igneous rocks that excavators had carved down to the quarry floor. It was Saturday, the pit was closed to the outside world and back home all her family were occupied. Tara knew she'd have all the time she needed.

Climbing to the rim of the crevasse, where part of the rise had collapsed, she surveyed its surface below. The shallow cave ran in a 'v' back from the edge, decreasing in size as it went. She dropped the bag in then at the mouth, close to the edge, sliding over holding the sides, finding small depressions where her hands could grip. It was perilously close to the lip of the quarry and the seventy metre drop to the rock floor. But it was large enough for her to climb in and then stand slightly bent.

As if I am bowing or praying, she thought and somehow that seemed just right. She crouched, scrambled a further two metres in, then sat midway down the cave's length. Tara ran her hand across the sandstone wall; a soft shower of gritty sand fell. Opening the book at the marked page, she studied it for a minute, occasionally looking at the wall in front of her. Taking up tools, she began to chip at the rock face. The sandstone came away easily, perhaps a little too easily. Sometimes large seams collapsed across bigger spaces than she wanted, destroying the shape she planned to carve. She slowed down, setting a series of perforations so that the stone would fall away as she wanted. From time to time, she referred to the illustration and then carved lines with the edge of the chisel, using it like a pencil. The image would be twice as large as she had originally planned but that was fine. The bigger the better, for what she had in mind. She worked on the creation until long afternoon shadows fell across the crevasse. The image now sat in the fading light, complete and commanding. Totally absorbed, Tara didn't notice the lengthening of the shadows till one of them moved across the cave wall and she looked up.

'What are you doing?'

It was Cory peering over the lip of the cave and taking in the bas-relief that stretched across the cave wall. The body looked much like what she had taken from the book on cave art. Tara stood back and took the whole rock face in, satisfied that it would serve her purposes.

'That's cool,' he said, looking from the illustration to the image made solid.

Standing together, admiring her handiwork, there was just enough room for them both. When she turned, she was eye to eye with Cory.

'You're not to tell anyone, you understand?' Cory nodded with a sense of the importance of what was happening. 'Especially Mum and Dad.' Once again, he nodded.

'Yes, but what is it? Is it part of the Broken Shield?' Tara shook her head.

'No, it's a temple, to a horse... To a horse that's going to come.'

"To do what?'

Tara turned to him and said with great earnestness, 'To save Mum and Dad.'

Cory looked puzzled and was just about to speak when she added, 'You'll have to trust me. I am going to make it happen!'

Admiration shone out of Cory. She knew he would not question what his sister, the leader of their adventures, was planning. *What the 'Falcon Wielder' commanded, must be obeyed.*

Cory bent down and one by one threw the chipped rock, that lay at their feet, into the chasm below.

TEMPLE SUNDAY

25

Tara spent all morning on the internet but there was so much information on 'White Horses of Myth, Legend and Religion' that she became lost in all of it. As far as she could tell the white horse had been around for thousands of years and it seems in almost every culture and religion. But for all the strange names and powers these white stallions and mares had, it was not clear to Tara what was coming and how to bring it forth. In the end she thought she might try another approach.

The sign said they were open every day except public holidays. The carved columns stood at the top of the long rising steps leading to a wide stately entrance, the name above written in English but attempting to look like carved Latin or Greek. It's trying to look like an ancient building like the Parthenon or the temple to the Oracle at Delphi, Tara thought, and so this, she was sure, was the right place to further her investigations. Perhaps here she'd find what she was looking for … here at the big library, that stood on one side of the large city square. The friendly librarian showed her where the section she wanted was.

'You can read here but you can't take these books out. I can make photocopies of anything you want.'

Tara smiled, nodding. For a few minutes she walked up and down the rows of the Reference Section, running her hand along the spines of the cloth and leather-bound books. Beginning to look in earnest, Tara took out each tome, searching the contents and then the index and returning it when it did not provide the answer she sought. More than a dozen books failed her and then there it was. It was about the unconscious and someone called Jung. She wondered if he was the same nationality as Dr Woz. He was European, a Swiss. And before the war too. She read that the Nazis had burned his books.

She found some lines in the book that came close to what she was looking for - *'Signifies freedom and possibility in many cultures. In some it is seen as a sign of both death and rebirth, ...particularly potent as a dream symbol.*

This was a start but she needed more. Tara pulled out volume after volume. There was so much written by him and about him. Some of the language puzzled her but there was enough she understood to convince Tara that she was on the right track. After a while she again felt overwhelmed until with closing time only half an hour away Tara made a decision. She closed her eyes and hovered her hand over the seven books lying on the table. She landed on Letters of C.G. Jung Volume Two, picked the book up and placed it in her lap and let it fall open to any page that chance would allow. And there it was - a reply to a Mr E.L. Watson from 1954 who had asked Jung about a dream he'd had about a white horse.

As she walked back down the stairs, a photocopy of the page in her hand, the keywords kept repeating themselves inside her... *"You integrate your animal. Your parents, all the people who you love They all live in you. And you are no more separated from them."*

Tara found what she was looking for. A reply to a man old enough to be her grandfather but more importantly a reply to her from across the decades.

THE THIRD MONDAY   LATE AFTERNOON

Standing by the kitchen sink, Tara took the box of wallpaper paste, pouring it into a large bucket as she read the instructions. *Add warm water and stir till the correct consistency for application. Solution should not be watery or lumpy,* it said. For several minutes she stirred, watching it roll off her brush until she was sure it was just right.

She carried the bucket and the wide paint brush up to her room where her great find waited, Tara smiled at the teetering pile of glossy paper that came up to her knees. An hour before she'd stood looking in the window of the butcher's three blocks from home. She had often walked the long way home after school but this time she spied it.

'Do you have any more of those?' Tara asked pointing to the calendar on the wall behind.

'Do I!'

Returning a minute later, the butcher carried an overflowing box, full of glossy paper bundles.

'How many do you want?' he said with a grin that implied he was glad to be rid of them.

'Printer got the order wrong didn't he. Four hundred I said; he gives me fourteen hundred. Always put things in writing, girlie, that's the lesson there.'

Tara took one from the top of the pile and studied the picture closely, her mind making one jump after another with the possibilities of this new treasure- a picture of a horse with a calendar of the months of the year below. Inspired by this holy icon, she struggled toward the butcher's door; the box being much heavier than she'd expected.

'School project, is it?' he said holding the door open for her.

'Something like that,' Tara replied as she waddled down the road labouring under the weight of the complimentary calendars.

'Come back tomorrow, I might have another box out the back.'

* * *

Half an hour to separate the horse photos from the months, Tara judged and then she could start to paste. It was simple, pleasurable work. Two hours later, the display surrounded her on every wall and she felt almost delirious with the result. Every stick of furniture, the bed, the wardrobe, the desk, the bookshelf now stood butted up in the middle of the room, like an island of wood and cloth. And all around them was the panorama of white heads on sky blue background, looking down with a look of animal wisdom, in constant holy repetition, like a chant sung on glossy paper. Across each wall, from floor to ceiling, stood the three-quarter profile of a white horse. that looked left to right out of the picture, covering every available space. The head was strong and noble with the kind of eyes that suggested they knew things humans were still searching for; white from chest to ear tips except for a fine smudge of grey on its forehead.

Her arms and shoulders ached but the effort was worth it. The effect was potent; she could place the room in her special line of worship now. She'd read what high priestesses in ancient times practised and hoped that this too would be something that pleased the Gods she was calling on - whoever they were. Something much more powerful than what she first conceived when she created the cave art, at the quarry, this would transmit like a beacon from home. There would be nothing to stop the great arrival.

She was so engrossed with her masterwork that she did not hear the car pulling in, her mother calling from downstairs or her entrance to the room.

'Oh my God, what have you done?'

Tara's smile beamed at her mother, although she knew, at that instant, that her mother was displeased, horrified actually. But she determined to stand her ground, to stiffen her resolve. *I don't care what she thinks; it is what I need to do.*

'What is this? Are they...?' Kate fingered the paper on the walls, lifting the edge where the glue had not quite taken. 'Why are you doing this?'

They stood facing each other, the questions hanging in the air, more accusation than inquiry. What had only a moment before been Tara's holy sacrament was now being looked on as a major crime. And her mother's anger was rising to meet the weight of that crime.

'This is crazy. I thought you loved this room? Why?'

Tara watched her mother turn around twice, overwhelmed by the monstrous immensity of what she considered vandalism, a bewildered look on her face till finally she came to a stop, glaring at her daughter. No words were spoken but her look still said

'WHY?' The questions, the accusations glued themselves to each other just as strongly as this desecration. Tara could stand it no longer; she ran down the stairs and out into the yard where she hid behind the large spreading fig tree and buried her face in her arms.

From her vantage point Tara watched her father pull into the driveway. Kate stood on the veranda when he arrived, her arms folded, her body rigid. Tara read her mother as still angry and confused appalled at the desecration. Craning her head she leant forward to hear her parents' conversation.

'You need to go upstairs and see what your daughter has done.'

Her mother remained stiff backed, as her father disappeared inside. Tara was sure what his reaction would be. Moments later from the second storey the yell came that confirmed her father felt the same as her mother. I must not let them win, she thought, no matter what they say, this belongs to me; this is my room and I shall do with it whatever I like. Her father burst through the door, searing with anger.

'Where is she?

'I don't know, she ran outside. Hiding I guess.'

Her father looked around, wildness in his eyes, searching the yard as Tara pulled back further behind the trunk. Finding nothing he strode toward the garage, returned with two paint scrapers, handing one to Kate. 'She's your daughter too!'

Ray slammed the back door as he went leaving Kate standing there, scraper in hand. Tara tried to guess what her mother was thinking as Kate lingered, though the body language was clear enough - a mix of bewilderment and rage.

Please don't let them destroy this. Please don't let this be for nothing. Just a couple of days, that's all I need. Tara sent out a plea, though she was not sure where it was going or who would answer it, but she had to believe that what she was creating would work.

Her mother clenched her jaw and then followed her husband back into the house. Tara waited, caught between her desire to flee and to defend her work. She gathered herself up, trying to ignore the knot in her stomach and followed her mother.

At the bottom of the stairs, she could hear the sound of metal against plaster and paper. *I have to confront them, I can't let them have their way. They're wrong I know it.* With each scrape came the angry grunts of her father.

The beauty and wisdom of her enterprise was lost on Tara's parents, now only anger filled the space. Noticeboards and framed pictures that leaned against the furnishings were now flat on the floor. The shelves that Tara had waddled out from the wall spilt books and toys across the room, as if her father had angrily tossed them aside.

Ray pushed the scraper with such violent thrusts that the paint and sometimes the plaster came away with the print; the more he continued the more frantic his actions became. Kate had not yet joined him, instead his frustration created a kind of no-go area. Her child's action puzzled Kate but now it was her husband's frantic movements that filled her with a growing sense of alarm. He moved like a man possessed.

'DON'T TOUCH THEM!' Tara stood at the door, bristling with defiance as this transgression, this sacrilege cut into her.

Kate stopped in her tracks and stepped back from the wall, but her father, never once making eye contact, kept on with the task at hand, hacking away, harder, faster. Tara could feel the fury radiating from him. *You are angry about me I know it, but I am trying to fix us, can't you see?* Finally, exhausted, he stopped and lay his head against the wall and softly cried out, 'Tara?'

Tara moved to the largest wall and spread her arms out to protect the vast expanse of pictures.

'Tara this is insane, how could you do this? Why did you do this?' said Ray.

'I did it for all of us.'

'What do you mean?' asked Kate.

Ray and Kate looked at each other, bewildered and concerned. Tara retreated back even closer to the wall, realising she had said too much, that the situation was too far gone; it was already too late, she had stepped over the threshold now. She knew inside that she had entered a world of her own making. A world where she would not depend, like a child, on the strength of others, where she could prove herself, if only they would not stand in the way of her decisions.

'I...I.can't tell you....it won't work if I do!'

'What won't work?' demanded Ray. He waited for her reply but instead the silence grew more accusatory, the gulf between them all widening with every moment.

Despairing he shook his head. 'Tara, this is crazy talk.'

Tara would not put into words what she knew inside, what she plotted, how she would make this work. If she told them, if they laughed or scorned her ideas, she knew that the future she planned would disappear. The silence stretched out as they anticipated her reply but Tara said nothing. Ray turned back to the wall and began again, there was less frenzy this time but just as much determination.

'No please don't!' Tara dashed across the room, but Ray merely stepped around her and found another place to attack.

'Mum, make him stop!'

'I'm sorry Tara but you brought this on yourself.' Kate turned to leave, unable to look at her husband or her child. By the door she came across Tara's jar of coins.

'And I'm taking this until this mess is paid for.'

They locked eyes for a moment then Tara pushed past her mother and fled down the stairs.

'You're all stupid. You'll ruin everything!'

Tara looked back from the bottom of the stairs, her father was now glaring down at her from the balcony, but he wasn't chasing after her. Anger, frustration, accumulated loss, the disintegration of his life; Tara looked up and watched her father and for that instant she could see he looked lost. Tara fled the house.

Kate reached out to him and touched his arm. Ray recoiled for a moment then returned to the room, determined to remove this insanity. But the sheer size of the task stopped him in his tracks, instead, he placed his head once more against the pictures unable to scrape any longer, defeated. The world he was trying to hold together was coming apart at the seams. It was no longer Tara but his failures that overwhelmed him.

'I'm sorry Kate. I'm sorry! I'm really, really sorry!'

Kate put her hand out and touched his face. He turned and buried his head in her shoulder.

'It's ok Ray. It's alright now!'

A warm evening breeze arose and fluttered the torn papers, as they held each other, both of them as broken as the room.

TUESDAY MORNING

Pinning pictures to the display wall in her classroom, Miss Cork admired each one, pleased with the results of the children's theme of 'Imaginary Worlds.' She was standing on a desk when Kate Winslow entered; seeing her reflected in the window she said, 'Just take a seat Mrs Winslow I will only be a minute.'

They pulled up children's chairs and sat across from one another at a table where their knees barely fitted under. Kate felt as awkward as she looked.

'Well, firstly let me say that I don't think there's much to worry about. I'm not as concerned with Tara now as I was when I phoned and spoke to your husband.'

'Really?' puzzled Kate. This was not at all what she expected.

'Yes, she was a little lost for a while there, but she's come good just recently. Since last Tuesday she has been focused and bubbly.'

'You mean since she came back from the doctors?' Kate asked, almost fearing the answer.

'Was that the day? Yes, yes, I guess it was, a week ago today. Now I remember, she came back at lunchtime.' Kate sat bewildered trying to retain her poise, as the questions and ambiguities resounded within her. Her home was under siege, from a daughter who refused to explain her actions, and yet at school everything seemed to be stable. How was that possible?

'Miss Cork, I know that this may seem a little odd, but have you noticed Tara showing any interest in horses?'

'Horses, no.'

'God, it's like an obsession at home.'

'Oh, that's just a phase. Lots of girls go through that!'

Kate seemed unconvinced.

'It's just a borderline puberty thing, often. Soon it will be boys.' Out in the corridor Mrs Campbell walked by and Miss Cork went quickly to the door, determined to catch her.

'Trish would you step in here a moment. Tricia, this is Tara Winslow's mother. Mrs Campbell is our librarian.'

'Hi, I'm Kate,' she said offering her hand and rising from the children's chair.

'I was just telling Kate that girls often develop crushes on horses.'

'Oh, God yes. Every year there's at least three or four girls going through that one,' offered Trish Campbell laughing at the predictability of it all.

'It's perfectly normal,' Miss Cork added.

'Though I must say Tara is very interested.'

'Oh?'

'She's exhausted every book I have on the subject.'

'You see! This is what I mean!' Kate would not be mollified now. She looked around mid-conversation, in an effort to gather her thoughts and through the window Kate saw Tara, in the playground, playing with a group of friends – she was the only girl in a game of piggy back fights. Pulling and pushing each other as clouds of dust rose, she dislodged the other boy from his mount.

The librarian broke into Kate's observation with, 'Not the novels though. No "Black Beauty," no "Pony Club". She only wants the non-fiction. All the reference books we have.' Kate turned back from the window, puzzled, 'The reference books?'

'Yes, she appears to be looking for something, but she won't say what! She's been back every lunchtime. I've never seen a child so determined.'

HEADSTALL 21ST CENTURY

26

Tara lay in bed all of Saturday morning, at sea on a gentle tide of anticipation. It was coming, she could feel it, it was only a matter of time. She'd been punished, that much she expected, for her parents wanted answers and she gave them nothing. They understand none of it but that was as it should be. Even her brother had not buckled under pressure; he managed to keep a secret this time. It pleased her that her faithful lieutenant had remained silent for the seven days since she had repapered her room and had not mentioned the temple at the quarry either. She'd done everything she set out to do. The horses were now fixed to the walls apart from where her father had scraped away some of them.

The old house creaked and moaned and spoke to her as it always did. The shadows in the corner of her ceiling shifted, forming into shapes that looked like …like horses' heads and bodies. 'Madame' was giving her approval. *Be ready old house*, she thought as she conspired with the walls around her, *you must be ready for her arrival.*

Her arrival? Tara paused mid-thought to marvel at this. *Yes, the horse was female,* she was certain of that too, after all it was a mare the last time. The inevitability of it all filled her with a peace she hadn't known for months.

The callus on her hand, the one she earned, Saturday a week ago, from chiseling the effigy on the temple wall, was hard and rough. She rubbed it with enthusiasm, connecting her to the effort she put into this venture. Contented, she pulled the curtains across the windows, darkening her room as best she could, and returned to bed. She'd decided not to enter the day but to linger a little longer, reveling in all she had created. Her brother was already up but it was the weekend, she had nowhere she had to be. Anyway, it was best to stay out of her parents' way for now; she didn't want to be cross-examined again. Echoes of the everyday world - the kitchen radio sounding muffled and indistinct, a distant mower disturbing the quiet, they filtered through but she was determined to keep them as far away as possible. Enveloped by her large, downy pillow, she pulled the sheets and the light cotton blanket up to her chin and closed her eyes. She'd slept well but this lie-in was such pleasure, that Tara wanted to enjoy it for as long as she could. She began to drift.

Wind spilled through the canyon carrying a whirling tumble of leaves ahead of it. Clouds moved in, rolling and flexing, turning over each other at the base of the cumulonimbus, dark and violent. Tara could see herself standing on a large cairn of stones in a wide sea of waving grass, facing the mouth of the canyon. In her left hand she held the handmade silver sword with which she fought the Riders of the Broken Shield and the Dark Army. Her right arm reached up into the sky, as if she wished to pull its power down to her. Her fingers were bleeding and rivulets of red ran down her outstretched arm and gathered in the creases at her elbow. The hot dry wind, that raced in front, dried the blood to her skin.

At the canyon's mouth sheer cliffs rose into the sky tearing at the base of the thunderhead, spilling the first of the coming deluge. Intermittent spots showed across the rock platform. Then the gentle splatter of rain began to rise in pitch and volume, finally becoming a roaring tumult lashing at her horizontally. The rain buffeted her body as she bent into it, bracing against the intensity.

White and shadowy it came, appearing out of the storm, stark against the battle grey cloud-bank that now rolled along the ground, flattening the grass all the way to the platform where Tara stood. The mare rose up on her hind legs and dropping down raced headlong towards the rocky outcrop. As it galloped toward her, steaming reems of water flew from its flanks. At the mound of stones, the horse rose again, hooves sparring before Tara, as sheet lightning shimmered in vast pockets inside the now purple-black mass. The mare came down on all fours and stood unmoving, while the storm raged. Tara met the horse at eye level but neither moved while the downpour passed as quickly as it came. The grass slowly rose back up in the stillness.

Silence hung in the field that was glistening wet and eerie. Tara bowed to the mare and the horse in turn dropped down on one knee and splayed the other out in front for balance. Elegantly, it lowered its head in supplication.

Tara awoke with the image of the horse's neck burnt into her mind.

'My, God!' She knew what she had not done, how badly underprepared she was. She leapt from her bed and ran to the landing. The knowledge twisted up inside her. *How could she have missed such a vital part? How could she have been so foolish?*

She felt she might still save the situation, after all it was Saturday and they would be open. All she had to do was get the money. Downstairs, the house was deserted whilst the radio still played to no-one in particular. One last look around, to be sure she was alone then she made her way into her parents' bedroom.

*   *   *

As Kate turned the engine off, and slumped in the driver's seat, the weariness she'd kept at bay, finally caught up with her. It was mid-morning; she'd already held two property inspections and was feeling overwhelmed. She had no desire to enter the house though she knew Ray was away, he too was working overtime - both working on a weekend when they should be with their children. He was defying her, preparing to sell the business.

It was obvious what he wanted to do, although Ray would never admit it. Run a surfboard shop, maybe even fashion and shape boards, she thought, sell the business and live like a beach bum. That was Ray all over; probably end up surfing all day and make no money at all. *Well, I'm not carrying the can for all your pipe dreams.*

His business was failing because he just didn't work hard enough at it, she felt. He was more determined to sell it than save it. *I'm just as determined to stop him*, she tried to tell herself. These thoughts played in her head, playing like a song that wouldn't let go. A song of anger and frustration. Although there were moments of steely reserve, usually the ones she showed to Ray, alone she couldn't maintain them. The consequences seemed to grow disproportionately as all their lives seemed to be getting out of hand. Ray and his lack of backbone, her children and their willful …What could you call it?… *fantasy madness*. Even she couldn't be as sure of herself as she pretended, especially when she scrutinized her own less than perfect job.

Damn him. Things would come to a head soon, sometime in the next few days. Was Ray, right? She wanted him to be wrong about his life and about theirs but there were so many unanswered questions. What kind of life is this, doing her paperwork after hours when the office was empty meant she could avoid her boss, she told herself - a boss who couldn't keep his hands to himself but why should she have to avoid him? It angered her that her job felt so intimidating now but even that was only the half of it, for it was bigger than that. Some immense screw up was happening, that brought her to this point, the emptiness that was her life, *this life* was not what she had worked to create. *I never saw it coming. Did I ask for this? Has it just crept up on me? Was it really Ray's fault?* She wanted to believe it was, she *had* believed it was for so long but it became harder to maintain her level of animosity.

Her anger didn't extend to Tara or Cory though she knew they were plotting something, something strange she couldn't fathom. It was childish and compulsive but apart from the damage to the room, which could be repaired ... hey, it needed a repaint anyway. Really what harm could they possibly do? She sat in the car and watched Cory playing alone in the yard, moving across the lawn, as if he was in the middle of some great adventure. *What must it be like to live completely inside your imagination? To be in a place that was more real than all of my grown up, screwed up world?* She sat for a few minutes longer enjoying his fantasy and then it struck her that she was once like that and it was gone. Kate felt a sense of loss and deep sadness that she would never be like that again. She slammed the car door and walked inside.

'Tara, Tara!' Kate called from the kitchen but got no answer. On the kitchen bench sat the jar, lying on its side empty, that once sat in her room. The jar she'd confiscated till the damage to the walls was paid for, though she knew the collection of coins would never cover the cost. The money was gone, Tara had defied her and gone into her bedroom.

But she wasn't just angry, this defiance worried her. *What the hell was all this?* Why did Tara want to get herself into more trouble? This was truly obsessive. Kate knew she was kidding herself, the nightmares may have gone but they have been replaced with this - her daughter's compulsion. *Don't be a fool Kate, something is going on here.*

Searching each room of the house, Kate called out but got no reply. Tara was either hiding somewhere, refusing to answer or she was gone; gone when she knew she was grounded. She strode across the lawn and confronted Cory.

'Have you seen your sister?'

Stopping mid-movement, Cory looked miffed that his mother had broken into his battle-scene, pulling him back to reality.

'No. She went out an hour ago.'

'Where?' Kate demanded.

'I don't know. She took her daypack.'

Cory moved away, falling back into the other world, his body forming martial stances. Did Cory know more than he was letting on? Should she be just as angry with him? No, this was more of his sister's mischief and this time she would get to the bottom of it.

PACKAGE 21ST CENTURY

27

Tara took the package from her backpack and held it reverentially above her head, as if offering it up to the Gods, and then reached up placing it in the bough of the fig tree, before going inside. As she entered her mother looked up from the kitchen table.

"Where have you been?'

'Out,' replied Tara with a practiced indifference that pretended to be innocent although they both knew she was not allowed to leave the house.

'Where?'

'Just out … that's all.' Only then did Tara notice that the empty jar was now sitting upright in the middle of the table.

Kate saw that split second of recognition and the guilt it implied, rising from her chair with an anger that brooked no opposition.

'Put the bag on the table,' she demanded. Tara stood there just long enough to smack of defiance, then casually rolled the backpack off her shoulder placing it gently in the middle of the table. All the while mother and daughter locked eyes, continuing the battle of wills that had been escalating for the past week.

'Open it!,' Kate barked, any pretense of polite exchange was gone now. Tara rankled at her mother's display of authority. How dare she talk to me like this; if she just knew what I was doing for our family. But of course, she must not know. Tara unzipped the bag and mockingly turned it upside down with a gesture like a stage magician, who had just caused a white dove to appear from a top hat. The display irked her mother, which was exactly what was intended.

Kate never missed a beat but instead tossed the bag from the table and demanded, 'What have you done with the money?'

'My money!' Tara said, returning fire.

'You lost that when you destroyed your room.'

'Exactly... *my room*!'

They both glared at each other, neither speaking nor giving ground. Finally, Kate spoke in a low but determined manner just barely holding a threat of violence in check, 'Tara Winslow, you had no right to go into my bedroom. No right to take what no longer belongs to you. If you know what is good for you, you will tell me the truth.'

Again, the standoff remained as Tara matched her mother's aggression and then almost mirrored her mother's delivery with one long, slow word.

'No!'

Kate stepped out from the other side of the table, the anger pulsing in her body. Catching the corner of the table cloth, it followed in her wake, dragging the jar over the edge. Glass shattered across the hard wooden floor, scattering into all four corners of the room. The atmosphere at that instant changed, as if the rising anger had exploded and dissipated as well. Both stared at the floor but when they raised their eyes, Tara couldn't tell whether her mother was going to scream or cry. Kate pushed past heading out to find Cory, not saying anything but still the message was clear; Tara knew that she *must* go to her room.

The room was not as resplendent as it had been several days earlier. Tara's father having made attempts to remove the pictures a couple more times but conceded that they would have to be steamed off. For now, the temple was safe. At the bottom of the butcher's box copies of the calendar sat intact. She pulled one out and looked at the pictorial display at the top of the month of a sequence of lunar illustrations, in all their phases. Full moon was only three nights away, Monday night. It had to be soon; Tara was not sure how long she could keep her parents at arm's length, how long before she was discovered, before she or Cory broke down under pressure; the secret had survived almost two weeks now. She decided to stay out of her mother's way.

Ray arrived home for lunch and looked at his wife from the doorway. Kate sat slumped at the table again, lost in her own world, her eyes red from crying. She did not notice him as he studied her a moment from the safety of the veranda, then hoping that this time it wasn't his fault, he entered.

Kate immediately blurted out the confrontation she had with Tara. It was still not clear to Ray what was going on, what Tara's fixation was leading to now? He listened in silence as Kate described the theft and Tara's reaction.

'Have you spoken to Cory?'

Kate nodded and tried to gather her thoughts. 'Nothing! I don't know what to make of it but Cory knows what she's up to, I'm almost certain.'

Ray and Kate found Cory in the yard and ordered him inside. Kate stood back, her arms folded and admired the measured way her husband handled their children. Why did all her exchanges end in confrontation, she wondered? Her anxiousness always created an edge that meant that every difficult conversation she had, with either of them, spiraled out of control. But there he was communicating on the children's level, almost immediately.

'Cory, Tara's in trouble. You know that don't you?

Cory looked down at the floor and shuffled uncomfortably. Ray waited for a response but got none but Kate could see that even without speaking Cory was more at ease with his father, than with her.

'I don't mean the stealing. No, something is going on, she is doing something to her room, to herself? Do you understand what I mean?'

Cory shook his head. 'Oh, I think you do Cory. I think you know exactly what's going on?' Ray spoke softly but assuredly; there was a certainty in his voice that made Cory want to talk. He was just on the edge of confessing, both Kate and Ray could see it.

Cory looked up at them and was almost about to tell all but remembered the oath he had made to Tara. She was the Falcon Wielder, she was the captain of their exploits, she would never betray him and he must be faithful to her. She had told him that everything depended on it and he believed her; he must not reveal their secrets. But his father was insistent; he had to give him something.

'Cory, why did Tara take the money? Why Cory?'

Cory's lower lip trembled and both his parents knew he was compromised and on the verge of tears.

'What did she do with the money, Cory?'

'She bought a bridle.' There it was out. But for Cory there was no relief, instead his stomach twisted with the immensity of his betrayal. His parents stood there dumbfounded while Cory hung his head, saying nothing, hoping his father would ask no more of him.

GONE 21ST CENTURY

28

THE FOURTH MONDAY MORNING

The events of the last few days and weeks tumbled through Kate's head as she tried to make sense of it all. First there were the nightmares that went on for over a month, twenty maybe thirty she had lost count, none of which Tara would share with her. Until there was the one where Cory drowned in an underground tunnel while Tara cried out. That one Tara shared with a stranger - a professional admittedly but it still bothered her that she shared it with him and not her. Was that supposed to *mean something*? Was any of it?

    She had to wait till the Monday to see him. Determined to get to the bottom of this, Kate had taken the morning off work. Somehow it all had to do with the Doctor, with Wozniak. She should have confronted him the last time, should have asked, what sorcery had he done when Tara came out of his rooms transformed?

The traffic was slow even for a Monday morning. Then there was the room covered in pictures of horses? The absurdity of that and Tara's defiance confused and frightened her. Finally, Cory's revelation, of just what the stolen money was for, kept going through her mind, all the way to the doctor.

'Why, why Cory? Why is she buying a bridle?' demanded Ray. Cory remained mute for some time but Ray would not let up. In the end Cory broke down and gave in.

'Because ... because of what the doctor said' And then he would say no more. Having confessed he backed off but resolutely refused to say another word. Ray despite his best attempts could get nothing more from him. This revelation disturbed Kate most of all. When Tara heard of Cory's confession she seethed with anger but inside was glad he had said nothing more. For the rest of the weekend, she spoke to no-one.

Outside the downtown medical office, Kate gathered up her apprehensions that now grew into fear of some kind of madness. In her mind, she could still see Cory's face wracked with guilt and shame. No matter how much they both threatened, begged and pleaded Cory would give them nothing more. Just like Tara, she thought. What on earth were these two trying to do? She had always seen their fantasy world as harmless, had always indulged it. But now, now she could not even guess what was going on in their heads. A family with such deep secrets, it bewildered her. At first Ray wanted to go with her and confront 'this crackpot' as he put it.

'No, stay here. Keep your eye on Cory. And make sure Tara doesn't do anything stupid.' *I must do this myself.*

When the elevator doors opened on the second floor, the corridor was full of the "Old World." The long oak table, the big leather chairs, the display case empty now, the old pictures all wrapped in padding were now lining the hall leading to the office. In the reception area, a red eyed secretary was filling boxes with medical files. A man in his sixties came out of the adjoining rooms. He looked like a younger version of Wozniak, Kate decided.

'Can I help you?'

'I was hoping to see the doctor,' Kate said, realising that something was wrong before she had even finished.

'I'm afraid that's not possible,' he said. The secretary broke down at that moment and excusing herself, grabbed some tissues and left the room.

'My daughter is one of his patients.'

He reached out a hand, offering, 'I'm Michael Wozniak.'

'Kate, Kate Winslow.'

'I am sorry Mrs Winslow but I thought we notified all the appointments. We must have missed you. You see my father passed away … two weeks ago. The funeral was last Thursday, once our relatives arrived from America.'

Kate stepped back, shocked. 'I'm sorry. I shan't bother you anymore.' Kate turned and made for the door. Michael studied her as she hurried out.

'Mrs Winslow, is there anything I can help you with?'

Kate stopped on the spot and gathered herself, deciding that regardless of his death, there were questions she had to ask. By now the secretary had returned and was standing next to the son. 'Yes, yes perhaps you can. Did Doctor Wozniak ever talk to you about my daughter Tara?' She meant the question for both of them.

'No, no that wouldn't happen. My father never talked about his cases. That would be unethical.'

'Yes, yes of course. Stupid to ask, I guess. Thank you!' Kate backed away, unsure what to do in this situation. She should leave she knew, without answers. But no, it wasn't enough, there had to be more, surely these two must have heard something. She turned back to them, 'This is going to sound very strange ... but did Dr Wozniak ever talk about horses?'

'Horses?' they replied in unison.

'Not that I recall. What about you, Ruth?' The secretary shook her head whilst dabbing her eyes with the tissues. Kate waited a little too long hoping that one of them would remember something. The embarrassing silence meant that now she was obliged to make a quick exit. Back in the elevator she slumped against the wall. *Still no answers.* As the doors were closing, it came to her. She pushed the open button, returning to the office doorway. The secretary and the son looked up, puzzled expressions again on their faces.

'Forgive me for asking. You say your father died two weeks ago, what day?'

The secretary replied, 'Tuesday.'

Kate stood there her mouth open, almost afraid to ask the next question.

'Who was his last patient?'

'Why your daughter Tara,' said the secretary. 'Then he went home ...' Ruth began to sob. 'And died in his sleep that night.' Her shoulders heaving, she collapsed into the son's arms.

Somehow Kate knew that was going to be the answer; she offered a quiet thank you and left.

* * *

'What do you mean, you don't know?' asked Ray as he followed Kate up the stairs, the tension rising between them again, as it always seemed to. Together they stopped on the landing, outside Tara's room. Before she knocked Kate turned to her husband with a brutal finality, 'I mean, he's dead Ray. I didn't get any answers.'

This fact cut the conversation completely, Ray could say nothing to that. They looked at each other, with that studied defiance that had been the measure of their exchanges, for months now. Kate knocked hard and waited but no-one came to the door.

'Tara! Tara, come downstairs. We need to talk.' Still no answer came.

Ray tried the handle, it wasn't locked but as the door swung open, it revealed an empty room and a window half open. A moment of puzzlement then they entered. Ray went to the window and looking out saw the trellis that met up at the lower sloping roof and eaves that covered the first-floor veranda.

Shaking his head he said, 'I don't want her climbing off the roof. God, these kids are out of control.'

Kate slumped on the bed as Ray turned back and sat on the edge of Tara's desk, looking hard at his wife and wondering where they went to now for answers.

'Tell me again, what happened? From that last visit'

Kate looked up, a mixture of confusion and fear. Her face carried the weight of a life losing balance, by the hour. She looked at the rooms furniture all clustered in the middle, the room as chaotic as all their lives had become, then she scanned the torn and tattered cavalry, that covered the walls. She turned in on herself, clutching her body, her shoulders slumped, saying nothing.

His wife was losing her grip, Ray felt certain of that. He asked the next question softly, with more reassurance. 'We'll look for Tara in a minute. Just tell me what happened. The doctor's dead, what else?'

Kate nodded but struggled to put into words what had transpired between her, the son, and the receptionist. It sounded like nothing when she thought about it. He passed away in his sleep, people do that, after all he was an incredibly old man. Yet there was something more to this, she just knew it. What had he told Tara?

'All I know is what I told you before. She came out changed and she said he told her "Just stories."'

'What?'

'Just stories. That's what Tara said he told her that day ... that Tuesday ... just stories' It didn't seem threatening but somehow it was. '*I wanted to ask him* but his son was there, packing the place up. They buried him last Thursday .... Tara believes this story, whatever it is, and Cory too.'

Kate stared into the distance, lost in thought as Ray shook his head, it was clear the whole situation made no sense to him also. Her intuition about this was the only thing that did.

'We've got to look for her.' With that Kate got up and Ray followed, uncomprehending but willing to accept his wife's concerns.

Tara climbed back in, soon after they had gone. Hidden in the alcove, beside the open window, her father might have found her, had he swiveled around to the left. It made her sad to think that the old doctor was gone. But it pleased her that her parents were taking her efforts seriously.

Downstairs late in the day, her parents confronted Tara but it did no good. Like Cory she simply folded her arms and stared off, the more they persisted with questions the more resolute Tara became, sure now that she was on the brink of something momentous. Kate watched the body language and wondered about the similarities between Tara and her brother. *It's like they belong to some secret society.*

In their frustration, they banished her back to her room, which to Tara didn't seem like any punishment at all. Tara used the afternoon to restore her furnishings to their place and glue her tattered pictures back to the wall with school glue. All except the ones where it was too high to reach. It was no longer the glorious homage she wanted but she had done her best.

She went to bed early and watched from under her sheets, as the room slowly lost light. The bedside lamp stayed off as she waited for total darkness. It would be another hour before the moon came up and began to spill its milky glow across the floorboards. The full pictures and the torn half frames of horses all looked her way.

'It doesn't matter that the temple is less than perfect, the horse will understand,' the words echoing as they addressed the room.

Closing her eyes, she began to hum the tune she'd found in her "classroom" dream. The "Old World" music that none of her classmates heard, though she wished that Katya had. Music from a by-gone world, a place where families who'd lost each other to all kinds of wars were reunited once more. Violins and concertina in waltz time.

MOON 21ST CENTURY

29

MONDAY EVENING

Kate fell into her bed emotionally exhausted but instead of sleep came questions and fears chasing each other inside her. Ray lay beside her, already deep in slumber. As always, he seemed to drop the worries of the day and sleep through every terror of the night.

But tonight, right now something was building; she could feel it in the fibres of her being, as the strangest thought of all possessed her. *'The doctor he did it on purpose. He died on purpose.'* Even in her agitated state she could see the absurdity of the thought but still it staked an unrelenting claim on her. People don't just choose to die one Tuesday and then leave. Or do they? She wanted to wake Ray and run this past him but he was already snoring. It was another hour, of going through the litany of obsessions and strange behaviours, before she was tired enough to fall asleep.

For Tara it was a different matter. The moonlight spilt into her room, lighting all the white heads, torn or whole. She lay there humming to herself, continuously that Romany-like melody. Where did it come from? From her dream, yes but before that? It was familiar. Was it Polish? Did she know any Polish songs? Vibrating with excitement, she decided to stay awake all night. But she too drifted off to sleep, as the tiredness caught up with her.

MONDAY/TUESDAY MIDNIGHT

The house was the first to become aware of the hooves; 'Madame' softly hummed in reply to the sound that rose up from a distance. But they came for Kate also, galloping, rhythmic and commanding, drumming, and dragging her out of her restless state, to the very edge of sleep. And there, the creature stood waiting, snorting and whinnying. Kate lay in the darkness, certain that someone, no *some thing* was nearby, her eyes wide open and very much awake. The house was singing now, low, and melodic - a tune of creaking timbers in three- four time.

Tara drifted between ecstasy and exhaustion, hearing the sound approach from a vast distance, as if it was traveling across the great eastern bush lands - the kingdom of the Falcon Wielder. Hoofbeats drumming on the hard land growing louder as they came. Hoofbeats coming toward her.

She opened her eyes, the horses all stared at her, in the vivid light. The moon at this hour, had dipped to an angle where it shone directly into the room. Hymn-like the house moved up a register.

And Tara knew. *She's here*.

Through her open window came the warm musky scent of hair, hoof and breath. Grabbing her padded jacket, she pulled it over her nightdress, then slipped on a sock but then anxious to go, she put both runners on without the other one.

'I'm coming!' Her voice echoed in the emptiness of her tattered bedroom.

Kate sat up, rigid with fear, certain the time had come. Movement in the house, movement outside, no both. Strange sounds almost musical but coming from where? By the time Kate reached the landing, at the end of the hall, she heard the back door close quietly.

'Steady, steady now girl.' Tara approached the mare with soft words and slow, gentle movements. The creature was more beautiful than she had imagined, shimmering with silver light, its eyes dark, alert and penetrating, its chest and flanks rippled with muscle and sinew. In her mind, Tara had been rehearsing this for days. Must not spook her, she thought. Getting the bridle over her head would be a task, she was a tall horse, maybe sixteen or seventeen hands, but putting the bit into her mouth would be the real challenge.

'That's the way. That's my girl,' whispering she almost sang to her. As if it understood, the mare splayed out one leg and lowered her head.

Watching from the back porch, Kate tried to make sense of what she saw. Tara had something in her hands, she was holding it high in the air, as she spoke to … nothing. There was nothing at all in the yard except her daughter.

'Tara!'

Tara turned to where the voice had come from and in that moment the horse shied, galloped across the yard, down the driveway and away toward the bushland.

'Tara, what are you doing?'

She glared at her mother and then ran after the fleeing horse, out onto the street and into the night.

By the time Kate arrived at the front gate, the street was empty.

'Oh, my God!'

'What is it?' it was Ray, he was fully dressed, 'why are you out here?'

'It's Tara, she ran off.' And then the enormity of what she was doing hit Kate hard. 'My God, the bridle!' She stood there frozen, lost in the terror of the madness that was unfolding.

'Ray, we have to find her,' Kate demanded.

'Of course we have to find her. It's after midnight.'

'No. We really have to find her. She had a bridle. Something terrible is happening! I know it.'

Ray felt her urgency. 'Where did she go?' But Kate stood there helpless, pointing down the road toward the bush.

'I don't know. Where would she go in the middle of the night?' She crouched down, overcome by the gravity of it all, she placed her palm down on the ground to steady herself. Forces were in play, monstrous forces, a kind of insanity was swallowing their family; a madness she couldn't explain. In the distance the Forest Mistress turned towards the house and closed her eyes. And then Kate had an answer or at least the promise of one.

'Cory. Cory will know.' She ran back to the house, leaving Ray to peer into the white-blue night, the silent street, and the dark bushland beyond.

Ray had a torch in his hand and the car out, with the engine running, by the time Kate returned, dragging Cory by the pyjama sleeve, with his dressing gown over one arm. Cory looked bewildered and still half asleep.

'Cory! Where has your sister gone?' It was a question but the almost hysterical demand in her voice frightened Cory.

'I don't know.' He was awake now but confused and picking up on his mother's panic. Ray wasn't sure whether to intervene.

'Yes, yes you do, Cory. You and your sister have been planning this for days. Now tell me, where did she go?' Kate yelled as Cory struggled to pull away from her. Ray took Cory's arm out of his mother's powerful grip and crouching down, held him firmly with both hands at the shoulders, meeting his son at eye level.

'Now listen very carefully. It's late, Cory. After midnight. I don't know what game you're playing but it's dangerous. Do you understand?'

Cory said nothing but instead turned his face away so he did not have to look at his father…Kate stood behind, desperate, shaking her head in disbelief, trying to hold the hysteria at bay.

More firmly Ray said again, 'Do you understand?' Cory nodded, head downcast.

'Good. Now where was Tara going?' Cory looked puzzled, as if he wanted to give an answer but wasn't sure which one.

'She had the bridle, Cory. Where was she going? You have to tell me, Cory? Where?'

Cory's face came alive, he looked into the distance knowing that the time had come. 'The quarry. She's gone to the quarry!'

'Oh God!' Kate looked at Ray but he was already moving. He scooped up Cory and flung open the back door and almost threw his son in. Kate ran to the other side and seconds later they were racing down the road.

Kate was out of the car first, no longer lost in the nightmare, she was resolute - frantic but determined to find her child. She shook the gates but the padlock held. Ray beside her, scanned the fence to see if he could scale it. The top was covered in barbed wire that ran the perimeter in both directions. Cory was already walking away; then he took off running.

'This way. Follow me!' he shouted, a note of excitement in his voice. And then he vanished into the darkness of the trees ahead. By the time his parents arrived a hundred metres above the gate, Cory was standing on the other side, his hands on his hips. Noting their puzzled looks he declared, pointing to the ground, 'It's not magic. There's a hole just behind that bush.'

The incline was steep and the loose stones kept giving way under their feet as Cory led the procession but the closer, he came to the top, the less like an adventure it seemed. The moonlit rocky terrain and the dark abyss at the edge began to frighten him.

'Where are we going, Cory?' his father asked. Cory said nothing.

'Stay close to him, Ray…the edge.' Ray clasped Cory tightly and they both stopped and waited momentarily. Kate came up beside them. Together, hand in hand and single file, Cory led them up and across the top of the escarpment.

Cory stopped abruptly, all playfulness gone from him now. It was maybe fifteen metres, but there was Tara standing at the edge, her head raised, bathed in white light. Kate wanted to call out but Ray squeezed her hand hard and she stifled it.

'Say nothing,' he whispered. Kate and Cory nodded, as Ray left them and keeping low, moved forward slowly.

He could hear Tara talking softly, as she stood silhouetted in the moonlight. Ten metres now.

'It's alright girl. Nothing to be scared of. Let me take you home.'

Five metres. Tara raised the bridle once more and held it up into the air, as she stood at the mouth of the cave. Her cave, the Temple to the White Horse. One foot touched the rim and a small cascade of pebbles dropped into the darkness below.

Two.

'Here we are.' Her arms and the bridle raised higher into the air.

One.

The horse whinnied and turned to see Ray, as he leapt across the distance. Tara tumbled forward as Ray met her in mid-air. It was the corner of the goal post, she was his ball and he came crashing down into the cave, with her held in his arms, the bridle falling from her hands. He hit the rock wall hard and the bas-relief of the cave horse, fell away into rubble. The bridle teetered on the edge then tumbled into the abyss, clinking and crashing as it hit the sides and finally the quarry floor. It rang out against the walls chiming like bells on the hard volcanic surfaces.

Ray cried out with a sharp gasp as his body shot full of electric stabs. Moaning, he clutched his daughter, holding her tight to his chest. Tara looked around, *the horse was gone.*

Kate and Cory came clambering to the rim of the crevasse, some distance from the edge, staring down. Tara lay bewildered, as if she'd just woken, with her father wrapped around her.

Slowly Ray gathered himself and staggered to his knees refusing to let go of his daughter, no matter what his body endured. He raised her above his head, handing her to Kate and Cory, though the effort was agonising. Climbing out, Ray crumpled as hot bolts of pain spiked through his swollen shoulder, then collapsed, his head between his knees as wave after wave of sensation shook his upper body.

Kate locked Tara close in her arms, rocking back and forward, whispering 'I love you. I love you both.' Cory held his mother and his sister.

Finally, Ray spoke. 'We need to go.' His shoulder ached almost to the point of blacking out, as the adrenaline and the pain mixed together. He knew he had broken his collarbone. The last time was back in his football days in Liverpool, he thought. It felt the same.

Ray lifted his daughter into his arms and grimacing; he began the descent. Kate, realising something was wrong, threw her arm around him for support and with the other she held Cory to her side. Together they walked down as one, like some many legged creature.

At the bottom, they stood staring at the hole in the fence. It was too small; they would have to separate but Tara clung to her father and Kate clung to all three. It was Cory who noticed it, a hundred metres further down.

'Look, the gate's open.'

They walked along the perimeter fence, still unwilling to let go of each other. As they passed through the quarry gates, Cory looked around. Who had done this? Was it security or the foreman who had chased them off many times before? No-one was around.

By now, the injury was starting to overwhelm him and Ray allowed Tara to slip to the ground and walk beside him. They all clung to each other, afraid to lose the unity they shared now. They stood before the car, still as one and faced the same challenge.

'Are you alright?' Kate asked. He nodded as she held him up. She could see he wasn't.

'I'll drive' she offered but Ray had already turned away from the car. Kate and the two children were being steered up the road. Ray, despite the damage was in control. Kate understood and, in that instant, moved in tandem with her husband. They could not let go of each other now for something alchemic was happening. It was a half a kilometre down the moonlit road and they all knew the way back. Ray felt, that no matter what, he must walk his family home.

Tara held to her father and felt her mother holding her. The night air was chillier now, as she slipped one hand into her jacket. Something hard sat inside. She brought it out. It caught the moon as she held it up.

Tara stopped, the family stopping with her, all looking down at the object catching the pale light. Kate gasped. It was a pewter cavalry-man on a charger with a raised sabre. Tara stared at it as if it was a message but also a sleight of hand, a piece of magic from a distant past.

I wonder who put that there? Then Tara smiled; she felt, yes, yes, *she knew.*

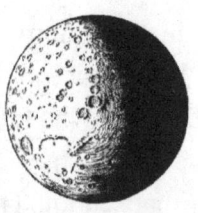

MOUNTAIN?

30

The gates closed and the padlock clicked into place. Behind him the great horse stamped with impatience, luminous, shimmering in the moonlight. Her midnight breath rose mistily in the air.

Clothed in a large leather jacket covered in reworked leather patches, he wore a fawn denim shirt and moleskins that met huge working boots, buckled at the knee. He climbed up onto the seat and flicked the reins. Pulling to the left the dray turned away from the group some half a kilometre up the road. They were almost home, he judged. One more flick and the mare picked up speed, turning away, delivering him into the distance and the night.

ACKNOWLEDGEMENTS

I am indebted to the Jewish community of Sydney and the Jewish Studies Department of Emmanuel School, Randwick. To the participants in 'Project Heritage' who told their powerful stories to the children of Year Five during the 1990's, when I was lucky enough to be a teacher at that school. Those revelations about the 'Shoah'- the Holocaust are the underpinnings of this novel. As an idea it has haunted me since my childhood, when I first heard of my matrilineal great grandmother Miriam [also called Mary] Isaacs. Finally, I felt I must tell a version of these stories for myself.

I am indebted, more than words can convey, to Geoff Quick, Lucy Jones but most especially to my writing tutors and mentors at the University of Technology, Claire Corbett and Anthony Macris. Equally, accolades must go to Laurel Cohn whose editing skills guided me through drafts thirteen and fourteen.

Several insensitive terms used through-out this novel may offend some readers, at first. In Polish, these include 'glupi' and 'postak'. In English, these include imbecile, simpleton and idiot. All are used in reference to one of the characters masquerading with mental health issues. No offence is intended and as a 'Special Education' teacher [for part of my career] I thought long and hard about their use. These are the terms that would have been current at the time the book is set. I felt a need to be accurate to those times. We can be glad that the accompanying attitudes, associated with those words, have moved on.

My special thanks go to Markus Moors of the Kreigsmuseum Wewelsburg for the time he gave me while at Castle Wewelsburg, the site of one of the SS strongholds.

I am grateful also to Pavel and Adam my drivers in Lower Silesia who offered their knowledge of the Gross- Rosen concentration camp and the 'Project Reise' tunnel complexes in the Owl mountains. And a momentous thank you to the intrepid captain of our expedition Ulass Paul Bell who was always heading in the right direction, with compass in hand, across Germany, the Czech Republic and Poland.

Thank you to the Cafe Hernandez, my sanctuary during the winter and spring of my second last year of writing the initial drafts, when I needed a place to write, at any hour. Ana, Paloma, Juliana and Eliana were always there with coffee.

Regards   Luca Collins

APPENDICES

I have attempted where possible to be as accurate to the memories of those who told their stories and to anecdotes within research texts, however it must be acknowledged that this is a work of Historical Fiction. A few characters and incidents have been amalgamated and events that may have spanned days, weeks, months or years have been truncated into briefer sequences for dramatic effect.

POLAND - AN OVERVIEW -1939 to 1945.

The Nazi regime had specific designs for Poland in the same way it had for Jews, Romanies and others it deemed unacceptable. These plans had been conceived in the final years of the 1930s. Poland was to form part of a Greater Germany, its populace was to gradually be used as slave labour, and systematically worked to death. Farms, businesses, and homes that became unoccupied, due to the death or removal of their owners and workers, were then given to relocated German families. This practice was well underway, within the first years of the war. Though some German families moved into Poland, the take up was not massive. Many Germans were reluctant to re-establish themselves in what was now considered the 'living space' of Greater Germany.

Much of the population of Poland remained as it was, though it was now geared to serve the Nazi war machine. The division of Poland between the U.S.S.R. and Nazi Germany created deep resentments among the Poles. These were exacerbated when Hitler invaded Russia and Poland became a battleground for these opposing forces over the next four years. German forces were now fighting on both an eastern and a western front. Beyond the extermination and the slave labour camps, the larger plans for Poland were held in check whilst the war was being fought.

Now that the war had begun, for Nazi Germany there was a 'pecking order' of those they wished to eliminate. The Jews, Romanies, political opponents, Communists of any nationality, those considered sexual deviants or those with intellectual or physical disabilities were to be exterminated. Jews who practised the faith and lived in their community, were the first to be rounded up.

Later birth and death records were examined in Germany, Poland and across Europe. Individuals who had given up their faith or simply lapsed, who had been accepted into the mainstream population, found themselves transported to ghettos. Some were to discover they had an undisclosed Jewish ancestry for the first time. The process could be thorough and often merciless. However, there were instances where a Jewish background was ignored. The scale of administering greater Europe and waging war meant that there were anomalies.

All Slavic nations were to be dominated and brought to heel. These nations were to be the worker-slaves of the Reich. The Poles were the first to fall to the 'New Order.'

This was a gradual process but could not be fully implemented till Hitler had won the war. In the meantime, 'everyday' Poles continued their lives, under the Occupation and under curfew, until they could be dealt with. The killing of Poles was often arbitrary and indiscriminate. Obviously, Poles with skills that could aid the war effort might find themselves working in protected industries and forestall their own or their families' transportation to the camps, such as Harry Nowak - Bron's father. But even here Poles' fates might change on a whim or the discretion of a Nazi district commander.

Much of Poland existed as heavily forested areas. Impenetrable marshlands also offered some sanctuary from heavy vehicles, like troop transports and tanks. It was to these forests and swamps, to the north and east, that many Poles fled.

THE PARTISANS

Armed freedom fighters gathered into units according to their political persuasions. Left- and Right-wing groups had a common enemy in the Germans but were only loosely aligned with each other, for the duration of the war. Some groups were openly hostile to their fellow countrymen and betrayed them to the enemy, for some 'hoped for' political advantage, when the war was over. Hatred of the others 'political ideology could run deep enough for groups to execute their fellow countrymen and women.

Centuries old Anti-Semitism meant Jews would often form their own groups. However, Jewish partisans, such as Jakub, were accepted into already established units of various political persuasions, in small numbers. Nothing it seems is clear cut in times of war.

The numbers living in the forests of Poland ran into the thousands. It is believed as many as 20 000 partisans resisted the Germans, in the Naliboki Forest in the east. Of which, 3 000 were Jewish men women and children living in rural communities, deep in the forest.

The two groups mentioned in this novel come from opposite ends of the political spectrum. They would not have co-operated with each other to any great degree.

In fact, Zegota [Tobiasz and Agneta - Chapter One and Four] was strictly speaking not a partisan group. The organisation saw itself as Christian [principally Catholic] and therefore bound to risk their lives to do humanitarian work. It was an aid group, helping Jews to hide and eventually escape, much like the 'Underground Railroad' aided African-American slaves to escape from the South, before the American Civil War.

Many Jews, particularly children, received falsified documents that gave them new identities. Many were absorbed into Christian households and became members of these families. However, Zegota being Christian and nominally Catholic meant that they were nationalist and right wing, in the eyes of Ludowa.

Ludowa [Jakub and Marek] were a socialist partisan group who did not co-operate with right wing groups, such as the AK [Armia Krajowa] or Home Army - a nationalist militia. The AK was the largest of all freedom fighter groups. Ludowa had some Jews within it but they were in the minority and probably did not announce themselves to their comrades.

Jews also formed the Jewish Military Union and the Jewish Combat Organisation. The first worked with the Home Army [AK] while the JCO, a pro-Soviet group, did not.

All groups were vying for dominance, determined to steer Poland in their own ideological direction, after the Nazis were defeated.

This was a time when you might keep your beliefs, your allegiances, your religion, your ethnicity and especially your circumcision under cover.

THE CAMPS

Much of the world knows of the infamous extermination camps, their names are burnt into history. However, a number, often satellite camps around the major installation, were run as labour camps. The intention was to work prisoners to death. Despite less than 500 calories a day, freezing conditions in winter and heat in summer, inadequate clothing and brutal treatment some PoW's did survive. Of the 150 000 souls who came through the Gross-Rosen camp 30 000 survived and were liberated. Bronek and Michal find themselves in such a camp.

THE TUNNELS - PROJECT RIESE [Project Giant] 1943-45

Running for over 30 kilometres, the tunnels were built in the last two years of the war. There are seven complexes dug beneath the Owl Mountains in Lower Silesia, in what is now part of Poland. In the last months of the war Albert Speer - Minister for Armaments sent more concrete to this project than was being used to fortify against the Allies and the Red Army.

Obviously, the Nazis considered this a vital programme, though all records of what they intended to build have been lost, perhaps destroyed on orders from above. There has been much conjecture on what was the purpose of the tunnels. Surviving prisoners have talked of secret weapon tests. Others have recalled visits by members of the Nazi High Command.

Some tunnels have in part collapsed but the intact ones can be visited and are large enough to drive tanks through. Some tunnel entrances have sentry posts and pillboxes to hold off intruders. Many had ducting spaces that were intended for air, electricity, and water. None of the tunnel complexes connected with one another, though they were only a few kilometres apart.

It is possible that the intention was to build an impregnable bunker in which the Nazis might hold off their enemies, until the German Army rallied and came to liberate them. In the end they ran out of time and it was some of the poor wretches that built the complexes that were liberated.

OCCULT OBSESSIONS WITHIN THE THIRD REICH

Few war historians have discussed or understood the deeper intent of Nazi plans. It was not simply about the domination of Europe, the National Socialists intended to change the culture of the Western world.

During the 20s and early 30s they assaulted, intimidated, and killed their opponents. They framed the communists with the burning of the Reichstag. In 1933 when they came to power, they began to put their long-term plans into action beginning with the building of their first concentration camp - Dachau. Built inside Germany it was intended to house political prisoners, those that opposed them.

Soon after came the sterilisation of people with mental or physical disabilities. Later these people would be systematically euthanized. Doctors and nurses that opposed this were imprisoned or dismissed to be replaced by more compliant medical staff.

Himmler created the SS as a group of supposedly Teutonic Knights - an Aryan Warrior class. SS men were only to marry pure unsullied German women. Their wedding ceremonies made no mention of any of the traditional trappings of marriage, either Catholic or Protestant. Instead, they referred to Wotan [Odin] and to Norse Mythology. Wagner's Ring Cycle, the Sigfried Saga and German folklore all found their way into the overarching new Nazi culture.

The Hitler Youth and their female equivalent the Band of German Maidens raised on a diet of patriotism, violence and superiority would have embraced this new order in much the same way that the young Chinese did during the Cultural Revolution.

There was resistance to the regime from Church elders but enough were arrested to silence the more vocal. For the time being Hitler and the Nazi leaders tolerated the existence of the churches. To arrest and remove the churches would have destroyed the support Hitler had. To achieve that aim he would have to wait till after they had won the war.

This was what was intended - to destroy any notions of compassion and empathy, eradicate the concept of love and forgiveness and replace it with a religion, indeed an entire culture built on 'blood and iron', of the Norse myth of might and plunder.

After the war the next occupants of the camps would have been the church men and women. Much of this is laid out in the writings of Alfred Rosenberg- a shadowy figure who had been with Hitler since the 1920s.

THE DEATH OF HEINRICH HMMLER

High ranking Nazi leaders attempted to escape retribution by disguising themselves as common foot soldiers, as other nationalities, as German civilians, even ironically as Holocaust survivors. After the suicide of Hitler in his Berlin bunker, no Nazi was more sought after than Himmler, the architect of 'The Final Solution.' The official story of his capture was that his identity was discovered during interrogation and it was during questioning that he killed himself with a cyanide pill. This version of his capture appears to be designed to place British authorities in a good light.

While it was true that he was caught by the Russians on the 20th of May 1945 and handed over to the British where he was interned at Luneburg, it appears that both the Russians and the British were unaware of his identity, presumably because he was dressed as a common soldier. The actual events of his unmasking have not been revealed in any detail.

The version I use here is based on a newspaper article that cites the war-time diary of a British guard, at the Luneburg internet camp. The diary was known only to his family and has not been revealed publicly, until after his death. The incident was only ever discussed within his family during his lifetime. This suggests that the anecdote has veracity.

My version of these events is seen through the fictitious character of Horst an onlooker to the actual Corporal Harry Jones' account. However, like all the characters and events within the novel, it is based on an amalgam of true incidents and real people's lives.

Source - Daily Mail U.K. August 2nd 2010

REFERENCES

* Survival in Auschwitz - Levi Primo Pub. Touchstone Simon and Schuster   New York 1996

   * The Bitter Road to Freedom - A New History of the Liberation of Europe - Hitchcock William I. Pub. Free Press Simon and Schuster New York 2008

   * The Devil's Diary - Alfred Rosenberg and the Stolen Secrets of the Third Reich - Wittman Robert K. & Kinney David Pub. Harper Collins New York 2016

   * Victory in World War II - The Allies Defeat of the Axis Forces - Cawthorne Nigel Pub. Arcturus Publishing London 2017

   * World War Two 1945 - The Final Victories - Schupf Margot Pub. Time-Life Books New York 2015

   * Nazi Secrets - An Occult Breach in the Fabric of History - Lost Frank   Pub. www.euromyst.com 2013

   * Magic History- Theory- Practice - Schertel Dr Ernst Pub. COTUM - Catalogue of the Universal Mind. U.S.A. 2009

   * Hitler's Monsters - A Supernatural History of the Third Reich - Kurlander Eric Yale University Press U.S. and London 2017

   * The German War - A Nation under Arms 1939 - 45 - Stargardt Nicholas   Penguin Random House 2015

   * Psychology -Themes and Variations [Seventh Edition] - Weiten Wayne. University of Nevada Pub. Thomas Wadsworth U.S. 2007

* Disobeying Hitler - German Resistance in the Last Year of WWII - Hansen Randall   Faber and Faber 2014

* Berlin The Downfall 1945 - Beevor Antony Penguin Books 2003

* Night - His Record of Childhood in the Death Camps - Wiesel Elie   Penguin London 1958

* Last Stop Auschwitz - De Wind Eddy Pub. Black Swan 2020

* Mala's Cat - Kacenberg Mala Penguin Random House London 2022

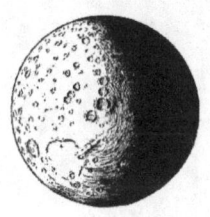

Dancing With The Midnight Mare   Luca Collins

www.ingramcontent.com/pod-product-compliance
Lightning Source LLC
Chambersburg PA
CBHW010824070526
44583CB00022B/2926